Reconceptualising Authenticity for English as a Global Language

SECOND LANGUAGE ACQUISITION

Series Editors: Professor David Singleton, *University of Pannonia, Hungary* and *Fellow Emeritus, Trinity College, Dublin, Ireland* and Dr Simone E. Pfenninger, *University of Zurich, Switzerland*

This series brings together titles dealing with a variety of aspects of language acquisition and processing in situations where a language or languages other than the native language is involved. Second language is thus interpreted in its broadest possible sense. The volumes included in the series all offer in their different ways, on the one hand, exposition and discussion of empirical findings and, on the other, some degree of theoretical reflection. In this latter connection, no particular theoretical stance is privileged in the series; nor is any relevant perspective – sociolinguistic, psycholinguistic, neurolinguistic, etc. – deemed out of place. The intended readership of the series includes final-year undergraduates working on second language acquisition projects, postgraduate students involved in second language acquisition research, and researchers, teachers and policy-makers in general whose interests include a second language acquisition component.

Full details of all the books in this series and of all our other publications can be found on http://www.multilingual-matters.com, or by writing to Multilingual Matters, St Nicholas House, 31–34 High Street, Bristol BS1 2AW, UK.

SECOND LANGUAGE ACQUISITION: 102

Reconceptualising Authenticity for English as a Global Language

Richard S. Pinner

MULTILINGUAL MATTERS
Bristol • Buffalo • Toronto

Library of Congress Cataloging in Publication Data
Names: Pinner, Richard S., author.
Title: Reconceptualising Authenticity for English as a Global Language/Richard S. Pinner.
Description: Bristol; Buffalo: Multilingual Matters, [2016] |
Series: Second Language Acquisition: 102 | Includes bibliographical references and index.
Identifiers: LCCN 2016004826| ISBN 9781783095674 (hbk : alk. paper) | ISBN 9781783095667 (pbk : alk. paper) | ISBN 9781783095704 (kindle)
Subjects: LCSH: English language—Globalization. | English language—Study and teaching—Foreign speakers.
Classification: LCC PE1073.P566 2016 | DDC 428.0071—dc23 LC record available at https://lccn.loc.gov/2016004826

British Library Cataloguing in Publication Data
A catalogue entry for this book is available from the British Library.

ISBN-13: 978-1-78309-567-4 (hbk)
ISBN-13: 978-1-78309-566-7 (pbk)

Multilingual Matters
UK: St Nicholas House, 31–34 High Street, Bristol BS1 2AW, UK.
USA: UTP, 2250 Military Road, Tonawanda, NY 14150, USA.
Canada: UTP, 5201 Dufferin Street, North York, Ontario M3H 5T8, Canada.

Website: www.multilingual-matters.com
Twitter: Multi_Ling_Mat
Facebook: https://www.facebook.com/multilingualmatters
Blog: www.channelviewpublications.wordpress.com

Copyright © 2016 Richard S. Pinner.

All rights reserved. No part of this work may be reproduced in any form or by any means without permission in writing from the publisher.

The policy of Multilingual Matters/Channel View Publications is to use papers that are natural, renewable and recyclable products, made from wood grown in sustainable forests. In the manufacturing process of our books, and to further support our policy, preference is given to printers that have FSC and PEFC Chain of Custody certification. The FSC and/or PEFC logos will appear on those books where full certification has been granted to the printer concerned.

Typeset by Nova Techset Private Limited, Bengaluru & Chennai, India.

Contents

	Acknowledgements	vii
1	Introduction to the Book	1
	Premises of this Book	2
	Relevance of Authenticity to Language Learning	5
	Structure of the Book	6
2	Existential, Philosophical and Theoretical Underpinnings	10
	Introduction	10
	Existentialism and Authenticity: The Meaning of Life and Self?	10
	The Innateness of Language and the Nature of Authenticity	17
	Complex Dynamic Systems and Chaos Theory	28
	Conclusion	32
3	English as a Global Language	34
	Introduction	34
	Globalisation and English as a Disembodied Language	35
	Global English	36
	Ownership and the Pareto Principle	42
	The Affective Effect of Authenticity	47
	Authenticity and International Models	55
	Conclusion	62
4	Authenticity in Language Teaching	63
	Introduction	63
	Historical Overview and Development	65
	The Numerous Definitions of Authenticity	69
	Authenticity as an Approach	77
	Authenticity and the Dearth of Empirical Research	83
	Conclusion	97

5	The Authenticity Continuum	99
	Introduction	99
	A Pivotal Period in the Evolution of Authenticity	100
	The Authenticity Continuum	101
	The Paradox of Authenticity	127
	Conclusion	130
6	Authenticity in Bilingual Educational Contexts	131
	Introduction	131
	The Changing Face of Language Education Programmes	133
	Authenticity of Purpose: Bilingual Educational Models	135
	Conclusion	142
7	New Media as a Catalyst for Authenticity	144
	Introduction	144
	Language Education and Communication Technology	148
	Authenticity Online	150
	Increased Social Contact and Awareness	155
	Increased Opportunities for Exchange	156
	Increased Exposure to Language and Culture	160
	Games and Authenticity	162
	Conclusion	163
8	Conclusion	165
	Directions for Research	167
	References	170
	Author Index	188
	Subject Index	191

Acknowledgements

I would like to thank various people for their input and support in the realisation of this book. First, I would like to thank Ema Ushioda for not only being a supportive and incredible colleague, but also for encouraging me in this 'extra-curricular' endeavour, and for her insightful comments and suggestions on several of the early chapters. I would also like to thank Zoltán Dörnyei for his comments on early drafts, and for telling me that 'authenticity is going to be big'. I also send very heartfelt thanks to my dear friend, colleague and mentor Makoto Ikeda, whose help and wisdom have taken me to places I never thought I would reach. Thanks also to my good friend and colleague Robert Lowe for comments on the section about native-speakerism, and for encouraging me to write more on the issue. Similarly, I thank Dr Erkan Külekçi for his input and for sharing his deep knowledge on this topic. I am also grateful to Nick Andon for initially encouraging me in this direction. Thanks also go out to my mum, Susan Keidan, not just for her maternal support but also for her comments and suggestions on the book. I would also like to thank the anonymous reviewer for his/her insightful, kind and critical comments. I am genuinely grateful for your comments as they helped me to improve the book. I would also like to thank David Singleton and Simone Pfenninger for their editorial contributions, and for having also helped me to improve the work and bring it up to a better standard. It is fair to say that without each of these people, this book would not be what it is. Each person has encouraged me and helped me to formulate my ideas in a way that I hope will make better sense to others.

I would also like to give a special thank you to Laura Longworth at Multilingual Matters for all her support and encouragement, her understanding and her humour throughout the process of proposing and then writing this volume. It was a real pleasure to work with you.

Finally, I would like to thank Oscar and Kimie for helping me to be an authentic person when I was not working on this book. I have tried to make sure this book did not keep me away from either of you, and being with you both has helped me to remain whole. You were supportive when I was away, and without you I would not be half the person I am today. Oscar was good at keeping my mind off work, and Kimie was just fantastic at helping me to keep improving upon myself and to be motivated throughout the process of researching and writing this book. Thank you both so much.

There are of course other people I should like to mention and thank, whether you were someone who came to see one of my talks or a dear friend who argued with me over strong coffee about existential philosophy many years ago. I would also like to thank anyone who reads this book. I put a lot of myself into it and so I hope others can get something back out of it.

1 Introduction to the Book

Authenticity is vital in second language acquisition because it connects the individual learner to the content used for learning. It connects the students to the teacher, and also to other learners, and influences classroom dynamics of interaction, which in turn affects how learners engage with tasks and how much they invest themselves in the learning. It is also an integral part of how learners conceptualise themselves in relation to the wider social context in which the target language will be used. In other words, authenticity is a powerful affective component of perceived validity which bridges the individual and social worlds of both learning and teaching. It is a fluid component of identity and part of the dynamic system of motivation. As such, it is both essential to language learning and at the same time highly elusive and hard to define.

As many scholars have pointed out before, most notably Widdowson (1978), Breen (1985) and van Lier (1996), authenticity is not something absolute, but rather it is relative to the learner and their unique and individual beliefs. Therefore, any discussion of authenticity needs to take place within a flexible framework, one which can bend itself to meet the ever-changing identities of learners and teachers in a rapidly evolving social environment. In this book I have attempted to unpack these concepts and to examine them holistically. The title of this book, *Reconceptualising Authenticity*, might seem to suggest that I will present a new theory of authenticity. Perhaps a more descriptive title would have been 'synthesising and unpacking the concept of authenticity as a dynamic, contextually dependent component of a complex system'. However, I opted for the shorter version in the spirit of the book itself, which is partly intended as a summary of the diverse and complex strands of thought on the topic of authenticity, and partly as an attempt to consolidate these discussions and move away from static definitions. This book presents the various strands of thought that so far seem to have made little impact in the domain of authenticity as a practical issue in the classroom, or as a puzzle that can be at the heart of an empirical inquiry. Many teachers and students of foreign languages around the world still cling to the view that authenticity is a linguistic trait, inherently the product of a target language culture, as evidenced by staff-room discourse, the widely disseminated methodology books carrying such definitions and learner preferences that greatly influence unfair employment practice, particularly in the English language teaching industry (Mahboob & Golden, 2013). I refer to this definition as the 'classic' definition, and will provide further justification and proof of its ubiquity in Chapter 4. This situation is further exacerbated by the fact that research into authenticity is rather scarce. I will try to explain why I think this is and also suggest ways that the issue can be addressed.

My aim in writing this book is to replace the 'classic' definition with a reconceptualised version, which is more inclusive to other varieties of English. The concept of authenticity is currently in a state of turmoil because the rather abstract concepts, which are inherent in the construct, are either not fully acknowledged or they are debated up until the point where authenticity becomes an 'illusion' (Widdowson, 1990: 44). In asserting this I realise that I am taking a rather dangerous and paradoxical approach, saying that we need to get away from an oversimplified version of authenticity, when the issue is already fraught with complications. This is part of the paradox of authenticity: at one end it is too complicated to have a single definition, and at the other end practitioners talk about 'authentic' materials when they generally mean newspapers or other items that have simply been extrapolated from a target language speaking community. As a result of this rather reductionist view of authenticity in language teaching (particularly where materials are involved), the inherent complexities have been largely ignored, or at least avoided, in the mainstream of English language teaching (ELT) materials and teacher training courses. I think authenticity is in need of unpacking again. There is a lot of old baggage within the concept of authenticity, even fairly modern publications such as Harmer (2008) and Richards and Schmidt (2013) still define authenticity along the lines of 'newspapers'. I agree that newspapers can be authentic, but so can almost anything else. Similarly, some things that we may take for granted as being 'authentic', such as a newspaper, may actually not be very authentic at all in certain contexts. In this book I would like to invite the reader to reconsider authenticity from the perspective of English as a global language, and to examine authenticity as it relates to individuals and their positions within society. As the English language becomes ever more abstract as a result of its employment as a tool for international communication, the necessity to personalise it and to make it relevant to the Self becomes more pronounced.

Premises of this Book

The majority of books dealing with the concept of authenticity in language teaching tend to take a practical approach to the subject. Authenticity is a concept that is familiar throughout the language teaching world; students, teachers and researchers are aware of it and, generally, view it as a desirable component of teaching. Practical books on authenticity often present lesson plans and ideas that incorporate authentic materials, and these materials tend to be 'cultural products', as Mishan (2005) calls them. The long-standing practical definition of authenticity is basically materials that were not designed for language teaching originally, but some other use in the target language community (Harmer, 2008; Hedge, 2000), with the 'classic' example being a newspaper. Works that deal with the theoretical side of authenticity are much less common than such practical works. Henry Widdowson is perhaps one of the most well-known proponents of authenticity in language teaching; however, his many discussions on authenticity have tended to belong to larger works dealing with other topics. For example *Teaching Language as Communication* (1978) is about communicative language teaching, with Widdowson primarily arguing that traditional language teaching, which focuses on grammatical structures, fails to prepare learners to communicate effectively. Authenticity is a central tenet to his vision of communicative language teaching, but the book is not solely about authenticity. Rather, authenticity orbits the entire theme, sometimes manifesting itself as a basic assumption of the approach. *Aspects of Language Teaching* (1990) is even broader in scope, dealing with the issue of theory and practice, as well as approaches to language teaching and considerations for syllabus design. Authenticity is defined as 'natural language behaviour' (1990: 45) and Widdowson writes that it is hard to imagine another definition of authenticity. However, Widdowson himself has provided numerous definitions and positions in his writing, with Mishan suggesting that he actually 'metaphorically throw[s] water on the flames he himself had helped to kindle' (2005: 17) by suggesting that 'Inauthentic language-using behaviour might well be effective language-learning behaviour' (Widdowson, 1990: 46–47 following Breen, 1985; see also Widdowson, 1979). Here, Widdowson points out one of the widespread assumptions about authenticity as a 'means to an end' and in doing so he (either intentionally or unintentionally) introduces a sense of drudgery into the use of authentic materials, as the idiomatic use of 'a means to an end' can imply an undesirable way of achieving a necessary outcome. This is somewhat at odds with what Csikszentmihalyi (1990, 1997, 2013) calls 'flow theory', and also recent educational innovations such as game theory (Lazzaro, 2009) and language play (G. Cook, 2000), where enjoyment of the actual process of learning is viewed as crucial. All of these concepts deal with the idea of authenticity in learning, and this is one of the reasons why authenticity is commonly associated with motivation. Widdowson, also, seems to fundamentally agree that the learning process should be rewarding in itself, and his basic argument is that foreign language learning should serve some fundamental communicative function. These issues will also be addressed in later chapters.

The issue of authenticity is often referred to as the 'authenticity debate' (Mishan, 2005) and there are various definitions and positions available in the literature, some complementary and overlapping, many contradictory and confusing. Gilmore (2007a) summarises over a century of literature on authenticity in his state-of-the-art paper, providing an in-depth overview in which he identifies eight different and overlapping definitions. His paper for the journal *Language Teaching* cites 240 other works, but of these only 29 mention authenticity specifically in the title, two of these referring to authenticity in language testing. This shows two things: first that authenticity is implicit in a large number of these papers even though it is not directly mentioned in the title; and second that relatively few papers deal exclusively with the thorny issue, perhaps showing a general reticence in tackling authenticity directly in our field. This is not to say that authenticity is under-theorised. In fact, complaints about the complexity of authenticity and the unhelpfully diverse number of definitions have been a feature of any serious discussion of authenticity for some time.

Concepts that have long been central to second language acquisition (SLA) such as motivation and culture are evolving to reflect the 'fluidity of today's learning contexts' (Ushioda, 2013a: 5), and I would argue that authenticity is also in need of an updated examination. The concept of authenticity needs to be discussed in light of emergent theories of language acquisition such as chaos/complexity theory and dynamic systems approaches as these seem to represent our best way of describing the complex phenomena of second language acquisition in an ever diversifying social context (Kramsch, 2011; Larsen-Freeman, 1997; Larsen-Freeman & Cameron, 2008a; Mercer, 2011; Tudor, 2003).

In this book I present the case for authenticity as a complex dynamic construct that can only be understood by examining it from social, individual and contextual dimensions, in relation to actual people. I will talk about existential philosophy to show that authenticity is a problem not just for language acquisition, but one which affects us as individuals belonging to society. I will examine authenticity from a chaos/complexity theory perspective and resist the urge to reduce it down into something that can be printed onto a textbook in order to sell more copies. I believe that in doing so I am actually making the issue more manageable by opening it up and unpacking it in all its complexity. I aim to examine what people mean when they talk about authentic language. In today's world, in which technological developments have led to a situation where cultures are in constant interaction, with the English language working as a binding agent for cross-cultural exchanges, how does the concept of authenticity fit in?

One of the fundamental opinions I have about language teaching is that a good teacher naturally attempts to build a rapport with his or her learners. Good teachers or educators in any discipline try to get their students to engage with the content and to engage in a process of personal meaning-making. Ushioda explains that 'the notion of engaging our students' identities is something many experienced language teachers have intuitively recognised as important' (2011b: 17) and she goes on to state that doing so is not new or surprising, but is in fact what many good teachers do instinctively. Intuition and 'gut feelings', far from being vague or unscientific, are actually a vital part of a teacher's work (T. Atkinson & Claxton, 2000). This is because teachers draw on their own personal beliefs and experiences when constructing environments which they feel are most conducive to learning in real time. The application of intuition when responding to the students' needs and navigating through the learning process is one of the ways in which the teacher creates a culture of authenticity in the 'small culture' (Holliday, 1999) of their own classroom and teaching context. This has much in common with ecological approaches to language learning (Tudor, 2003; van Lier, 1998), which I will discuss in further detail in Chapter 2.

Relevance of Authenticity to Language Learning

Although this book deals primarily with authenticity as it relates to second language acquisition, I pay particular focus to English as a foreign language instruction. This is because English is somewhat of a special case in the world today, and also the most widely taught as a foreign language. English is part of the reason we have what Fairclough termed the 'globalisation of discourse', which he illustrates with an example of World News coming from global television channels such as CNN in the USA, also the BBC in the UK would fit this example. He explains that although these channels claim to be global in their scope, and are broadcast and viewed globally, the locus of the content is still fixed on the country of origin, what Fairclough terms a 'parochial' view of the world. In other words, globalisation is responsible for the dissemination of an Anglo-global world view. Fairclough calls the globalisation of discourse a 'constant external point of reference' (2001: 206) from which many nations collectively view the world in order to make comparisons and to market ideas. This reference point could potentially invoke the concept that 'the grass is always greener on the other side', although Fairclough uses caution and explains that the globalisation of discourse does not necessarily mean the homogenisation of discourse, but rather that there is an awareness of 'the other' and its relation to 'the Self' on the scale of national identity. As the English language is pushed and pulled in ever more diverse directions, as we see an increase in what Vertovec (2007, 2010) has labelled *super-diversity*, in which it becomes not only impossible but also undesirable to state where one language or culture ends and another begins, as the English language especially starts to resemble a handful of grains of sand rather than a single solid rock, it is important to ask ourselves what authentic language is. Globalisation is often associated with the term 'global village'; however, Blommaert (2010: 1) notes that this is actually not the case, and rather the world is a complex web of villages, neighbourhoods and communities that are all interconnected in various material and symbolic ways. For many learners and teachers around the world, the English language is an abstract yet terrifyingly real phenomenon. It is the world's second language and as such there is tremendous social pressure and political momentum behind getting people to learn to speak it.

Furthermore, English can affect where learners go to school or university, which has a knock-on effect for other aspects of their career. A person who wishes to do well in the field of biochemistry will eventually have to learn to read complicated academic journal articles, requiring a very high level of English proficiency, because most of the research in the scientific fields is published in English first, even though it may not be written by those who speak it as their first language (Ammon, 2001). The English language is therefore something which can be seen and heard all over, but understanding how it relates to one's own needs and requirements is not always so apparent. For some learners, English is easy to connect with and to use in authentic ways for purposes beyond learning or studying for a test. For example, Henry (2013) points out that in Sweden, learners are so proficient in English because they use it all the time to watch television, go online or even participate in online gaming (a highly enjoyable social and collaborative form of communication) that they tend to just 'coast' through English classes as an easy option. In other contexts, like mine in Japan, for many students the English language is just a *subject* that is taught at schools and spoken about in political and higher education circles well beyond the learner's locus of control. For many of them, English quite often just boils down to the USA or American culture. Yet for others, English is a second language because they lived abroad for months or years, usually because one of their parents was sent there for work. Others yet may have parents who come from abroad, and so their home-life might be conducted in English, as is the case with my own son. All these contexts and differences mean that to talk about the authenticity of a certain piece of language is like describing the colour of glass; each individual's perspective and stance will influence their perception. But authenticity *is* an essential component of the language classroom and it *does* connect in a very real sense with other important factors crucial to learning, such as motivation and autonomy, as I will attempt to show in the following pages.

Structure of the Book

In this book I will explore the theoretical issues surrounding authenticity in depth. I will propose that authenticity be considered as a continuum, which attempts to reframe it in a way that is more inclusive to L2 varieties of English. Using the continuum, I will explain how authenticity is partly a socially constructed shared experience and partly a sense of validity, which comes from the individual self about the teaching/learning situation. This is an idea that is grounded in sociocultural approaches to learning, but also marks a return to what existentialist philosophers such as Kierkegaard and Heidegger were referring to in their discussions of the authentic self. The continuum is an attempt to incorporate the majority of speakers of English into the concept of authenticity while also allowing for such important factors as identity, affect and agency. Another purpose of the continuum is to allow for the importance of Self and the process of engagement with the language and learning materials. In this way the continuum incorporates autonomy and identity, which Ushioda (2011b) notes are vital in motivating learners. Authenticity is often referred to as a motivational force in language teaching, and the continuum attempts to better establish the conceptual links between authenticity and motivation. Ushioda advocates a *person in-context relational* view of motivation (2009), and in many ways the continuum tries to encompass both the individual identity of the learner and bridge that with the often distant reality of the target language culture, whatever it may be. This is especially important in EFL contexts, where learners may not know much about the culture and they may be learning in compulsory language classes. I hope to demonstrate how authenticity and motivation are closely related and I believe that learners would find the materials and tasks being used in the classroom more motivating if they can relate to them personally and as individuals. In other words they can engage their true selves and, ideally, exercise a certain degree of control over the learning process. This also strongly ties in the concept of autonomy, which is an essential ingredient in motivation. I believe that in order to understand authenticity it must be viewed in relation to other factors with which it is in constant interaction. In this way, authenticity is envisaged as a dynamic component of a complex system. Finally I will explain how authenticity is being amalgamated into the burgeoning domain of bilingual educational models, such as Content and Language Integrated Learning (CLIL) and English as a Medium of Instruction (EMI), since in such learning environments there is what Coyle *et al.* (2010) refer to as *authenticity of purpose*. In this book I aim to show how these important developments are contributing to a pivotal stage in the evolution of what we mean by the term *authenticity* in second language acquisition.

Chapter 2 deals with authenticity as an existential issue related to the Self. I will examine how the concept of the authentic self is made manifest in the language classroom, and the complexities of this self-image when negotiating identity in a foreign or second language. I discuss both the individual and social aspects of this process, and in the latter part of the chapter I explain how chaos/complexity theory might be a useful way of gaining a more holistic insight into the dynamics of second language acquisition. In Chapter 3 I overview the history and development of English as a global language, with particular focus on issues of ownership and the inherent prejudices of the English language teaching (ELT) and English as a foreign language (EFL) industries. I will examine how this prejudice relates to authenticity, and how this in turn relates to both learners and teachers. Chapter 4 presents an overview of the concept of authenticity within language learning and teaching. I examine the numerous definitions that have been posited over the decades long 'authenticity debate' and provide a critical examination of the 'classic' definition, which seems to be the most pervasive and problematic definition of all. In this chapter I will also look at authenticity in relation to other important concepts such as autonomy, motivation and materials. The final part of this chapter discusses the research, or lack of research rather, that has been done into authenticity and makes suggestions about how to address this in future agendas. Chapter 5 presents what could be considered the heart of this book, the Authenticity Continuum, which is a framework for approaching authenticity as a socially mediated and contextually dependant dynamic process of investment. I attempt to validate such a framework with practical examples and a small sample of my own research. Chapter 6 looks at authenticity in bilingual educational models, and examines how the landscape of foreign language education (particularly English) is changing to meet the advanced requirements of today's more global societies. In Chapter 7 I look at how new media and communication technologies have greatly influenced language use and I discuss how authenticity is also affected through increased exposure and opportunities for international exchanges to take place. In the final part of this book, Chapter 8 will offer a conclusion and summary of the main arguments put forward, as well as making some suggestions for the direction of future research.

I would also like to add a final comment about my own writing style, and some of the research I will present here. Mostly, this book has developed out of my own reflective practice, making it a very personal quest. I therefore have tried to be as *authentic* as possible in the writing up as well, conveying personal observations from my journals and also combining them with other evidence which arose from my experiences. In writing this book I have been engaged with a process of what Barkhuizen (2011) calls 'narrative knowledging' – a process where the researcher/writer makes sense of things in the act of detailing the narrative. I have often noted a prejudice against such data, with comments coming back from journal editors that such observations are merely 'anecdotal'. However, this is a misguided view, grounded on a mistaken assumption that evidence based on reflections from personal experience is not useful or scientific. In fact, the data I have collected in this way are based on an ongoing process of reflective practice (Edge, 2011; Farrell, 2011; Schön, 1983), and based also on the well-established research discipline of Narrative Inquiry (Barkhuizen, 2013; Barkhuizen *et al.*, 2014; Clandinin & Connelly, 2000; Johnson & Golombek, 2002; Pavlenko, 2007). In fact, when investigating something as subjective and personal as the concept of authenticity, I see such a constructivist approach to the inquiry as being essential. Not all the data I will present come from my own self-observations, and I will also present research based on questionnaire studies and interviews that I have conducted over the past few years. However, the act of writing this book has also been heavily entwined with the process of me analysing and making sense of the data of my own lived experiences, which includes the reading and secondary research I engaged in when going over the literature. In this way the book is part of an ongoing process. It is my hope that readers will engage in that process in their own way as well, rather than looking for static answers locked in the ink of these pages.

2 Existential, Philosophical and Theoretical Underpinnings

Introduction

This chapter aims to explain existential philosophy and to outline how some of the 20th century's greatest thinkers discussed and conceptualised the idea of authenticity. Primarily, I will explain how these theories are of importance to language learning and second language acquisition, with special reference to second language identities, as authenticity in the existential sense primarily refers to the Self. It is easy to think that the discussions on authenticity in language teaching have had almost nothing to do with the discussions about authenticity in existential philosophy. However, I will point out that there is a surprising amount of overlap between the two. Our society is changing rapidly, and tidy, clean-cut theories simply do not have the scope to describe what we now recognise as complex dynamic phenomena. In this chapter I will outline first what the existentialists thought authenticity meant to them from a philosophical perspective as it related to the individual in society. I will explain how and why these ideas have relevance to second language acquisition and I will also attempt to show that these arguments have already been voiced in the SLA literature. I will also explain the theoretical underpinnings of this book, focusing particularly on identity, the social side of authenticity and leading finally to a brief explanation of complex dynamic systems and chaos/complexity theory.

Existentialism and Authenticity: The Meaning of Life and Self?

The search for authenticity is often described as a *quest*, and since I became interested in the subject I have certainly come to understand why. In wrestling with the subject I have been brought into contact with controversial philosophers and highly pragmatic educators, with big ideas and minute details, with simple truths and perplexing definitions. The study of authenticity has also brought me closer to myself, as I question what makes me who I am and how that shapes my work as an educator and a learner. As I explained in the introduction, many of the books on authenticity in language teaching are *practical* books; dealing with actual materials or tasks that can be applied directly from the page to the classroom. This is an excellent thing, one which first drew me to the subject. However, as I noted in the introduction to this book, the way practitioners talk about authenticity is not always aligned to how it has been discussed in the literature on SLA. Defining authenticity is like trying to explain the colour of glass; we all know it is there but it changes depending on how you look at it. It is for this reason that Mishan noted she was not particularly trying to 'establish... a definitive definition [but rather] a workable criteria for authenticity' (2005: 11). In this way, she was acknowledging the complexity surrounding the issue of authenticity and attempting to sidestep 'the increasingly tortuous search for a finite definition' (2005: 11). The choice of word 'tortuous' is an interesting one, particularly in the context of this chapter where I will examine the existentialist thinkers, many of whom did seem to entangle themselves through a preoccupation with understanding authenticity.

The authentic self

Rather than getting into this important issue by explaining abstract theories and philosophical points, I will try and explain through a simple example of how authenticity and existentialism are highly relevant to the language classroom.

Being British, I am often asked by students if I like football. This question always causes me a bit of a dilemma, because the student asking me is usually one I have just met with a big smile and a strong passion for football, looking for a connection with me. So I usually say yes, I like football. If I was being my authentic self I would tell the student that I actually strongly dislike football with a sort of listless passion. But if I say this I will break face with the student and lose a valuable chance to form a bond with them. However, having once told the lie that I like football I am often required to further expand on it by naming my (non-existent) favourite team. If I am really unlucky the student may know some players and I will nod along until the conversation moves to another topic. The worst part is that I think quite often the student can tell I am lying, and so they are left wondering why I was insincere. This is what the existentialists were mainly concerned with in their discussion about authenticity and the difficulty we all face in being true to our authentic selves. Society often puts us in situations where we cannot be authentic or true to ourselves, for one reason or the other. We know what we are doing is not being true to ourselves, and yet in order to conform to social conventions we must be inauthentic. It feels bad and it can even create tensions later on. This issue can be further complicated by the concept of multiple selves, so we might never know what our authentic self actually is, because we invoke different versions of the Self depending on context and who we are with. This is why the concept of authenticity can be seen as a journey rather than a destination, a process rather than a state. Authenticity is a dynamic concept, one which evades definition by definition. Usually authenticity is more easily defined not by what *is* authentic but by what is *not* authentic (Golomb, 1995: 7).

Jean-Jacques Rousseau (1712–78) argued in his famous treatise *The Social Contract* (1762) that 'Man is born free and everywhere he is in chains'. Rousseau is credited as having invented the idea of modern authenticity (Lindholm, 2008). Basically, for Rousseau 'authenticity is derived from the natural self, whereas inauthenticity is a result of external influences' (Yacobi, 2012: 28). We lose our authenticity by trying to be accepted by others, especially in societies with hierarchies and established socially acceptable codes of behaviour.

> Rousseau earnestly believed it was necessary to demand absolute honesty from the world and from himself, and he was the first writer to present the reading public with a completely positive picture of someone who lives an authentic life by indulging his own inner emotional demands regardless of the opinions of others. (Lindholm, 2008: 8)

Rousseau's posthumously published book, entitled *The Confessions of J.J. Rousseau* (1781) presented his authentic self; 'shamelessly revealing himself' to be a rather pathetic and self-serving individual who also liked to be spanked (Lindholm, 2008: 8). He wrote in his confessions:

> Let the numberless legion of my fellow men gather round me and hear my confessions. Let them groan at my depravities and blush for my misdeeds. But let each one of them reveal his heart at the foot of Thy throne with equal sincerity, and may any man who dares, say, 'I was a better man then he'. (Rousseau, 1781, cited in Lindholm, 2008)

I have no intention of advocating that any of us make similar demands on ourselves, or our learners for that matter. However, the ideas put forward by the existentialists have relevance for second language teaching, if we drill down into them a little.

The existential philosophers have a somewhat negative image, with many of the most famous arguments being associated with death or social decay. Personal authenticity and the existential strand of thought connected with the authentic self is 'out of fashion', not just within analytic philosophy but with other traditions too (Golomb, 1995: 4). A quick look at the existentialist philosophers who discussed authenticity does not encourage a positive outlook. Martin Heidegger (1889–1976) discussed authenticity at length in much of his work. He was an eminent thinker and philosopher who mistrusted society's faith in technology for its own sake. Although he did not dislike technology per se, he believed that it was very dangerous and he saw humanity's rising technological abilities as the dawn of a new technological era. His ideas on authenticity and language were very insightful, but he was discredited and temporarily banned from teaching owing to his public support of the Nazi party in World War Two. In 1946 he suffered from a mental breakdown (Guignon, 1993: xx), although he later returned to academic life as a professor emeritus at Freiburg University. Owing to these controversial aspects of his life, he is often seen as a somewhat troubled figure. Friedrich Nietzsche (1844–1900) was another important existentialist philosopher interested in the concept of authenticity. Nietzsche questioned the idea of almost everything that people at the turn of the 20th century took for granted; such things as truth and morality, even God. He argued that the idea of an objective, single truth was unrealistic, and he also explosively announced the death of God (Nietzsche, 1974). A reclusive yet tortured genius, near the end of his life at the age of 42 he went insane. At first it was believed that his mental collapse was due to syphilis, but now the more popular belief is that it was brain cancer (Matthews, 2003). Other existentialist thinkers who are bound up with authenticity are Søren Kierkegaard (1813–1855), who wrote a scathing attack on Christendom and died at the age of 42, a month after collapsing in the street. He described his own life as having been filled with suffering in various letters, and it was a theme in much of his writings (Hannay, 2003). Of course, no account of the Existential movement would be complete without the great French philosopher, writer and curmudgeon Jean-Paul Sartre (1905–1980); a chain-smoker who turned down the Nobel Prize for Literature and perhaps the main reason for the stereotype of the existentialist thinker as a depressed and incomprehensible figure shrouded in tobacco smoke and mystery.

Of course, by explaining all this I am attempting to dust away any such stereotypes of existentialist philosophy by acknowledging the *ad hominem* flaws in that argument. By this I mean that the stereotype of existentialism is based on a fallacy which attacks the people, not the arguments they made. In fact, all these rather sad men were trying desperately to be happy. They wanted to understand their position within society. They said interesting things about how the media is an 'intervening agency' that prevents us from having true experiences (Holt, 2012). They questioned religion and faith at a time when doing so was socially unacceptable. They were wary of technological advances that could have a depersonalising effect on society. Consider the quote attributed to T.S. Eliot, that television 'is a medium of entertainment which permits millions of people to listen to the same joke at the same time, and yet remain lonesome' (cited in Edidin, 2005). This is something more salient today than perhaps ever before, as more and more people find themselves connected to technology at the expense of a connection to the moment. Heidegger discussed this issue when he talked about *Dasein*, or 'being there', a discussion I will return to again in Chapter 7. Although these discussions may well be relevant to daily modern life, how are existentialist theories relevant to second language acquisition, and if they are, why have they not been incorporated into the literature already?

In fact, the work of these existentialists is already featured in the literature on authenticity. Although not always prominent, existentialist versions of authenticity feature richly as an underlying theme in much of the important work on second language acquisition, especially works dealing with identity, social context and affective factors. Leo van Lier cited Sartre in his book, choosing the following quote to open his section on authenticity.

> If you seek authenticity for authenticity's sake, you are no longer authentic.
> Jean-Paul Sartre (1992: 4, cited in van Lier, 1996: 123)

Leo van Lier's famous work *Interaction in the Language Curriculum: Awareness, Autonomy, and Authenticity* (1996) is at the time of writing almost 20 years old, but the concept he puts forward of authenticity as a 'personal process of engagement' (1996: 128) is very much a point of departure for this book. Van Lier was one of the first scholars to my knowledge to connect existentialist ideas of authenticity with language teaching and learning, although he was closely following Breen (1985) and especially Widdowson's (1978: 80–81) ideas about the process of *authentication*. Basically van Lier was not interested in viewing authenticity as an inherent linguistic trait, but rather he saw it as 'a goal that teacher and students have to work towards, consciously and constantly' (1996: 128). Authenticity is something that manifests itself through interactions, through engagement and as a product of meaningful exchanges where people speak as themselves, something which Ushioda notes that many good teachers already encourage in their students intuitively (2011b: 17). This is something which Menezes (2013) also finds central in her view of language as an essential part of human nature. She draws a connection between creation myths and science to situate the importance of individual identity and social autonomy in language education. She approaches this position from a chaos/complexity theory perspective because identity is constantly negotiated in the construction of societies on the macro level, while also forming the building blocks of self and the individual at a micro level. Benson (2013a) also finds the existential view of authenticity useful when making the distinction between *independence* and *interdependence*, specifically in relation to learner autonomy and the attempt to bridge the social and individual aspects of autonomy as it relates to SLA (see also Benson and Cooker (2013) and G. Murray (2014) for edited volumes providing further discussion on this issue). In his chapter, Benson draws on the work of Bonnett and Cuypers (2003) who are themselves building on the existentialist idea of being true to one's self as an essential component in educational authenticity. Also in the field of general education, Alan Glatthorn constructs his argument using existential views of authenticity in the same way, specifically from the teacher's perspective, making the case for the teacher *as a person* (1975, 1999). In much the same way, Ushioda (2009, 2011b, 2015) argues that we should view our learners *as people* who are learners in context, rather than just as learners. For Ushioda this is not only essential in terms of motivation, it is also an important ethical consideration when conducting research. In her attempt to personalise and humanise the interactions between learners and educators, Ushioda invokes the concept of *transportable identities* (Richards, 2006; Zimmerman, 1998), the idea that different people play different roles in different situations, which I will examine in the next section. In an interesting article published in the journal *Philosophy Now*, Yacobi (2012) explains that the search for personal authenticity is rather futile, precisely because of the dynamic nature of life and identity. Even if one were to find their authentic self, advances in technology only serve to cloud the issue by changing what it is to be human:

> The merging of human and machine may necessitate new definitions of what a human being is, and generate new problems related to human nature and identity, the nature of society, and the meanings of existence and human authenticity. (Yacobi, 2012: 30)

It seems that one reason why the existentialist philosophers struggled with the concept of authentic self was that for many of them (such as Rousseau) the concept of a true self was singular. In other words, they were searching for a single identity which they could see as being the authentic one. Despite this, Jean-Paul Sartre's basic argument was that there is no such thing as a permanent, stable essence of the Self. He claimed that 'authenticity requires taking full responsibility for our life, choices and actions' (Yacobi, 2012: 28). This idea of authenticity relating to taking responsibility may strike a chord with those familiar with autonomous learning, which is why Mishan states that 'in the language learning context, autonomy and authenticity are essentially symbiotic' (2005: 9).

Returning to the field of applied linguistics and SLA, two edited books, Rilling and Dantas-Whitney (2009b) and Dantas-Whitney and Rilling (2010) are the most recent published volumes that I know of which deal solely with the theme of authenticity. Both these books are grounded in sociocultural approaches and, like me, they view authenticity as essentially being a 'process of appropriation and agency, shaped according to the needs of [the] social context and situation' (2010: 1). Dantas-Whitney and Rilling draw on definitions from existentialism and anthropology for their own definition of authenticity in language learning, which situates authenticity as a social phenomenon and one which is constantly redefined by the interactions which take place.

It is interesting to note that, although the idea of authenticity in the existential sense is often referred to in the literature on second language acquisition, it seems to be rather played down or referred to indirectly. When I encounter the word 'authenticity' in a book, I often recognise that the word is being used in the existential sense, meaning basically 'true to one's self', and yet the authors rarely point out that they are using the word in this way. For example, in Gregersen and MacIntyre (2013), a book which draws together both theory and practice and provides suggestions on how to *capitalise on learners' individuality*, the authors mention that language anxiety (to which they dedicate an important chapter) arises partly from 'a learner's cognisance that the authenticity of self and its expression cannot be communicated as readily in his or her second language as in the first' (2013: xiv–xv). This is an important point in itself, and one which I will turn to in the next section, but for now I will limit my focus to the authors' use of the word 'authenticity'. Just a few pages into the introduction of their book, authenticity as an existential concept is introduced in a way which clearly underpins the work and leaves us in little doubt as to the saliency of the term. They mention the word 'authenticity' frequently from cover to cover, with more than 15 references. On top of its use in the existential sense, the word 'authentic' is used in reference to materials, to tasks, to interactions, to purposes for using the target language and even in reference to helping 'students develop a sense of authentic self-esteem' (Gregersen & MacIntyre, 2013: 222). And yet, the word 'authenticity' is left out of the index at the back of the book (hence my uncertainty as to how many references there are exactly). 'Autonomy' *is* indexed, and it appears on apparently just four pages. So, although this book uses the term 'authenticity' frequently and even as, I would argue, a central justification behind the work, it seems to have been left out as one of the key words appearing in the index. True, the authors may well have just forgotten to index it, but I fear that what is actually the case is that authenticity is not given its due in the existential sense in SLA literature. Looking at the collection of books I currently have on or nearby my desk, many of them part of my research into authenticity, I have been troubled by the fact that authenticity is seldom mentioned in the index. This is because authenticity appears frequently in books about language teaching, but it is rarely one of the main themes.

The authentic self is not something which need only concern a few lofty thinkers and philosophers; every human being has a good reason to be interested in finding their authentic self because this entails learning more about themselves, finding their true self and understanding how that person fits into larger society as a whole. Because the way we speak is an essential form of expressing ourselves, I argue that understanding more about authenticity is an essential component in good language teaching. It is also important to acknowledge that we have multiple selves and various, contextually dependent identities and it is the teacher's job to engage his or her students' identities in an ethical way which does not lead to any discomfort or emotional stress. For this reason, authenticity is not just about the individual but also about the socially constructed identities that depend so much on context.

The Innateness of Language and the Nature of Authenticity

Language is often cited as one of the main things that distinguishes humans from animals. Language is how we build relationships, how we maintain closeness with people, how we instruct or request or reprimand or plead. The importance of language to human existence is rarely understated, and this of course has powerful repercussions for SLA, since:

> language, after all, belongs to a person's whole social being; it is a part of one's identity, and is used to convey this identity to other people. The learning of a foreign language involves far more than simply learning skills, or a system of rules, or a grammar; it involves an alteration in self-image, the adoption of new social and cultural behaviours and ways of being, and therefore has a significant impact on the social nature of the learner. (Williams & Burden, 1997: 115)

Even though Williams and Burden do not use the expression directly, they are talking about the *authentic self* here, in the existentialist sense. By extension, this means that as language teachers, one of our jobs is to enable our learners to find how to express their authentic self through another language. Therefore, finding authenticity may also entail the creation of a foreign language identity, and this L2 identity may or may not be the same as the L1 identity (Block, 2007). The importance of identity in language teaching has been explored in depth by a number of scholars, as I will examine later in this chapter. Identity in the language classroom is strongly connected to motivation, and recent theories of L2 motivation have begun to draw heavily on self-concepts (Dörnyei, 2009; Dörnyei & Ushioda, 2011, 2009; Nitta & Baba, 2015; Ryan & Irie, 2014). Again, the connection between authenticity and motivation is hinged on the idea that language is about expressing the authentic self, and that good teaching therefore allows learners the chance to express themselves in an authentic way.

> [L]anguage is a medium of self-expression and a means of communicating, constructing and negotiating who we are and how we relate to the world around us – that is, of giving ourselves voice and identity. A foreign language is not simply something to add to our repertoire of skills, but a

personalized tool that enables us to expand and express our identity or sense of self in new and interesting ways and with new kinds of people; to participate in a more diverse range of contexts and communities and so broaden our experiences and horizons; and to access and share new and alternative sources of information, entertainment or material that we need, value or enjoy. (Ushioda, 2011a: 203–204)

Indirectly, Ushioda is talking about authenticity in the existential sense, and here situating the use of language as being innately authentic and individual. As Freda Mishan points out in her seminal work, 'language learning is a natural – an *authentic* – activity' (2005: ix). The idea that language is innate to humans is one of the most ground-breaking and essential contributions to the understanding of human language to have arisen in the last century. It has caused a kind of revolution in our appreciation of the importance of language. This, coupled with recent developments in communicative technology, have changed the face of our society and created a surge in interest about the nature of language and communication. The greatly increased interest in language in the 20th century was probably attributable to a number of simultaneous occurrences that I think did not happen by coincidence but as a chain of interconnected events. In linguistics people joke about BC not to mean before Christ but to mean before Chomsky (Harris, 1993: 54), but it was not actually his original proposal that language is an instinct or something innate to humans; that accolade can actually be traced back to Charles Darwin from *The Descent of Man* (1871). Despite this, it was while positing that humans must be born with a language acquisition device as part of an attack on behaviourism, specifically aimed at B.F. Skinner's 1957 book *Verbal Behaviour* that Chomsky was brought into the world of televised debates and international fame. However, while Chomsky and Skinner were battling it out, arguing over the nature of language, the world was watching and before long there were a lot of new departments being founded. Chomsky himself was at Massachusetts Institute of Technology (MIT), which at first was just an engineering university with no linguistics department. That changed when Chomsky became a celebrity. As it states on the MIT Linguistics Department homepage 'the first class of PhD students was admitted in 1961' ('Linguistics at MIT', 2014), which was also the year Chomsky was made into a full professor. Suddenly there was a lot more going on in the field of linguistics, and with it a growing emphasis on language education.

Yet, even before the Chomsky vs Skinner debate, there had been pioneering work in the field of language education. The first journal dedicated solely to the discipline of applied linguistics, *Language Learning*, appeared in 1948. The difference between applied linguistics and linguistics is that applied linguistics is more concerned with practical issues and problems such as the way languages are used, as well as the teaching and learning of languages.

Both are still considered to be relatively new fields, and later led to the birth of the field of second language acquisition in which appeared in the late 1960s and early 70s, again on the back of the competence/performance distinction highlighted by the Chomsky/Skinner debate (Howatt & Widdowson, 2004: 334–337). These new fields are all interdisciplinary, and as such there were many theories being put forward by scholars, a large number of which overlapped and many of which contradicted each other. When he identified up to 60 theories in SLA, Long (1993) mentioned that such variety is a feature of fledgling disciplines. Rod Ellis also voiced concern for the numerous and overlapping theories of SLA. However, in the second edition of his epic book, *The Study of Second Language Acquisition*, he explains that perhaps diversity is something to be celebrated as a sign of the field being in good health (R. Ellis, 2008: xxii–xxiii). Mishan (2005: 21) explains that the 'pluralist' view of SLA in which multiple theories can coexist seems to be the only practical one, especially within the context of authentic language teaching. I will examine this in more depth when I come to look at research and empirical studies that focus on the issue of authenticity in Chapter 4.

The individual side of authenticity

A person's idiolect is the unique way of speaking possessed by an individual. Everybody who can speak a language, be it Russian, Chinese or American Sign Language, possesses an idiolect that is as unique to them as their fingerprint. However, unlike with a fingerprint, the idiolect is not so easy to see and map. Idiolects change too, as a person goes through stages of personal development and identity growth. Idiolects are the starting point for investigative forensic linguistics and involve a process known as *linguistic fingerprinting* (Coulthard, 2004). Unlike fingerprints though, it is very hard to give shape to a person's idiolect, although with the creation of a large corpus one might well be able to identify certain unique features. In his explanation of the idiolect, Coulthard (2004) mentions that it is a trait of the 'native speaker' of a language. Primarily, idiolects are conceptualised as being the domain of the L1, but that is not to say that they do not exist in the L2. In fact, I would argue that even a low-level learner has at least the notion of their idiolect when speaking in L2, as I discovered myself in my own efforts to learn Japanese, when I asked my Japanese teacher to correct my writing. I had created a free blog in which I would post articles I had written in Japanese, and as these were private lessons I was able to request that my teacher use them as the basis of the lesson and correct them with me. She would rephrase many of my sentences, even though what I had written made sense. Not all of her corrections were based on grammatical issues, many of them were about word choice or word order, and she had a particular phrase that she would often use – '*nanka gaikokujin-poi*', which means 'somehow [it] sounds like a foreigner'. I would often return home with the corrected article and not make some of the changes that she had insisted, because I felt they did not reflect how I wanted to sound. For example, she often made me change the word *shikashi* (however) to *demo* (but). I found this grating because to me it did not sound the way I wanted to sound, and I had an intuitive reaction that my teacher was infringing on my own way of saying things. This was actually more acute in my L2 because I was struggling to find an authentic voice for my language learning and I already lacked confidence in my ability. Kramsch discusses this in more detail when she talks of *Textual Identity* (Kramsch, 2000; Kramsch & Lam, 1999), and this is argued to be one way in which learners of an L2 can begin creating a solid L2 identity within the target language. I make this point because I am hypothesising that the L2 idiolect is an important component in a speaker's ability to experience authenticity in the target language. In order to be authentic in the sense that you can be yourself, it is essential that you are able to speak like yourself. This is further complicated by the fact that our self is always changing, and quite often the act of learning a new language becomes a catalyst for greater identity change. For example, in Japan the learning of English is often a liberating experience and can become a tool for identity transformation and as a means for achieving better gender equality and social mobility (Takahashi, 2013). For immigrants, refugees and those who leave behind their home country in search of another life, learning the target language is directly entwined with the creation of a new and potentially very different identity (Block, 2007; Norton, 2013; Norton & Kamal, 2003; Pavlenko & Blackledge, 2004). If the learning of a language, particularly a powerful and potentially empowering global language such as English, fuels a significant identity change then this could have rather profound implications for the personal authenticity of the language learner. This is why it is essential to assist learners to express their own individuality (Gregersen & MacIntyre, 2013) or to cultivate an environment and provide scaffolding for them to 'speak as themselves' (Ushioda, 2011b), while at the same time being sensitive to identity changes that may be taking place both within and outside of the learning environment. The learner may not be able to fully grasp the changes in identity that are taking place, which would put them in a delicate position. This is perhaps one of the reasons why identity in the second language is a complicated issue (Block, 2007; Mercer & Williams, 2014; Norton, 2013), or indeed a fully fledged complex system (Menezes, 2013; Mercer, 2015).

The dynamics of second language identity

One important aspect of the Self in second language acquisition is the idea that self is a dynamic construct. For example, on an average day I may present myself as a teacher, a husband, a father, a dog owner and friend. I am a foreigner living in Japan, but when I go back to the UK I am an expatriate. These different selves are distinct, although they are also part of a larger whole. For this reason, the Self is sometimes seen as *fractal*. This means that there are many parts which make up a whole, and that although one may be foregrounded the other identities, part of us may remain in the background. Menezes (2013: 64) compares the concept of fractal selves to a matryoshka doll, because they all resemble each other, although each is separate yet part of a larger whole. While this may seem like an obvious idea, it does have a lot of implications for language learning. If one naturally switches their identities around, foregrounding different aspects of their self-image to fit the context or social situation, then foreign language proficiency will depend on the speakers' ability to express themselves *as themselves* in a large number of situations. However, in terms of language learning it is important to note that for many learners, the only self that they have access to in the target language is the learner-self. A student is only a student for a small percentage of their day, and an even smaller percentage of their lives. If the student's L2 self is composed solely during classroom interactions it will be hard for them to have enough self-images to compose an authentic self of identity in the L2. Therefore, language learning requires authenticity to have any hope of success. Methods of language instruction really do need to encourage learners to speak as themselves (Ushioda, 2011b). Any view of authenticity which does not take into account the learners' L2 self (and, by implication their L1 self too) will be unlikely to prove effective in the long run. Other research, such as Block's (2007) and Norton's (2013) studies looking at identity change and language use among migrants is particularly interesting. In these situations identity is often at crisis, when people are uprooted (either by personal, political or economic factors) and find themselves in very different cultural settings in which they inhabit different social roles and possess very different communicative abilities.

A related model for understanding the social impact of layered identities is the idea of contextually dependent identities in talk, which Zimmerman delineates into three types.

- **Discourse identities:** participants assume these when they 'engage in various sequentially organised activities: current speaker, listener, story teller, story recipient, questioner, answerer, repair initiator, and so on' (Zimmerman, 1998: 90).
- **Situational identities:** these are imposed by the context or situation of the discourse. Examples would be 'doctor/patient identities in the context of a health clinic or teacher/student identities in the context of a classroom' (Ushioda, 2011a: 205).
- **Transportable identities:** these are different selves which a speaker might choose to invoke at any given time because they are 'potentially relevant in and for any situation and in and for any spate of interaction. They are latent identities that "tag along" with individuals as they move through their daily routines' (Zimmerman, 1998: 90). An example which

I often use in my own teaching is to refer to the fact that am also a language learner, like my students. I also often refer to the fact that I am a husband and father.

Although each of these are relevant to classroom conversations, transportable identities are perhaps the most relevant to our discussion on authenticity. Art lover and father of two, Keith Richards, draws on Zimmerman's concept in order to examine to what extent teacher-fronted classroom conversations are possible, by which I take him to mean *authentic* conversations which follow natural patterns of discourse. Richards mentions authenticity several times in his article, usually in the existential sense, eventually connecting it with morality and using it to draw his article to a close in which he reflects on the extent to which teachers should have a personal involvement with their students and how much 'professional distance' is necessary. He concludes with the heart-warming and *authentic* sentiment that 'it seems almost perverse to assume—let alone insist—that [the Self] is something that should properly be left at the classroom door' (Richards, 2006: 74). However, there is of course a 'thin blue line' here, in the sense of asking students to reveal too much about themselves or expecting teachers to break apart their contextually imposed situated identities. It is easy to think of examples where invoking different identities or even eliciting that students invoke them could create uncomfortable situations or even overstep the ethical boundaries of normal classroom behaviour. This is probably especially salient in the foreign language classroom, where people from different cultures with different standards of socially accepted behaviour are put together in rather intense situations where they may be struggling to express themselves. I will always remember a particularly uncomfortable lesson about capital punishment which I had with a multicultural group of advanced learners in London. There were Spanish, French, Italian, Korean, Turkish and Saudi Arabian nationalities in the classroom, each with their own political views, which may or may not have aligned with their home country's policy on the death penalty. However, it depends on the class as much as the task and the content being discussed, '[a]s all teachers know, every class has its own "personality", which emerges fairly quickly in the course of lessons and relevant out-of-class activities' (van Lier, 2007: 47). Conversely, some of the most successful lessons I have ever taught are ones in which transportable identities took over the classroom and the learners *spoke as themselves*, as Ushioda (2009, 2011b) advocates. For her the concept of transportable identities is a vital connection between classroom practices and motivation, and for her this also indicts research methods in applied linguistics, particularly where L2 motivation is concerned (2013a, 2013b).

One of the most well-known voices in L2 identity research, Bonny Norton, has also forged a strong connection between identity and motivation in what she terms *investment,* something she first observed in her paper for

TESOL Quarterly (writing as Norton Peirce, 1995), which she rephrases closely in the second edition of her seminal book on language and identity (2013). She prefers the term 'investment' to 'motivation' because for her, investment more closely describes the complex social and historical relationship of the learners to the target language, and captures the interplay of power and identity that accompany language learning. Investment is a term which Norton connects to the concept of *cultural capital*, first posited by Bourdieu (1977) as linguistic capital, and then later expanded on to include various forms of capital (Bourdieu, 1991), which translates as a type of power or currency; a system of exchange in social situations. I will explore the concept of cultural capital in more detail later in this book, for now what Norton means is that:

> If learners invest in a second language, they do so with the understanding that they will acquire a wider range of symbolic and material resources, which will in turn increase the value of their cultural capital. Learners expect or hope to have a good return on that investment – a return that will give them access to hitherto unattainable resources. (Norton, 2013: 50)

This sadly gives a rather transactional feel to the processes taking place in the language classroom, but it would certainly be naïve to insist that such acquisitive reasoning is not existent, if not indeed prevalent, in the learning situation. Norton insists that investment is different from extrinsic motivation, but again this will be discussed in more detail in later chapters. However, the main point is that there is a strong conceptual link between identity and motivation, and as usual the concept of authenticity seems to sit somewhere in the middle.

Although identity research is a thriving field of inquiry, it is also a multidisciplinary area with many diverse strands of thought. However, as Van De Mieroop and Clifton (2012) have noted, one 'unifying thread' that runs throughout current identity research is social constructionism. In other words, it is widely agreed that identity is not simply an individual trait but something dependent on social situations, broken down, reconfigured and reconstructed depending on different contexts. Since authenticity as a construct directly relates to the Self, it is therefore essential that any definition of language authenticity takes account of context, which is why I present authenticity as a continuum with both social and contextual axes in Chapter 5.

The social side of authenticity

Much of the discussion that I covered in the previous section on identity overlaps with the ideas I will review here, therefore I will try to limit the focus of this section to concepts that relate to learning and teaching specifically. However, the social side of authenticity also entails a much broader view as well, especially when discussing English language learning. This will be the main theme of Chapter 3, looking at Global English. At the moment it is necessary to connect the dynamic, socially constructed individuality of our learners' authentic selves with the socially mediated process of language learning. A particularly important concept here is what van Lier (1998, 2007) refers to as an ecological perspective. Van Lier was following in the still-strong tradition of sociocultural theory, which is an idea that sits on top of much of the work I present in this book. Sociocultural theory is built on the work of Lev Vygotsky and his pioneering research which led us to see learning as an essentially socially mediated process. These ideas have informed a great deal of the work in SLA, and therefore I only briefly mention it here as it was certainly a starting point for van Lier's discussion of ecological perspectives. The word 'ecology', van Lier clearly explains, was 'invented by Ernst Haeckel in 1866, to refer to the study of the relationships between an organism and all other organisms with which it comes in contact' (van Lier, 1998: 128). For van Lier, an ecological perspective to language learning means that 'consciousness and language, all elements, great and small, play an equally crucial role in the processes of learning' (1998: 138). Ecological perspectives are very much complementary to chaos/complexity theory and dynamic systems approaches (Tudor, 2003), in that learning needs to take place in a flexible, one would say *organic* environment where people socially co-create understanding and engage in personal meaning-making.

In the previous section I mentioned my Japanese teacher who changed my writing to reflect a more standard version of Japanese, one which I found at odds with my own idiolect and my emerging L2 self. Perhaps I should have listened to my teacher though, since she was a successful speaker with a shared sociolect which others would recognise as standard Japanese. However, I was not trying to be recognised as a speaker of standard Japanese. I want to fit into Japanese society, but I have no delusions that I can ever be identified as Japanese, and no desire to give up my British citizenship. This is because I feel I am accepted into Japanese society because of who I am. I play a role in society here, and I represent access to foreign culture from within Japan. Unfortunately, as a result I live in a sort of 'English bubble' that I have trouble breaking out of. My Japanese language ability allows me to read a menu, even catch the gist of a newspaper headline (about 40% of the time) and to read simple texts and stories. If I need to understand a more complicated document I need a dictionary and a few hours – usually I do not have the hours to spare and so the document goes un-read until someone asks me about it. However, I am still a long way from satisfied with my own communicative ability, and yet I have been in Japan for almost four years now. I recently came to see my lack of success as the fault of the vacuum I have created around my learning. I used to take private lessons from a

Japanese tutor (the one who bruised my idiolect). These lessons were mainly conversational, and there was only me and the teacher present, taking lessons in a quiet local café. There was no connection between me as a learner and the wider society with which I wish to integrate. In order to overcome this, I started writing a blog in Japanese, which I would publish and share on social networking sites. Many of my own students were able to see my blog posts and suddenly I felt a lot more connected with the language. I found that I was proud of my ability, and this pride acted as a confidence booster and made me throw myself into more social situations, which I might otherwise have felt unprepared to deal with. In my history as a learner, the events that stand out the most for me are the ones where I had a specific problem to solve in a social situation. Therefore, most of my learning seems to have taken place outside of the classroom and in the context of the target language use community. This means that most of my experience as a learner is rather opposite my experience as a teacher. As a language teacher I work with classes of between usually 15 and 30 people, mostly first-year university students. My teaching is very much institutional, whereas my own language learning has happened primarily in informal, social (non-institutional) settings. However, both my learning and teaching experiences are essentially attempts to bridge the social reality with the content used for learning, but with marked contextual differences.

Much of my teaching career has been characterised by my desire to bridge the gap between the classroom situation and the wider social context in which my learners can interact as themselves using the target language. For example, when I worked in London I would ask learners to create questionnaires and go onto the streets to speak with people who had nothing to do with the school. The task was designed to facilitate a reason for the students to interact with other people, and this could be quite challenging, even when living in a target language speaking country. Here in Japan, the situation is even more challenging. And yet I feel I have managed to incorporate authenticity into many aspects of my lessons. One practical example, which I would like to share here to illustrate the somewhat abstract issues in this chapter, comes from a course I taught at a Japanese university. The course was entitled *Discussions on Contemporary Topics* (DCT) and in the class I asked students to produce a collaborative video project related to one of the issues we looked at over the course of the semester. This was a class of students from the English studies department, all of whom had advanced proficiency, many of them being returnees who had lived abroad. My only stipulation for the project was that it somehow 'went beyond the walls of the classroom'. Although every group produced great final projects, the one which really sticks in my mind, and I would say became the starting point for my quest to understand authenticity, was a group of five girls who looked at the issue of world hunger. The group started off by researching statistics about world hunger, which they of course presented in their video. However, this group did not stop there. In the course of their research, they discovered that around 1.4 billion people live on less than $1.25 a day. They found this hard to imagine, and so the students actually tried to live on $1.25 for a whole day, and as part of their video project they recorded their meals. I think this is clear evidence of a level of commitment that certainly went 'beyond the walls of the classroom'. But this was just one part of their project. The group then went on to design badges which they had made especially to sell on campus (see Figure 2.1). By conducting their project, they raised around 5000 yen (about £33) and donated the money to a world hunger charity. The final video project was a documentary of all their efforts combined with their research and images from the internet, which they uploaded to YouTube (see Figure 2.2). They had over 400 views when I last checked, and even several encouraging comments from people around the world.

One of the students sent me an email at the end of the course, in which she explained that, because of the autonomy she had in the course, she was able to pursue something she was personally motivated to do.

> I thought making badges, doing charity, and actually trying to live like people suffering from hunger were the things I've been interested in and the things I wanted to do but never could. So I'm really happy that I had the opportunity to turn that into action. (Student A of DCT, English Major, 2012)

However, I think that this project clearly was very authentic from a social perspective, and the effort and motivation they put into the project is a clear

Figure 2.1 The badge made by the World Hunger group

Existential, Philosophical and Theoretical Underpinnings 27

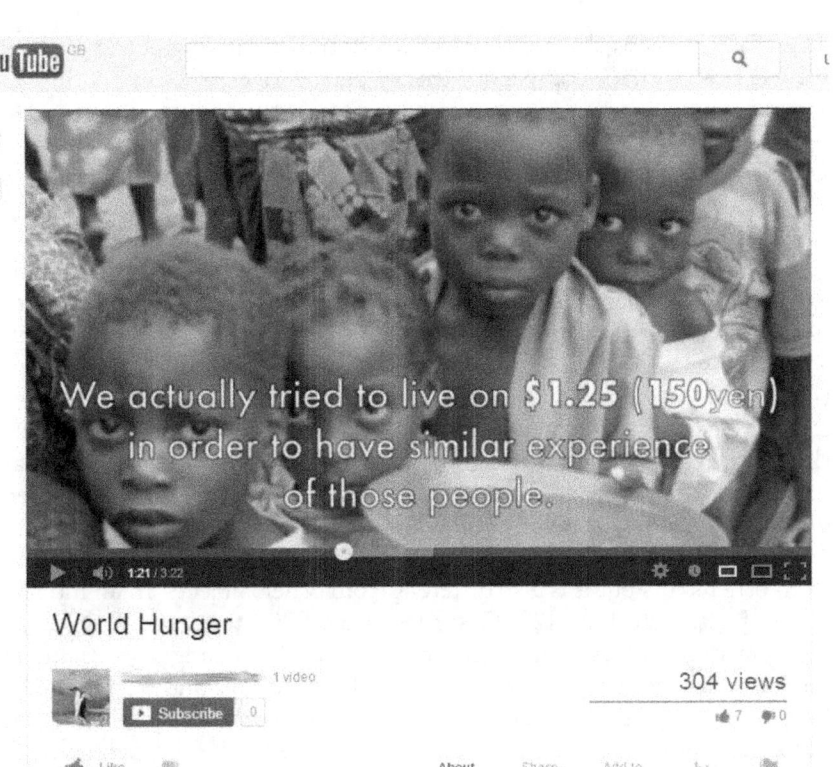

Figure 2.2 A screenshot of the final video project

indication of this. Partly, this magic combination of ingredients was achieved by the aspect of publishing the video online, part of it was achieved through connecting with the reality of the content (in this case, helping people in the world who are starving) and part of it was through the groups' ability to empathise with the situation, putting themselves in the shoes of those who are hungry and reaching out to help them. This, of course, was all facilitated by allowing the students sufficient autonomy to explore the content in their own ways. In this way, the learners have demonstrated that through 'their very engagement with the content and process of learning [...] what they learn becomes part of what they are' (Little, 2004: 106). In the authentic classroom, learners and teachers act together as social individuals, expressing their realities and co-constructing meaning. In order to get this to work, there are a number of dynamic components, interacting and changing as part of a 'personal process of engagement' (van Lier, 1996: 128), which very much relies on the whole and cannot be compartmentalised into isolated parts.

Therefore, perhaps the only way of really understanding authenticity is to view it from a chaos/complexity theory perspective.

Complex Dynamic Systems and Chaos Theory

Another important underpinning to this book is the idea that Mishan (2005) and others have already touched upon when discussing the 'plurarility' of SLA theories. That is the idea that there is no simple explanation or single panacea method for language learning, and that language learning is a process with multiple dynamic interactions rather than a simple property that can be 'learned' in the traditional sense. In other words, when one learns to drive a car, although through experience one might become a better driver, the main reason for learning to drive is to get a licence. Once we have a licence, we are said to 'be able to drive' in the legal sense, and from then on we are allowed to get behind the wheel of a car and drive around. Language learning is a fundamentally different endeavour, and it is not only different from other skills but it is also different from other subjects. In an interesting piece of research, Borg (2006) surveyed over 200 teachers, both language teachers and teachers of other subjects. He found that language teaching was seen as a distinct type of teaching, both from within and from outside the field. This is something that has been reflected particularly in the domains of L2 motivational research, which has developed quite independently from its parent discipline of psychology (Dörnyei & Ushioda, 2011). Another reason for the distinctness of language learning as a subject is perhaps the interdisciplinary nature of language teaching, and it is for this reason that chaos/complexity theory is particularly interesting as a concept that has great relevance to SLA in both teaching and research.

An important concept which is gaining momentum in the fields of SLA and applied linguistics is the idea that certain phenomena are constantly changing as a result of the dynamic nature of their constituent parts. There are several theories which overlap in this area; chaos theory (Larsen-Freeman, 1997; Menezes, 2013), complexity theory (Larsen-Freeman & Cameron, 2008a) and dynamic systems theory (de Bot, 2008), as well as the idea of complex adaptive systems (N.C. Ellis & Larsen-Freeman, 2009). These theories have developed recently from other fields such as biology, physics, economics, business management, psychology and even meteorology (see Larsen-Freeman & Cameron, 2008a for an overview). Although there are subtle differences between each, I will refer mainly to chaos/complexity theory and the idea of complex dynamic systems in the discussions throughout this book. First of all, it is important to note that the words 'chaos' and 'complexity' have a specific meaning in this context. Complexity means something more than just complicated or difficult, the defining attribute of a complex dynamic system is that behaviour, results and outcomes are the product of the interaction of its component parts. For example, an engine has many parts, and one might say it is complicated. However, an engine is not a complex system because (despite what a car mechanic might have told you) its behaviour is predictable and takes place in a controlled context. The weather is an example of a complex dynamic system because its components are multiple and in constant change, making it hard to predict its behaviour. Indeed, studies in the weather done by a meteorologist named Edward Lorenz are one of the antecedents to the emergence of chaos/complexity theory (Larsen-Freeman & Cameron, 2008a). Another example of a complex dynamic system is language (N.C. Ellis & Larsen-Freeman, 2009). The second term which needs to be defined is chaos, usually understood to mean something like random or lacking discipline. In the context of chaos/complexity theory it means that, owing to the large number of variables, behaviour is virtually impossible to predict (Larsen-Freeman, 1997; Larsen-Freeman & Cameron, 2008a). So, a teacher might describe her class as chaotic, but it is not quite the same meaning as chaos theory, which looks at modelling and understanding 'non-linear dynamical systems ... [which] are susceptible to even minor perturbations' (Larsen-Freeman & Cameron, 2008a: 4). Because of the fact that a small change can have a very significant impact and because the outcomes are non-linear, it is impossible to predict the behaviour of systems in chaos. Although Larsen-Freeman and Cameron generally use the term 'complexity theory', I will use the earlier term 'chaos/complexity theory' throughout this book, because I prefer the word 'chaos' and I find it useful as a reminder that when dealing with individuals (learners and teachers), certainly at the classroom level interactions are so complex and dependent on multiple factors that behaviour is impossible to predict. A well-known example of chaos theory is known as 'the butterfly effect', first coined by Edward Lorenz (1963) and probably based on a metaphorical example which was used in Ray Bradbury's short story 'A Sound of Thunder' (1952). In the story, set in the year 2055, a big game hunter named Eckels travels back in time to hunt dinosaurs, and is warned not to stray from his designated path. Of course, the hunter goes off course and accidentally crushes a butterfly. When he returns to his own time the world is completely altered. Although the story appeared 10 years before Lorenz's theory, it is most likely a coincidence and not related to the reason Lorenz chose that title for his theory (Stewart, 2011). It could also be that Lorenz was inspired by the Lorenz attractor-generated diagram, which resembles a butterfly. Either way, both the theory and metaphor have become part of popular modern culture, even spawning a film of the same name and a parody in the popular cartoon *The Simpsons*.

It seems like a cliché to say that chaos/complexity theory is by no means straightforward. It is anti-reductive, it embraces the unknowable nature of certain processes and therefore often necessitates a retrospective line of inquiry rather than a predictive one. It sounds rather abstract and very theoretical, but theory exists to explain real-world phenomena. A fundamental premise underlying chaos/complexity theory is that processes are in constant flux, that they undergo various change states and possess certain self-organising principles. Complex dynamic systems cannot be understood by building up a compartmental understanding of each constituent part, but they must be approached as a whole, and therefore context, time and change must be accounted for as well. Larsen-Freeman and Cameron state that applied linguistics would be 'well served with more dynamic models'.

> This is because a static algorithm cannot account for the continual and never ending growth and complexification of language as it is used and as it develops. [...] Complexity theory offers us an approach to understanding systems in change. It affords us a way to preserve the notion of a system without reification. By putting time and change back into our systems, we have new ways of understanding processes of using and learning language. (Larsen-Freeman & Cameron, 2008a: 97)

When I first read about chaos/complexity theory I could instantly see how these ideas would be helpful in describing the work I do in my classroom. This is not because my classrooms are disorderly or because I employ complicated tasks, but because I am interested in the motivation of my learners. Motivation is also a complex dynamic system, and this idea is making big waves in the field of L2 motivational research (Dörnyei *et al.*, 2015; Dörnyei & Ushioda, 2011; Kimura, 2014). Although it does not help us align our teaching to any particular methodology, the practical implications are that whatever the lesson plan or learning aims, changes need to be observed and responded to as they emerge because 'any particular moment in a lesson can be rich with learning potential and some directions to take may be better than others' (Larsen-Freeman & Cameron, 2008a: 198). This is connected with the idea of intuition (T. Atkinson & Claxton, 2000), awareness (van Lier, 1996), receptivity or basically being able to make decisions based on our experience, knowledge and beliefs about how something should be done (Gieve & Miller, 2006). This is a socially mediated process, and so when a teacher decides to allow more time for a task that students are enjoying rather than push on with her lesson plan, this is something acknowledged by chaos/complexity theory. Larsen-Freeman and Cameron connect this to Dick Allwright's idea of 'quality of life in the classroom' (2003), a concept that is at the heart of exploratory practice research. So, complexity theory validates awareness and responsiveness, reflection and interaction in practice. From a methodological perspective, it would seem to equate well with what Allwright and Bailey call *receptivity*, characterised as 'a state of mind that is open to experience' (1991: 157). It also connects well to research methods which are more situated in the process of teaching, such as exploratory practice and narrative inquiry. Narrative inquiry places great importance on context and situating research and individuals within a story environment that allows for a deeper understanding and therefore a more accurate analysis (Barkhuizen, 2011, 2013; Barkhuizen *et al.*, 2014; Johnson & Golombek, 2002; Pavlenko, 2007). Larsen-Freeman and Cameron state that 'a complexity theory view sees the individual and context as coupled' (2008a: 8), and this made me think of narrative inquiry being a good way of describing complex phenomena in the classroom and in language learning more broadly. Larsen-Freeman and Cameron also advocate Ema Ushioda's *person in context relational* view of motivation (Ushioda, 2009), and they extend it beyond motivation to the field of SLA in general, saying that research in the field tends to lack sufficient focus on individuals (2008a: 152–153). So this theory has quite important implications for research and practice in that it adds support to teaching practices which promote awareness and receptivity, prioritising interactions between people – individuals in a social setting. It also encourages research that seeks to understand people in relation to context, and to understand processes holistically. It allows us to bring together some of the disparate theories of SLA which have 'hitherto developed independently of one another' (Kramsch, 2011: 10).

If learning and teaching and researching is about quality of life, this means one aim of learning is to make it personal and rewarding for its own sake, which connects with Csikszentmihalyi (1997) and motivational flow theory, the idea that learning should be its own reward since this will lead to higher engagement and more sustained focus and thus the likelihood of maintaining the activity is higher since motivation certainly has a fluctuating temporal aspect, meaning it goes up and down over time and is never static (Dörnyei & Ushioda, 2011; Ushioda & Dörnyei, 2009). In this view, the 'classic' definition of authenticity is clearly far too reductionist, quite aside from the problems it has of being imbedded in culturist assumptions. It is for this reason that a reconceptualised view of authenticity as a continuum is perhaps the most compatible model for explaining the construct as it relates to such dynamic factors.

Because I view authenticity as something that is dependent on both individual and social aspects, a non-constant factor which is unique and individual but at the same time shared, I think that authenticity is a dynamic component in a complex system. I would not at this point say that authenticity is a complex dynamic system in itself, but rather a *part* of one. However, because the concept of authenticity is rather broad I believe it belongs to more than one such system. It may, at this point, be useful to summarise why these ideas are important, since on the surface they seem to describe something which is perhaps self-evident. Of course motivation is dependent on a number of psychological and contextual factors and always has been. Of course language is a system made up of other parts, such as syntax, lexis, phonetics and pragmatics, which change all the time as they evolve and adapt to contextual variations. Why do we need another 'complex' sounding theory to describe all this? The reason is that complexity theory aims at understanding the whole phenomenon, even though that understanding may never be complete. Complexity theory aims to realistically acknowledge and embrace this concept rather than over-simplifying and assuming that processes can be 'converted into objects' (Larsen-Freeman & Cameron, 2008a: 1). In many ways, I think this defines one of the main issues with authenticity in language learning and this represents exactly why a reconceptualised view of authenticity, particularly from the perspective of English as a global language, is important now. Authenticity has been defined in numerous ways throughout the literature (Gilmore, 2007a) and the theoretical discussions and practical implementation of authenticity are problematic and riddled with contradictions and pitfalls (Mishan, 2005). Perhaps it will help us to understand the idea more if we take a long step back and try to see it as something which moves, which changes depending on how you look at it. The basic idea is that what is authentic to one person is not necessarily authentic to another, and this is for a number of social, contextual and individual reasons. I think that by acknowledging complexity in authenticity we are actually able to simplify it again by seeing it holistically, and by avoiding reductive definitions which have thus far proved difficult to pin down.

Conclusion

It is important here to take stock of what, probably for many readers and indeed for myself, has been a very tortuous and 'complex' journey through the hostile environment of multiple abstract interdisciplinary theories from decades of research literature. At this point, many of these ideas may not seem to connect directly and yet the problem is that many of them merely overlap. However, I think that all of these ideas are of central relevance to language teaching and second language acquisition, because they provide a way of conceptualising the language learning process as a set of dynamic interactions, between individuals in society, constantly shifting and changing as they are influenced by micro- and macro-level considerations.

In summary, this section has been an attempt to trace the existence of authenticity as an existentialist concept in SLA literature, language teaching in practice and more generally in language learning as a whole. I have attempted to present the rich seam of work relating to existential philosophy's conception of authenticity running through SLA literature, which at times overtly, but more often implicitly, referred to authenticity in the existentialist sense. As I stated earlier, the concerns of the existentialists were not solely the realm of lofty intellectuals. They were worried about authenticity and self in a world and society which was rapidly changing its values and way of doing things. In many ways, although the existentialists are no longer fashionable or contemporary, their concerns about the nature of self and individuality as it relates to society are more apt than ever. One of the reasons for this is, of course, globalisation, or (if one finds that term overused and vague), as Canagarajah (2013) eloquently puts it 'a form of transnational connectedness, which scholars have labelled *modernist globalisation*' (2013: 25). This is the next destination on our quest to understanding authenticity.

3 English as a Global Language

Introduction

To say English is the world's second language is rather like stating that the Earth is round; perhaps at one point people may have held a different view, but that time is past. English is the world's only hyper-centralised language, as de Swaan (2001) calls it, English is a 'life skill' (Graddol, 2006) and the traditional hierarchies of English are being flipped upside down (Jenkins, 2015: 177–178). Thanks to powerful voices in the now various discussions about English's international status, more power and recognition is being awarded to diverse varieties of English and the focus is moving away from 'native speaker' dominated or 'standard' varieties. And yet, at the same time things are not moving quickly enough. There is still too much emphasis on the 'native speaker' and the truly international voices of this diverse language are all too often marginalised. Global English is a story of two sides; a bitter matrimony of power and convenience and also a hopeful metaphor for global human collaboration. Into the midst of this turmoil I would like to focus on the way authenticity is being lost and rediscovered from the perspective of English as a global language. I will first examine the history and meaning of globalisation; an overused and somewhat ambiguous term, mention of which seems to be almost a mandatory requirement in modern publications on language acquisition. I will then examine the discussion on Global English and World Englishes, again taking a historical overview which attempts to trace to what extent the idea of authenticity is compatible. I will then talk about the concept of native-speakerism and the damage that this has done to English teaching and English language learning. Finally I will discuss the issue of affect as it relates to Global English, moving on to a discussion of authenticity and international models.

Globalisation and English as a Disembodied Language

The term *globalise* first appeared in use amongst economists as early as the 1930s, found its way into the Merriam-Webster dictionary in 1951, but it came to a wider audience when Theodore Levitt (1983) wrote an article for the Harvard Business Review entitled 'The Globalisation of Markets'. The term 'globalisation' was intended originally as a negative statement, and although in the context I first encountered it I thought it must be a good thing, it is actually very much a double-edged sword.

> Government policy-makers sometimes attribute their country's economic woes to its onslaught, environmentalists lament the destructive impact of its onward march and advocates of indigenous communities blame the disappearance of smaller cultures and minority languages on it.
> (Ramanathan et al., 2009: xi)

Globalisation is synergetic with commerce, with economies of scale, with expanding populations and the demand for everyone to have access to the same things others have. Levitt (1983: 92) cites the genocide of the Nigerian-Biafran war where televised news coverage showed soldiers carrying blood-stained swords while listening to the radio and drinking Coca-Cola, perhaps to show the juxtaposition of products and ideologies that globalisation brings. However, despite globalisation having distinctly positive and negative connotations, as a language teacher I have always thought of it as a positive, even a desirable thing. The reason is because I associate globalisation with Global English. Entrepreneur Jay Walker (2009) asks in his TED.com video lecture whether English is a tsunami, washing away other languages. I have used this video often in my teaching, not just to provide a sample of 'authentic' listening but also in order to elicit my student's opinions of English and encourage them to reflect on why they are learning the language. This is a process I find essential in gauging their intentions and learning aims when English is, for many students, a somewhat disembodied language. By this I mean that English comes not with a single culture or even a single variety. Whereas many other languages are spoken across various communities and cultures, and although there are other global languages (such as Spanish, Arabic and French), English is certainly the language that is most often learned as a foreign or second language around the globe (V. Cook & Singleton, 2014). As a learner of Japanese for example, I am in some ways lucky because I know that only one country speaks Japanese. Although it is true that there are many varieties of spoken Japanese, and the culture of Japan is not a straightforward thing to grasp, at least I know that I am learning the language mainly in order to speak to Japanese people and to integrate into Japanese society. This is not so for learners of English; not only is English used as a *Lingua Franca* around the world, but also not every learner of English needs or wishes to integrate into an English speaking community. This was something that Matsuda (2011) found was echoed by Japanese high school teachers in her study, where many teachers highlighted that really their main aim in teaching English was to get their students able to pass exams, and that competence in the language was something very few of the students would actually need. In certain contexts this is now a defining aspect in the learning and teaching of the English language. Jay Walker goes on to conclude that English is not a tsunami, but rather English allows people to join a global conversation about global problems, such as climate change or poverty. He says 'English represents hope for a better future – a future where the world has a common language to solve its common problems' (Walker, 2009). I suppose that it was in watching this video many times with different groups of students that I started to ask myself more about my students' motivation to learn English, and as part of that I began to wonder what content or materials I should use to help them. If English is the world's second language, what would be an authentic example of English? Was this video of Jay Walker from TED.com 'authentic'? It features an L1 speaker who has been voted by *Time Magazine* as one of the '50 most influential business leaders in the digital age', but is this an authentic example of English in use? Is this authentic material? I selected this video for use in my classes precisely because my answer was 'yes', but I wanted to analyse more deeply what I felt made it authentic and whether my students would agree. One of the main things I felt that made this video authentic was that it was dealing with the concept of Global English, and it made the students reflect on their reasons for studying a language with the potential to allow them to be part of a 'global conversation'.

Global English

In the following sections I will outline in more detail some of the arguments arising around international uses of English. My discussion will not focus much on English as a *Lingua Franca* (ELF), as this type of language use is inherently authentic. In fact, the 'reality' of many ELF encounters is often very high stakes, and 'where ELF is the only means of communication available, [...] its use may well be, quite literally, a matter of life and death' (Seidlhofer, 2012: 146). Therefore my focus is on authenticity within mainly institutional learning settings and how it can be achieved, despite the fact that authenticity in the language classroom is 'bound to be, to some extent, an illusion' (Widdowson, 1990: 44), a theme I will also return to later and attempt to refute.

The Global English debate has grown exponentially in the last few decades, and now there are a number of sub-fields and overlapping acronyms which, as Rod Ellis (2008) said more generally of SLA theory proliferation, shows that the field is healthy and full of life. Before getting into the discussion I feel I should explain the terminology I will adopt, and give some historical background to the discussion. Usually in this book I refer to Global English to mean the English language as a global phenomenon. By this I mean the worldwide spread of English language education, with particular emphasis on the learning of English as a second or foreign language. I realise this does not exactly narrow the term down, but I wish to make a distinction here between World Englishes, which are the varieties of English spoken around the world, particularly in contexts where English has some official status. In this way, the Singaporean variety of English, known as *Singlish*, is a World English, whereas Global English refers to the fact that English is used, spoken and learned all over the world. Other terms such as ELF and English as an International Language (EIL) will be defined later when they arise in the discussion. The relevance of these areas of inquiry to SLA is hard to ignore, although in some respects it *is being* ignored (Canagarajah, 1999a; Holliday, 2005; Pinner, 2014b; Suzuki, 2011). And, herein lies one of the central tenets to this book; the idea that on the one hand we have English as a global tool for communication, used and understood and accessible to everyone, and on the other hand we see English education being magnetised towards and by the 'native speaker', as discourses around authenticity tend to gravitate towards the centre of Galtung's Centre/Periphery distinction (Blommaert, 2010; Holliday, 1999; Pennycook, 1989, 1994; Phillipson, 1992; see Chapter 6 for further discussion). Many languages are used for international communication, such as Swahili in Africa, Hindi in India and Arabic in the Middle-east. Still many languages are used as *Lingua Francas*, with French and Spanish being common examples. This is of course not even a recent phenomenon, in fact Cicero wrote his philosophical works in Latin rather than Greek partly as a way of making Greek philosophy accessible to a wider audience, and partly to show that Latin was not, as some of his contemporaries believed, an inferior language which was incapable of expressing higher trains of thought (Harlow, 1998). Here, Cicero was using Latin as a *Lingua Franca*, which indeed it was for thousands of people under the Roman Empire. However, English now has a special status in the world of international language use, to the extent that de Swaan (2001) has labelled it the world's only hyper-central language, which means it occupies the top position on his *Hierarchy of Languages*.

The Quirk–Kachru debate

Although the issue of World Englishes can be traced back as far as Prator (1968), who was one of the earliest scholars to argue the case for second-language models of English being used for teaching, for this section I will start at one of the most defining moments in the Global English movement, or the World Englishes debate. Perhaps the most famous exchanges to bring the issue of World Englishes into focus were the discussions between Kachru and Quirk in the journal *English Today*.

Braj Kachru, a Kashmiri scholar of linguistics, posited that a pluricentric look at the way English was learnt and taught around the world was desirable in order to validate other varieties and reflect the way it was spoken around the world. He put forward a diagram of three circles of English (1985, 1988) which was designed to reflect the reality of English usage around the world (see Figure 3.1). He pointed out that:

> Linguistic interactions in English are now of three types: native speaker and native speaker; native speaker and non-native speaker, and non-native speaker and non-native speaker. The non-native speakers not only outnumber the native speakers; they also increasingly use English of different varieties in cultural contexts not traditionally associated with the language. Kachru (1988: 3)

Kachru pointed out the two possible views of the diversification of English.

> A variationist looks at this diversification and its implications as a blessing. However, for a purist or a pedagogue it is a nightmare. And both have their reasons. The sociolinguist may derive satisfaction from the

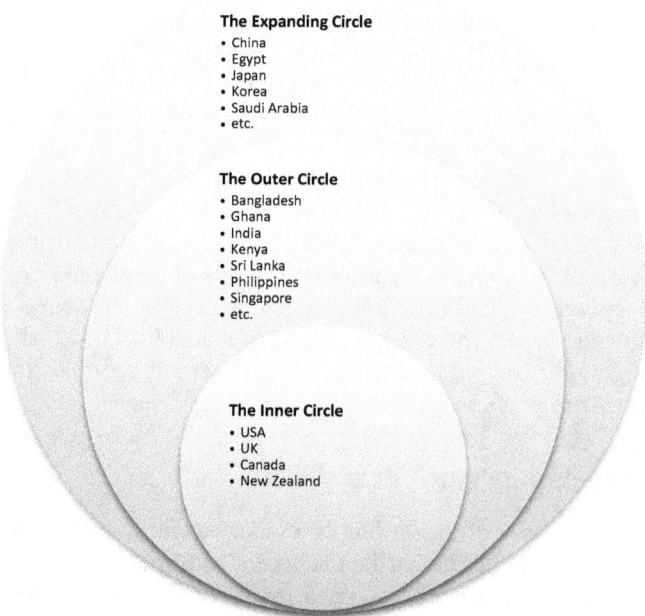

Figure 3.1 Kachru's circles (1988; adapted)

fact that, at last, we have an international language which provides access across cultures and national boundaries. The purists view the diversity as a mark of divisiveness, as a sign of the decay of the language, and perhaps more upsetting, as a threat to Eurocentric, Judeo-Christian ethos of the language. And therein lies the controversy. (Kachru, 1988: 3)

Kachru's argument was famously taken up by Sir Randolph Quirk, a distinguished linguist who, with David Crystal and others, had worked on the Survey of English Usage in the 1960s – one of the first ever corpora in linguistics which predated computers and went on to help form one of the first descriptive grammars based on English in actual use, *A Comprehensive Grammar* (Quirk et al., 1985). The communications between these two scholars on the World Englishes debate drew a lot of attention internationally, with Quirk (1990) claiming the need for a single, standard variety of English as oppose to Kachru's call for recognition of a diverse set of equally valid Englishes. Quirk proposed a taxonomy of varieties of English, which put an emphasis on the use and functions first, then moving on to the actual speaker. However, his distinction still fell down to 'native' or 'non-native' speakers, two terms which the Global English movement and many modern language teachers, including myself, find highly problematic (Canagarajah, 1999a; V. Cook, 1999; A. Davies, 2003; Paikeday, 1985).

Quirk's taxonomy has not been as widely accepted as Kachru's concentric circles have. Kachru's circles are generally acknowledged as 'the most widely accepted as the model with the best "fit" for English' (Mesthrie, 2008: 30). As Seargeant (2009: 10) succinctly explains, 'The basic battle here is between pluricentrism (Kachru [...]) and monocentrism (Quirk [...])'. Seargeant goes on to point out that paradoxically the two scholars were both advocating very similar things but in very different ways. Both Kachru and Quirk had at the heart of their argument a concern for L2 speakers to be validated and to have improved social mobility and career prospects. Quirk believed that to do so, speakers must adopt a recognised or 'monochrome standard' (Quirk, 1985: 6), whereas Kachru claimed that English should be celebrated for its diversity and suitability as 'a flexible medium for literary and other types of creativity across languages and cultures' (1988: 8). However, as Seargeant points out, both were advocates of a single, international language, mutually understandable by L1 and L2 speakers alike – namely Global English.

The Quirk–Kachru debate served as springboard for others to add their voices, and now over 20 years later the debate has many various strands and divisions of opinion. British scholar David Graddol criticised Kachru's concentric circles for placing the inner-circle or 'native' speakers in the centre, implying that they still retain the main power and ownership of the language. He proposed a slightly reworked version that places the L2 users in the centre and attempts to '[make] it easier to see how the "centre of gravity" will shift towards L2 speakers at the start of the 21st century' (Graddol, 1997: 10). Later,

Graddol elaborated on the importance of English as a second language, again pointing out that English no longer belongs to those who speak it as their L1. He noted that:

> 1950, over 8% of the world's population spoke English as their first language; by 2050 it will be less than 5%. ... The future status of English will be determined less by the number and economic power of its native speakers than by the trends in the use of English as a second language. (Graddol, 2003: 157)

Other researchers and scholars who have made important contributions to the discussion include Jennifer Jenkins and her colleagues (Cogo & Jenkins, 2010; Dewey & Jenkins, 2010; Jenkins, 2004, 2006; Jenkins et al., 2011), who often work with corpus analysis to describe the interactions of L2 speakers in an ELF setting. Jenkins is most noted for her work on the *Lingua Franca Core* (2000, 2005), which sets out to find the essential phonological components required for L2 speakers of English to be mutually understandable to one another by looking at samples from L2 discourse, with specific emphasis on misunderstandings. Jenkins focuses on the phonological components of ELF, but other scholars are also working on different aspects of the language, such as pragmatics (House, 1999) and lexicogrammatical features (Cogo & Dewey, 2006, 2012; Seidlhofer, 2004). The work on ELF is very promising as a field, with many scholars using corpus analysis to accurately describe how English is used among L2 speakers and predict and validate language changes instigated by L2 users. For example, the marking of the present simple third-person –S, which is peculiar to English and rather unlike many other languages in the world (Trudgill, 2002: 104), might not even be worth teaching to students as it does not affect meaning and it is usually one of the last patterns for learners to be able to acquire and use. For example, if I say 'he go to the shops each day as he travel to work' it is unlikely that my meaning will be lost because I failed to add the third person –S. Trudgill (2002: 92) describes the third person –S as 'afunctional' and Breiteneder (2005: 5) goes so far as to call it 'communicatively redundant'. Findings in ELF discourse from corpus analysis may lead to a radical and, more importantly, descriptive reorganisation of textbook grammar presentation and curricula, focusing on learning what students need to know first in order to survive in English and for learners to be comprehensible between both L1 and L2 speakers. This could have rather large implications for 'authentic materials' if learning materials and taught lessons were to incorporate ELF language usages.

It would be interesting to work out which side of the Quirk–Kachru argument came out on top. Despite Kachru's being the most widely cited model, I will show later that Quirk's (1985) 'monochrome standard' still holds a lot of political power. What certainly is clear is that a small number of textbooks and publishers are now incorporating L2 model speakers into their materials and hailing them as 'authentic' (see section 'Authenticity and international models' in Chapter 3 for further evidence).

Global English is closely associated with other terms, such as International English, World Englishes or English as a *Lingua Franca*. There is a central idea behind each of these concepts which tries to take the emphasis away from native English speakers and give more power and flexibility to people who use English as their second language. According to Graddol (1997), over a decade ago there were 375 million native English speakers and 750 million people who speak English as a second language. Crystal (2003) estimates that for every four people in the world who speak English, three of them will speak English as a second language, and he later revised his estimate to 2 billion English speakers (2008). It is likely that the numbers are now stacked even higher in the L2 speakers' favour. This has lead scholars such as Crystal (2003); Kachru (1991, 2006); Kachru and Thumboo (2001); Nunan (2003); Graddol (2006, 2007); McKay (2002); Matsuda (2012) and Alsagoff *et al.* (2012) to argue that the way we learn and teach English should reflect the fact that there is no longer a clearly defined set of 'native speakers' who have ownership over the language or can say with any certainty whether a particular usage of the language is 'correct' or not, such as third person –S. Hu (2012) also argues that this should be incorporated in the way the English language proficiency is tested, since such tests work as 'gatekeepers' to access greater forms of cultural capital (Jenkins, 2014; Kanno & Norton, 2003; Norton, 2013). Therefore the idea of Global English is to have a more flexible approach to using the language and to give more power and ownership to second language learners. The concept is opposed to linguistic imperialism, thus promoting a more democratic understanding of the language. This could be in terms of phonological, lexicogrammatical or even pragmatic usage of the language.

I fundamentally agree that the way we teach and present models of English for learners should reflect the international status of how it is spoken by the majority of its users. I see the validity of each different type of English and I agree that 'the second-language varieties of English can legitimately be equated with mother-tongue varieties' (Bolton, 2008: following Prator, 1968). I also acknowledge that in EFL contexts such as Japan where I live and teach, there still needs to be a certain amount of consistency between the varieties in order for them to be comprehensible. For me, the primary aim of my teaching is for my students to be able to understand and to make themselves understood. I also want them to be validated as speakers, by others and by themselves. Each student will probably have a very different reason for studying and a different goal, and their motivation will alter and fluctuate over time and for a myriad of reasons (Ushioda, 1996). A central justification underlying this book, and the function of reconceptualising authenticity from a Global English perspective, is to gain a better understanding of the experience of learners and teachers of English and how they view their own identity in relation to the concept of authenticity. Therefore, in order to truly become successful speakers of English, even lower-level learners need to have a sense of entitlement to the social capital that access to English can provide. In other words, learners of English need to take more ownership of the language.

Ownership and the Pareto Principle

The 80–20 principle, also known as the Pareto efficiency, is the theory that 20% of cause can lead to 80% of effect. For example, it is estimated that roughly 80% of the world's wealth is held by 20% of the world's population (J.B. Davies *et al.*, 2008). So, it was no surprise when Canagarajah (2005) reported that 80% of English language teachers are L2 or non-native speakers. Further, with an estimated 2 billion L2 and only 375 million L1 speakers of English in the world, the 80–20 principle looks very relevant to English language teaching in the current era of accelerated intercultural interaction, and there is an imbalance here as well. Much as the wealth distribution seems unfair, especially for so much to belong to so few, there is also a persistent imbalance between the status of language ownership. In my opinion one of the reasons for this is the concept of authenticity. This imbalance is felt most sharply among language teachers:

> Fresh from graduate school, certified with a Masters or a doctorate in applied linguistics, and groomed for a career in language teaching by a reputed university, the non-native ESL teacher often discovers a gloomy professional future. This story confronts us with the absurdity of an educational system that prepares one for a profession for which it disqualifies the person at the same time. There are many ironies and contradictions here. (Canagarajah, 1999a: 77)

Canagarajah composes a sophisticated and honest attack on the gatekeeping practices of educational systems and institutional prejudice, and he specifically aims his attack at the practices of the West. His argument is validated by Jenkins' (2014) work in which she examines just how truly 'international' international universities are. The crux of her argument is that to enter into a university programme (one usually claiming to be 'global' and 'international') students must pass entry requirements for English proficiency which are measured by tests based on the so-called 'standard' variety of English. It seems that despite the power of Kachru's voice and the fact that this area is thriving in terms of research, sadly it seems to have made little impact in the reality of Global English as it is experienced by those who wish to engage with it. It seems that although Quirk's (1985) 'monochrome standard' idea was less popular within the academic community, there is a lot of political power behind such an idea, particularly in terms of cultural capital.

Why is Global English still essentially directed by a 'standard', 'norm-providing', 'monochrome variety', even when such terms have been proved to be untenable countless times? The problem is not simply a matter of the West maintaining the supremacy of the BANA (Britain, Australasia and North America) (Holliday, 1994b) varieties as being 'correct' or 'best'. Kramsch (1997) talks about how non-native speakers actually have certain privileges, although she fully acknowledges the fact that things are not stacked in their favour. Conversely, many L2 users elevate the 'native speaker' and in doing so they *create* the prejudice against themselves. In language teaching contexts, this is done specifically by being self-conscious of language usage errors (Moussu & Llurda, 2008), a process Reves and Medgyes (1994) have labelled 'self-discrimination'. Such practices reduce the L2 teacher's self-image, which subsequently damages actual language performance in many cases, creating a downward spiral in teacher self-efficacy, self-image and motivation. The claim is that although so-called 'native speaker' teachers of English often make language usage errors or are unable to answer a question about grammar, this rarely impacts on their self-image, whereas when a non-native English teacher makes a mistake or reveals that they 'do not know everything about the English language, their teaching abilities are often immediately questioned' (Moussu & Llurda, 2008: 323). This prejudice might in some cases also extend to the world of international publishing. It can therefore be difficult for non-native speakers to publish research, which was brought to attention in a famous study by Flowerdew (2001), who looked at attitudes of journal editors to non-native speaker varieties. Flowerdew interviewed 12 prestigious journal editors associated with the fields of applied linguistics and English language teaching, and found both positive and negative aspects expressed in the editors discussions of contributions from non-native English speakers, although generally editors were 'sympathetic' to those writing in a second language and 'supportive', although they did not divulge in any official policy as such (2001: 129). Editors also discussed the role of the reviewers, and several gave accounts of 'harsh' comments, recommendations that the manuscript be proof-read by a 'native speaker' or even 'disparaging comments about NNSs' language competence' (2001: 132).

Other evidence from the language classroom is even more concerning, for example Lasagabaster and Sierra (2005a, 2005b) discovered that students learning English in expanding circle contexts often show a preference to be taught by, or at least to learn, native speaker varieties. Suzuki (2011) looked at three student teachers in Japan who underwent a teacher education module aimed at raising awareness of other varieties in English and tried to, as Graddol (1997) would say, 'shift the centre of gravity away' from British and American varieties. However, Suzuki found that despite having positive views towards other varieties, the teachers concluded that they would not use outer-circle or expanding circle models in their teaching because it might confuse the students, or they were still viewed as being 'incorrect'. It is my belief that such 'language error nit-picking' and elevating the status of so-called 'native speakers' stems from the central concept of authenticity, as authenticity is a vital and established aspect of the language teaching tradition (Gilmore, 2007a). It seems that the concept of authenticity is in need of being realigned in order to offer a more inclusive concept which incorporates L2 speakers of English more overtly.

Within the culture of the English language classroom, authenticity remains culture-bound (A. Matsuda, 2003; Suzuki, 2011; Tan, 2005), and perhaps as a result there is still very much a gap between native and non-native speaker teachers of English.

> The native speaker still has a privileged position in English language teaching, representing both the model speaker and the ideal teacher. Non-native speaker teachers of English are often perceived as having a lower status than their native-speaking counterparts, and have been shown to face discriminatory attitudes when applying for teaching jobs. (Clark & Paran, 2007: 407)

This gap is very real, and yet those on either side of it (native and non-native speakers) would seem to be non-entities, since the terms 'native' and 'non-native speaker' are problematic, non-descriptive and vague (V. Cook, 1999; Paikeday, 1985), leading Davies to label the term both myth and reality (2003). It is for this reason that realigning the concept of authenticity to fully include L2 varieties is essential in order to move the mainstream of EFL learners and teachers into a position that aligns with the current status of English as an international language.

Native-speakerism

As I have already mentioned, the concept of the 'native speaker' is contentious, emotive and hinges on a distinction that is basically useless; both a myth and a reality (A. Davies, 2003, 2004), or as Paikeday (1985) memorably phrased it, *the native speaker is dead*. The 'native speaker' is mainly used to refer to L1 speakers of English, reflecting the hegemonic dominance of English as a foreign language teaching (Creese *et al.*, 2014: 938). Despite the problematic nature of even the term 'native speaker', there is another even more serious problem at the heart of this discussion, which is best known as native-speakerism (Holliday, 2003, 2005). Native-speakerism is the term for acknowledging the fact that there is an ingrained culturism running through the entire field of English language teaching; a deep vein of prejudice which flows toward the idea of 'native speakers' of English, somehow elevating the 'native speaker model', usually at the expense of those for whom English is a second language. However, there are also times when the native speaker teacher is negatively affected by native-speakerism (see for example Houghton & Rivers, 2013). The basic point of native-speakerism is that this is an endemic problem within the ELT industry.

Several notable scholars have attempted to tackle the uselessness of the 'native speaker' label, with unfortunately little impact. For example, over 25 years ago Rampton (1990) suggested the term 'native speaker' should be dropped, offering alternatives along the lines of 'expertise' and 'inheritance'. Vivian Cook prefers the term L2 speaker to 'non-native' speaker because the state of being a native speaker is unalterable. He points out that saying many learners fail to achieve a native level of proficiency 'is like saying that ducks fail to become swans' (Cook, 1999: 187). However, it has also been pointed out that seeing 'non-native' as a negative term indirectly assumes the superiority of the 'native speaker'. Turning the argument on its head, Paul Kei Matsuda claims that in examples such as non-smoker and non-toxic, the non- prefix loses any negative connotation.

> It is not really the non-part that people find unfortunate. For nonnative to be a pejorative term, its counterpart would have to be positive. Nonnative is unfortunate because native is supposed to be fortunate. Nonnative is marked, whereas native is unmarked. Nonnative is marginal, and native is dominant. Nonnative is negative, and native is positive. If anything needs to be changed, I do not think it is the term nonnative. Rather, it is the assumption that native is somehow more positive than nonnative that needs to be challenged (P.K. Matsuda, 2003: 15)

The term 'native' has been used as a derisory term in some contexts (think savages or barbarians) and a positive term in others. It is native-speakerist to assume that non-native speakers will be offended by their non-ness (Edge, 2011; Holliday, 2005). The issue of authenticity is linked to legitimacy, power and authority, and the idea of the 'native speaker' is heavily implicated here (Creese *et al.*, 2014). As I found in a study based on Japanese High School teachers of English, being an L2 speaking teacher of English is sometimes viewed almost like a handicap, and this can negatively affect the teachers' self-efficacy and self-image. I found this to also have an important impact on the teachers' concept of authenticity. In a study in which I conducted a one-day training workshop for in-service Japanese high school teachers of English, I tried to understand more about how non-native teachers viewed the concept of authenticity by asking them to write a reflection paper (see Pinner (2014a) for a full description of the study and methods). One participant, who I will refer to as Keiko, provided a classic response which confirmed my fears that for many of the participants they (as non-native speakers of English) did not see themselves as being able to provide an authentic model of English.

> Before I took this lesson, I thought that authenticity should be 'native'. I mean that the material should be written by native speakers. (Keiko, Osaka 2013)

This comment was typical of the participants on the course, and proved that although L2 speakers themselves, the participants held native-speakerist biases and prejudices which detrimentally affected their own self-image as teachers. Japan has been shown to be a context where such prejudices are strongly enforced by certain sociological factors (Houghton & Rivers, 2013; A. Matsuda, 2003, 2011; Seargeant, 2009, 2011). Some of the participants in my study, such as Momoko, held native-speakerist views at first but rejected them after the workshop, perhaps because the more international definition of authenticity which I promoted as part of the workshop had empowered her somehow.

> Before this workshop I just thought that 'authentic' means 'native'; using a newspaper in English class is better than using a textbook. But now, at the end of the workshop, I can talk more about authenticity, giving my experiences today as an example.... I have felt negative about myself as a non-native English speaker who teaches English. Now, I don't. Authenticity connects me not only to English but also learning. (Momoko, Tokyo 2013)

In the above sample, Momoko makes it clear that she felt authentic language was the sole product of native speakers and that her understanding of authentic materials was something like a newspaper, which I identified as the 'classic' definition of an authentic material during the workshop. This definition excludes Momoko from being an authentic model English speaker, although clearly after the workshop she has altered this definition and now takes a more positive view of her own identity as a non-native teacher of English. However, she does not go into great detail about this and her quick rejection of the old 'native speaker' based definition may not yet rest on a robust and reconfigured new definition with herself at the centre. More follow-up work would be needed to know how deeply the course was able to shift this view.

> My idea about authenticity has changed dramatically by participating in this workshop. Before I joined this workshop, my definition of authenticity was the language material source from native speakers. Now, I have learned what really makes material, lesson to be authentic is how we teacher use it. (Aiko, Tokyo 2013)

In the above quotation, Aiko puts the emphasis on the way the teacher exploits the materials through tasks, in other words the process of engagement which the teacher facilitates. This allowed the idea of authenticity to shift away from culturally embedded concepts and focus more on the way the materials are used, therefore decentralising the inherent native-speakerism of authenticity. During the workshops, the idea of authenticity having relevance to the learners seemed to be the take-home message, and one that was easily adopted and imbibed by the participants. This is probably because trying to make the classes relevant is something that teachers intuitively feel will make their lessons more successful and more motivating.

As mentioned in the previous section, other studies such as Árva and Medgyes (2000), Reves and Medgyes (1994) and Braine (2004, 2010) have found that, quite often it is the L2 or non-native speakers themselves who are critical and view themselves as being lower down on the hierarchy of language use. Either way, it certainly seems clear that attitudes toward the mythical 'native speaker' need to be re-aligned if they are to coincide with more global views of English usage, and the issue of authenticity is deeply implicated in the problem of native-speakerism.

The Affective Effect of Authenticity

Authenticity is a loaded term. If one thing is branded authentic and another is branded as inauthentic, clearly the inauthentic item is less desirable in ordinary circumstances. I would not want to be told that my Swiss watch was inauthentic, or that my relationship with a friend was inauthentic. Likewise, it seems apparent that a student would not want to hear that the language they were producing or learning from was inauthentic either. The extent to which learners and teachers view what they do in class as *authentic* is likely to have a huge affective impact.

Affect is a very important component of second language acquisition and it has a lot to do with motivation and identity. Affect refers to various emotional and psychological factors, which lie in the attitudes and beliefs of learners and teachers. For example, personality traits such as introversion or extroversion fall under the umbrella of affect, as do language attitudes and beliefs about learning. Self-confidence is another term associated with affect, and it is perhaps the complexity of some of the concepts associated with affect that led former president of the American Association of Applied Linguistics, Tom Scovel, to blame the difficulty of interpreting the relationship between language acquisition and the effect on the unwieldy number of variables, describing it almost like a giant carpet 'under which is swept a wide range of disparate constructs and behaviors' (Scovel, 1978: 129). Dare I add the term 'authenticity' to this already lumpy pile? Dr Scovel might be pleased to know that I will not be lumping authenticity under the 'rubric' of affect; however, I think there is a relationship between affect and authenticity and in the next two sections I will attempt to demonstrate how notions of authenticity can influence language acquisition in affective terms because of the strong connotations associated with the word 'authenticity' and because of the even more powerful notions of authenticity as it relates to the Self.

On learning

Learning a language is a long-term endeavour that requires a serious cognitive and emotional investment from the learner in order to succeed. However, the concept of 'being a successful language learner' is as fraught with difficulties as the native speaker vs non-native speaker issue. There are levels of language learning success, and various linguistic competencies such as communicative competence, inter-language ability, vocabulary size and sociocultural awareness to name a few (R. Ellis, 2008). To be a successful learner of a language, a person must have a reasonable ability in all of these areas. Perhaps a simpler definition of a successful speaker would be a person who is able to deal with real situations in the TL. This is the approach taken by the Common European Framework of Reference for Languages (CEFR), which defines language aptitude along a list of Can-Do statements including references to understanding native speakers, following lectures, understanding public announcements and being able to watch films in the target language (Council of Europe, 2002: 234). It seems clear from looking at the Can-Do statements that learners will be interacting in the target language and using it as a tool for communication in much the same way they would use their first language. Thus, the CEFR's Can-Do statements match a rather simplistic definition of authenticity, one which seems to over-emphasise the native speaker varieties as the norm providing model for both linguistic and social models of acceptability. This is fundamentally the assumption that Widdowson (1990: 44) argued against in what he labelled as the *means/ends equation*, in which authenticity is defined in terms of learning aims and outcomes. Authentic language material is a means to an end because the authentic 'real world' is the ultimate destination of the learner. The crux of the means/ends assumption is that learners need to be exposed to authentic language since they will need to comprehend authentic language when they use the target language in actual interactions taking place outside of the classroom, or 'natural language behaviour' as he calls it (1990: 45). So even at its simplest definition, authentic language input is essential to the learner and is part of the criteria for becoming a successful speaker of a foreign language. Of course, the issue is not as simple as that, because many people are learning foreign languages without there being a clear *means to* an *ends*. This is not just the case in English, but also in other foreign languages. When I was a high school student I was obliged by the British national curriculum to study at least one foreign language at school. One of my greatest regrets from my high school days is that I never made an effort with French and can now only just get by at a restaurant, despite several years of weekly instruction. The textbook in our French class was adorned with backpack-wearing and unstylish French teenagers who seemed to belong to a distant, outdated and undesirable universe. Mocking them was about the only interactions that took place in the classroom, of course very little of it in French. Needless to say, English textbooks have also been mocked around the globe for the same reasons, see for example Canagarajah (1993). Was authenticity an issue here? I believe it was. Even though I had been to France and could easily go there again, I had no way of connecting French language and culture with my own personal life at the time. Although now I live even further away from France, I still regret my lack of French and blame myself. But, in retrospect, maybe it was not entirely my own fault that I never worked hard at French. It seems that at least some of the onus should be on the institution and the ministry of education. Some of the blame also lies with the textbook, and perhaps even some with the teacher (although I am sure she did her best). By sharing this example I hope to illustrate that there are many learners who may not even realise that they are interested in learning the language until it is too late for them. These students do not have a way of connecting what they do in the class with their real lives and personal goals. The learning that happens beyond the classroom is highly important to language learning (Benson & Reinders, 2011; Nunan & Richards, 2015), and of course very relevant to the concept of authenticity. As I mentioned at the start of this section, learning a language requires a great deal of time and effort and a sustained motivational push; therefore, if learning is confined to the few hours a week spent actually in the classroom, it is unlikely that any real progress will be made. This is a situation affecting the majority of English language learners around the world, with those who we could label 'expanding-circle' speakers, comprising a conservative estimate of over 80% (Braine, 2010; Canagarajah, 2005). Therefore, it is essential that there is some way of encouraging learners to connect with the language in their personal lives. Even if the country is within swimming distance (as France is with England) and a close linguistic cousin (as French is with English), there is no guarantee that learners will make this connection, and I would argue this is especially the case in formal educational settings where the TL is a compulsory component of the curriculum. I am talking now about situations in which the language is not viewed as a living, growing, socially constructed tool for communities to communicate, but merely as a cold dead subject being taught as part of the curriculum. Because learners do not personally choose these courses and because teachers may have to work towards goals set by larger institutional or national bodies that are aimed at standardisation, viewing anything in this reductive way as an obligatory item to be learned will throw a spanner in the affective works. In other words, both autonomy and authenticity are on very harsh terrain in such contexts and it seems very unlikely that they would flourish, and as result motivation to learn is suffocated except in those few students who have a genuine interest and can motivate themselves despite the lack of authentic input.

This bleak picture can apply in general to much of the foreign language instruction in formal institutional compulsory settings. However, the case is more complicated with English in some ways. Although French is an international language with many varieties such as Canadian and Senegal, even linguistic offspring (such as Haitian Creole, French Guiana Creole and Bourbonnais Creoles), when I wrote earlier of speaking French I was referring mainly to France. This was a natural thing for me to do since the French I was learning would very likely have been intended for use in France. The same cannot always be said of English. Although NS varieties of English dominate instruction, many of the students learning English are planning to use it as an international tool for communication. Learners of English may well visit France and use English there, not French. French people may visit India, Japan, China or Lithuania and the language they are most likely to employ would be English. ELF and the idea of English as a Global Language exercise a profound and important change in the affective beliefs of English learners around the world. This is a language which people are led to believe they will be able to speak *anywhere* and be understood. This language is a key to the world, and it represents an opportunity not just internationally but also on their home soil as well. For example, in countries where the pay is generally lower than developed nations, being able to speak English will allow one to get a job at a call-centre where labour is outsourced internationally. The call centre industry in India was estimated to be worth over 9 billion dollars by 2012 (Yamagami & Tollefson, 2011), and the industry is now so large that other industries that specialise in training Indian call centre workers how to 'neutralise' their accents have started to appear (C. Cowie, 2007; see Morgan & Ramanathan, 2009 for further discussion of this issue). Another example is medical transcription, an industry which is now expected to be worth over 1 billion dollars a year in the Philippines alone (Yamagami & Tollefson, 2011).

In countries where the average wage is too high for such an economic relationship to appeal to people in general, such as Japan, the English language is *still* sold as an economic advantage provider and as a life-skill which will help one to achieve success (Seargeant, 2009, 2011). However, in low-wage countries such as the Philippines, English ability can directly benefit relatively low-level workers, such as those working in call centres or doing medical transcription. These are good jobs in developing countries, but in Japan:

> The major beneficiaries of English language ability [...] are a relatively small number of middle and upper-middle class individuals: employees in international companies, international organizations such as the United Nations, and some non-government organizations [...]. Thus the benefits of 'global English' in Japan are largely limited to a relatively small elite, in contrast to the much larger and rapidly increasing employment of English speakers in low-wage countries. (Yamagami & Tollefson, 2011: 32)

In Japan, success in the language means success in life. This hyperbole manifests itself in reality as a very complex beast, much like the Greek Hydra with many heads. For example, one obvious effect of this portrayal of English as a necessary life skill would mean that there is pressure all the way through the education system; Institutional pressure, social pressure, personal pressure. However, on some level for many students, the English language is not a tangible reality but rather something requiring a certification in order to get a better job. This 'othering' of the English language has been described as self-orientalism (Beppu, 2005; McVeigh, 2002), although this may be an extreme view based on generalisations that Japanese university students are generally hard to motivate to study English (see Apple et al., 2013 for examples). Perhaps English is only a living and breathing, authentic language for those who are already upwardly mobile enough to have had some genuine contact with it already, either through their parent's international work or through expensive international education. Of course, there are many students who are genuinely interested in English and see it as a living, breathing language, despite the paucity of prior contact. These students are, in my experience, the more autonomous and self-motivated ones who have, for whatever reason, been able to successfully conceptualise an imagined community to which they can one day belong. However, due to the abstract global shape of English, quite often this aspiration is simplified to Anglo-American orientations towards the language. As Yano points out 'when we learn a foreign language, we naturally want to understand, speak, read and write like a native speaker. Japanese thus have long learned English as the language of British or Americans, along with the Anglo-American societal and cultural traditions' (2011: 131). This chronic native-speakerism, or as Yano calls it the *native speaker syndrome*, has a negative effect on the Japanese teachers of English, as I will explain in the following section. It also manifests itself in employment practices of English language teachers, with many positions still asking for 'native speakers' (Kiczkowiak, 2015).

In China, the infamous National College Entrance Examination known as the *gaokao* was known for placing great pressure on Chinese high-school students to learn English, which made up a large part of its compulsory foreign-language section. However, recently the ministry of education has decided to alter the test's administration from an annual 'once in a lifetime' model to a less stressful system where the test can be taken numerous times at the student's best convenience with the highest overall score being used (Rui, 2014). As part of this reform the test will also reduce the number of points assigned for English from 150 to 100, whereas the value for Chinese language will rise from 150 to 180. This move is generally greeted with approval from the public, but it has caused a debate among education specialists. However, Rui argues that this move will perhaps mean that there is a greater emphasis on actually learning to communicate, rather than just studying to pass a test. She also points out that learning English 'has been widely regarded as a national, as well as a personal asset' because it plays a vital role in the internationalisation of China and has clear ties to the country's economic development.

The intense pressure to learn English could have both positive and negative affective impacts and I am sure it contributes to the complex issue of motivation in different ways at different times, making it hard to examine empirically. Another manifestation of English as a Global Language is that the issue of culture is blurred beyond recognition. One of my reasons for regretting that I do not speak French is that I like French food and wine and would like to impress my wife by taking her to Paris. I learn Japanese, not to be able to speak to Hawaiian shopkeepers and hotel staff but to be able to speak to Japanese people and to integrate with the culture where I live. Reductive as such a view of culture is, it still represents a valid reason for studying a language. Language and culture are so intertwined as to be inseparable. With English though, this cultural assumption is problematic and complex. Students of English may wish to speak with native speakers of the language, they may wish to visit the USA and buy a book by Raymond Carver and order a Long Island Iced Tea or listen to a speech by the President. However, there are millions of people with just as much claim to the culture of the English language whose culture has nothing to do with the USA or the UK. As an English educator now I feel it is part of my duty to inform my learners that these other cultures exist and that they have a claim on the English language. Also, the wider world is open to those who can speak English. The idea is that only one phrase book is necessary to travel the world. Furthermore, I feel I am more likely to be able to connect English with my student's real lives, and thus get them to 'authenticate' English, if they are conscious of the fact that they do not even need to go abroad to benefit from making progress in the language. This complicated myriad of reasons to study English are constantly simmering away in the minds of learners and because of the complexity, it is actually very likely that rather than being something real and tangible, the reason for learning English becomes mixed up in an ever-changing brew of reasons. It is for this reason that I find Norton's (2013) concept of *investment* a useful one, since for many learners the main and most influential contact they have, at least in their earlier lives, in through instruction in the language. Getting back to my French teacher at high school. She was a British lady who was fluent in French and seemed to be genuinely interested in the culture. Because she was native speaker of English, my memory of the French lessons is mainly that both teacher and students spoke in English and most of the French was confined to greetings at the start and end of class, readings and tape-players. It is no secret that students view their teachers differently depending on whether they are native or non-native speakers (Lasagabaster & Sierra, 2005a, 2005b; Matsuda, 2011). It is for this reason that I now turn to the affective impact of authenticity on teaching.

And teaching

As a teacher of English I have often felt that I am lucky to be from England. However, as an Englishman my identity comprises equal parts pride and guilt. I have had students approach me and tell me that they want to learn English from me because I am English and English is from England. This makes me very unhappy, usually because I instantly feel that this person who wants to learn from me has a very different and incompatible view of the English language. People have told me they want to learn The Queen's English and I nearly always have to inform them that from me they will learn a modified internationalised Yorkshire English hybrid. I would call this positive discrimination and, although positive, it still constitutes as discrimination. To complain too much about this might be counter-productive for me though, since I work in a Japanese university and I am hired because of my high level of English competence and because I represent a foreign (thus international) culture. My Japanese is still only around intermediate level and if I am honest I struggle to make much of a contribution to Faculty Meetings in Japanese. So, this positive discrimination is something I have used to my advantage to secure a good job and one which I feel I owe a great part to from an inherent trait with which I was lucky enough to be born, that of being a so-called 'native speaker'. I often envy non-native speaker teachers because they have walked a much stonier path and as a result they represent better models to their learners. The bilingual teacher also represents an attainable and realistic model speaker which the students can use in the construction of their L2 self, an ideal learner (Medgyes, 1994, 2005; Moussu & Llurda, 2008).

This problem seems especially apparent to me living in Japan, a country which is still validly classified as belonging to the expanding circle. Japan is on the outer-edges of that circle, where contact with English on a daily basis is rather limited, unlike in countries such as, for example, Sweden (Henry, 2013) or Finland, where ordinary television broadcasts are often in English and many schools have courses where English is the medium of instruction (Isokallio & Grönholm, 2007). However, countries where the idea of Global English is still something rather distant or abstract and where native-speakerism is still strong, many students could have a hierarchical structure in their minds concerning speakers of English (Myhill, 2003), and the 'native speaker' sits at the top of that structure (see for example Figure 3.2). The 'native speaker' is seen as the originator of authentic language, or the *most authentic* model (Jenkins, 2015).

However, Jenkins proposes that this hierarchy be reconceptualised, taking into account international communication and bilingualism, as shown in Figure 3.3.

This is an excellent proposal, one which I personally fully agree with. I think very few people who read this book or follow the discussions on

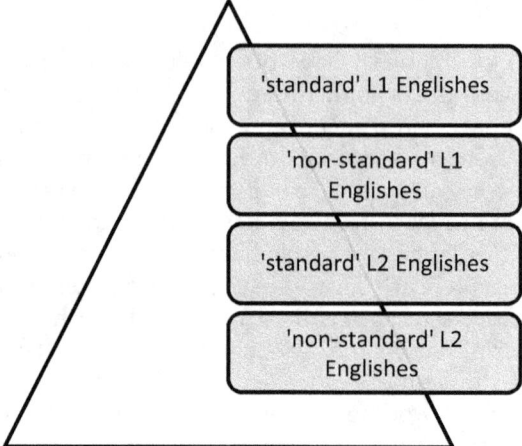

Figure 3.2 Jenkins' (2015) Traditional hierarchy of Englishes, adapted

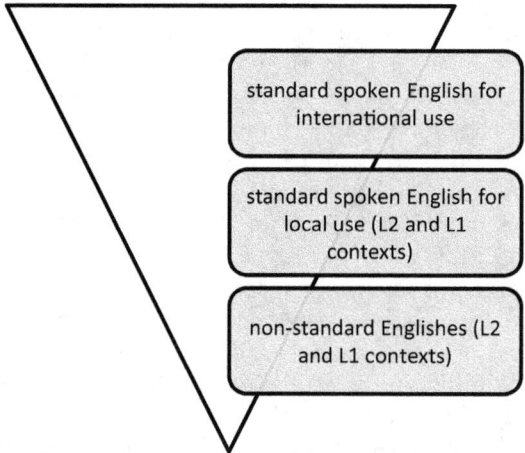

Figure 3.3 Jenkins' (2015) reconceptualised hierarchy of Englishes prioritising international use, adapted

Global English will disagree that this reconceptualisation is something which needs to happen, and furthermore needs to be reflected in teaching strategies and employment practices. However, resistance to this model comes not only from the top down, in terms of those with political influence over educational policy, but also from the bottom up, meaning those who are most directly affected by it, namely students. For example, at an informal round-table meeting set-up for teachers as a forum in a university where I was working, one Japanese teacher of English described his problems with a certain class when he tried to communicate with them in English. He explained that a student had asked him to 'speak Japanese' even though the class was supposed to be conducted in English. I found this challenge to be very concerning and I wondered how many other L2 teachers of English have been ignored by their students because they share a common first language. When I came from London to Japan I moved from teaching in multilingual classes of students from many different cultures to a monolingual classroom environment where nearly all of the students are Japanese. If a non-Japanese person is in the class, they are usually extremely fluent speakers of Japanese anyway. One of the biggest issues for me in making this transition was in getting the students to use English during communicative tasks. Quite often, students would do the tasks I set but using Japanese, which I felt could slightly defeat the purpose. This must be an even more marked issue if the teacher is also a speaker of the shared first language. My method of coping with the issue was to make grater allowances for L1 use and to create a bilingual atmosphere in the class, rather than strictly enforcing the use of English at all times. Most foreign language classes around the world are conducted in two languages I would assume, since 80% of English teachers around the world at non-native speakers (Canagarajah, 2005). However, this does create an issue and also brings us to the question of authenticity and model speakers.

Authenticity and International Models

As George Orwell famously put it in *Animal Farm*, 'All animals are equal, but some animals are more equal than others'. I would like to extend Orwell's clever irony and apply it to language teaching by stating that *All Englishes are equal, but some varieties are more equal than others*. I would like to point out that I do not agree with this, or think it is a good thing, but I am simply stating that in foreign language education the hierarchies of English varieties which Jenkins (2015) pointed out have not yet quite shifted to the more evenly distributed version which she envisioned. Myhill (2003) discusses the existence of an 'authenticity hierarchy' which he equates with the anti-Semitism of Nazi Germany, because it is based on a false ideology assuming the native-language to be one of the central elements of an individual's identity. Myhill discusses the German-speaking Jews who were not seen as true Germans under Hitler's regime, examining the propaganda that made their efforts to speak German seem like an attempt at subterfuge; a devious and intentionally inauthentic act. Myhill argues that although language and identity are linked, this ideology has been abused and he recommends a broader view of identity which is not solely dependent on the first language of an individual or ethnic group. The fact of the current status of English as 'the world's second language' and the continuing empowerment of second language speakers is the main reason why authenticity is coming back to the fore as an important concept that needs to be repositioned according to these global voices.

> English nowadays is just as often used for communication between non-native speakers as it is between native speakers, and this is recognised throughout Global. The 'Global Voices' sections give students the opportunity to listen to a wide range of native and non-native speakers of English. These are all authentic and unscripted recordings, and expose students to real English as it is being used around the world today. (Macmillan, 2010)

This is a particularly enlightening sample in the description to a textbook produced by Macmillan called *Global*, which, in addition to the Global Voices listenings described in the quote, also features materials written by David Crystal which specifically address the theme of Global English. Notice how the description specifically lists 'non-native' speakers as being part of the authentic listening samples. It is in fact made abundantly clear that not all the speakers are L1 speakers and this is presented as being a good thing and as reflecting the way English is used in the reality of a globalised world. Another defining aspect of the way the textbook presents authenticity is that the recordings are 'unscripted', which has connotations of the recordings not being contrived but being natural. Authenticity then, for the publishers of this textbook, means not being contrived and is not limited to 'native speakers'. I will return to this theme later, but I present this quote really to show how strongly connected Global English and authenticity are in language teaching. Textbooks are often criticised for being too generic or conservative (Bell & Gower, 2011; Meddings & Thornbury, 2009), or for being based on 'idealised data' (Tomlinson, 2011b) and so the fact that several major publishers have released textbooks that market themselves as being global and authentic (see also Cengage's *World English* and Hodder Education's *International English*) shows that even 'conservative' publishing companies are now feeling the international force of the second language speaker's voice.

I used this to my advantage when I designed a task for a teacher training workshop which I ran in 2014 at a Sophia University in Tokyo. In order to continue teaching in Japanese schools, every ten years all teachers from primary to high school level are required to renew their teaching licence by taking professional development courses that provide them with credits for renewal. For several years I have taught on one such course, an in-service training workshop for high school teachers of English as a Foreign Language, accredited by the Japanese ministry of sports, education and culture (for some reason abbreviated to MEXT). The course which I taught is entitled *Using and Adapting Authentic Materials to Help Motivate Students*, which is composed of four 90 minute workshops and a one hour assessment. As part of the workshop, I showed videos of speakers of different English varieties and asked the 40 participants to rate them out of ten according to comprehensibility and authenticity (see Figure 3.4).

What is interesting here is that although the British variety (for which I used a sample of Queen Elizabeth II from her 2014 Christmas Speech) was rated as the being the most comprehensible, the variety which the teacher-participants rated highest for authenticity was actually Indian English. This is strange because I thought that the most authentic variety in my opinion for that context was probably the video of Singaporean English, which shows an ordinary Singaporean man taking a busy commute to a sweaty office and having a bit of a hard day. Interestingly, the lowest scorer was the regional variety of British English spoken in Newcastle, known as Geordie. I did not tell the participants where the Geordie dialect came from, but it is certainly clear that not all native speakers are rated as having high comprehensibility or authenticity. However, the results are not particularly enlightening as they are merely quantitative responses from videos which I chose with the express agenda of proving that non-native varieties can provide better models than some native varieties of English.

I also conducted a similar experiment in 2014, in which I asked 25 students from an intermediate Academic English course to listen to different speakers and rate them according to which they felt was most authentic (see Table 3.1 and Figure 3.5). The students were all from different departments taking compulsory English classes which are part of the university wide Foreign Language Studies programme.

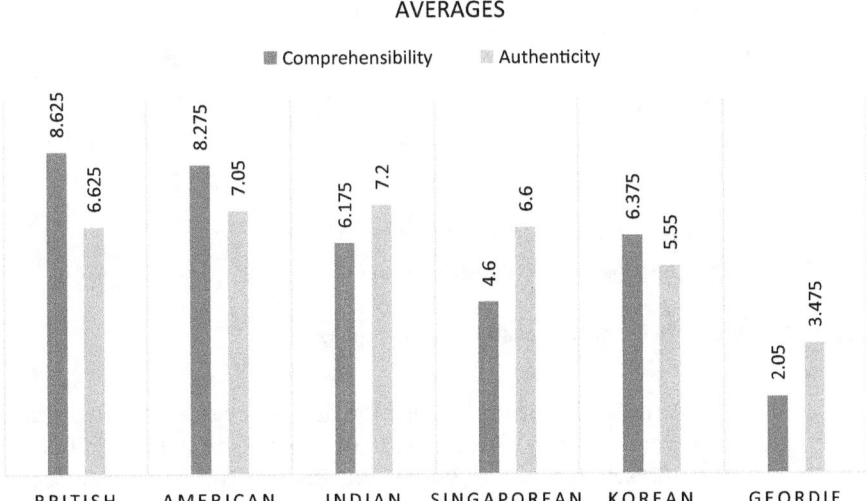

Figure 3.4 Comprehensibility and authenticity rating exercise from teacher training in Japan 2014

58 Reconceptualising Authenticity for English as a Global Language

Table 3.1 Authenticity of the speaker rating activity

No.	Speaker	English L1 or L2	Nationality	Video URL	Average	Overall
1	Ban Ki-moon	EL2	Korean	http://youtu.be/BQeUDcne3IE	5.12	133
2	Shinzo Abe	EL2	Japanese	http://youtu.be/3_FUnfw2grQ	5.77	150
3	Arnold Schwarzenegger	EL2	Austrian	http://youtu.be/EyhOmBPtGNM	8.58	223
4	Barack Obama	EL1	North American	http://youtu.be/ELrUi12cbrM	8.58	223
5	Dynamo	EL1	British (Northern)	http://youtu.be/YOaeXRZYNDs	6.58	171
6	Queen Elizabeth II	EL1	British (RP)	http://youtu.be/6E4v4Dw5Ags	9.00	234
7	14th Dalai Lama	EL2	China (Tibet)	http://youtu.be/1U7DYp6flPc	5.54	144
8	Naomi Watts	EL1	British/Australian	http://youtu.be/6Nd51Cq3deA	7.88	205

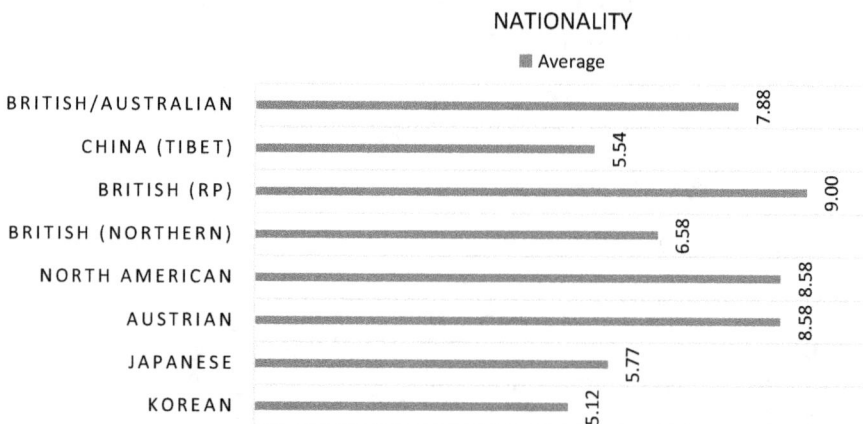

Figure 3.5 Authenticity of the speaker rating activity

This time the research featured a question asking for students to explain their reasons for each answer. One student (who was Chinese) rated Ban Ki Moon as a 4/10 and when asked to explain the reasons for giving that score, the student simply put 'He is Korean'. The same student also self-discriminated when he watched the Dalai Lama's extract, noting the reason for his low score of 3/10 was 'Chinglish'. One other student gave the Dalai Lama a score of 1/10, explaining that 'I don't like him. I think he isn't a gentleman'. Another student also graded the Dalai Lama lowly, giving only a 3/10 because 'He is a suspicious-looking person'. The Queen came out with the highest score here, although I doubt very much that the Queen's English is actually what I would imagine any of my students aspire to sound like, or are likely to encounter in their English-speaking careers. Reasons for the Queen's high score are exemplified by the following comments, with the score they assigned in brackets:

- I want like Queen Elizabeth II. I want to go to England someday. (8)
- Hers is royal. (10)
- Se [sic] is more 'authentic' because she must speak collect [sic] English. (10)
- She is queen. (10)
- She is the queen. (10)
- She's a Queen. (10)
- Because it is official British movie. (10)
- Her native language is English, and her end of a word is not clear. (9)
- Because she spoke dispassionately, so I felt it is difficult to understand what she wanted to say. (5)

As the reader will notice, the results only raise more questions than they are able to answer. However, a clear preference for unrealistic native models is evident here among my students, few of whom had lived abroad although the student quoted above who gave our beloved yet dispassionate Queen a 5/10 had been to Australia for a two-week homestay. The two students in the class who had lived abroad for a longer period of time, attending schools overseas, both assigned the Queen a score of 10/10.

For this task, I selected video samples of four non-native speakers and four native speakers for the purpose of a simple experiment. When I added up the average scores for non-native speaker (NNS) and native speaker (NS) the results are as follows (see Figure 3.6).

I should point out also that this experiment was conducted directly after several lessons in which I explained about the importance of Global English and in which I attempted to empower my learners as speakers of an international variety of English. I think that this shows just how ingrained the preference toward 'native speaker' varieties is. I should also point out that quite a few of the students thought that Arnold Schwarzenegger was a native speaker of American English, although to my ears (and relief) he has retained his trademark Austrian-German accent throughout his illustrious career.

It is not only students on the ground level who want the native speaker model, policy makers and governments also discriminate against their regional varieties. For example, it is interesting that in Singapore, the government issued a ban in 1993 which seemed to forbid the public dissemination

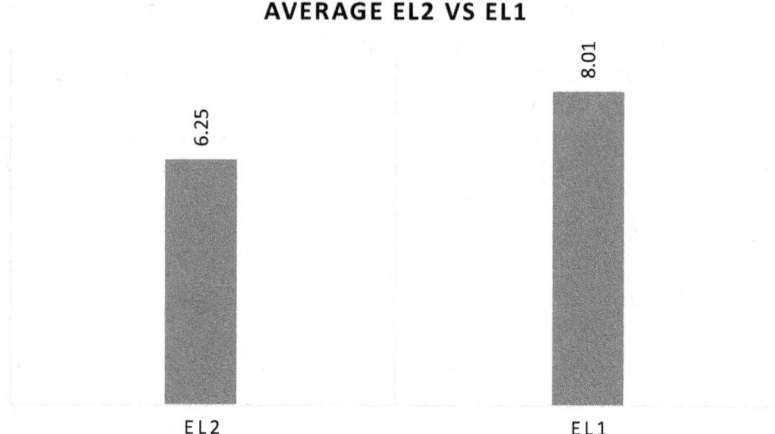

Figure 3.6 Averages for EL2 and EL2

of Singlish on broadcast media, although Singlish is recognised by many linguists as an independent variety of World English (Fong *et al.*, 2002; Gupta, 1994). One blogger (who I learned was a North American) commented that:

> Singlish is no longer allowed on public television or in movies. It is no longer the choice of any of those taking part in the production, distribution, sales, or displaying of a film whether it is allowed to be shown or not. If the film is in Singlish, the government will not allow it to be shown in theatres. (GB-GIL Trans-global, 2002)

Again, I find this quite disturbing as someone who is trying to establish the validity and authenticity of international models of English. A similar case appeared in the news recently, this time in Taipei, where a lawsuit has been filed by a coalition of organisations against the government's ruling that Mandarin should be recognised as the nation's only official language. Headed by Brian Qo, an expert in Hoklo and author of the Tong Long Taiwanese Dictionary and Tsua Gim-liong who is the Taiwanese National Party chairman, the lawsuit was filed on the 29 January 2015 to overturn what Qo said was 'an illegitimate policy, designed by the Chinese Nationalist Party to eradicate the nation's culture, identity and linguistic diversity' (Pan, 2015: 3).

An experiment by Suzuki (2011) found that even with training specifically designed at validating L2 varieties of English as part of a teacher training module entitled *Multicultural Education*, her Japanese teachers of English were very sceptical about presenting such a model in their classrooms (despite being L2 speakers themselves). One of her teachers said that he feared students would be 'disorientated' and, echoing Quirk, said that he felt the students needed a single, standard variety such as British or American English. This not only shows a preference for certain models, but also seems to assume a certain amount of homogeneity within these models, as though British English were one standard which echoes the RP of Queen Elizabeth. These comments have been echoed by both teachers and students I have met in my own experience. Recently, a student of mine submitted a paper in which she argued that:

> Of course, it is important to teach Standard English, because when students study many types of English, they might be confused, but there are also many problems in Standard English. (Student X of Sociolinguistics Class, Foreign Language Major, 2014)

However, a different student from the same class made the following remark:

> Today some people criticize American or British English dominate over the world languages and cultures. Although it is not that learning English itself degrades the linguistic diversity, but how and what kind of English to teach has significant influence on the learners' thoughts. Therefore, if learners are exposed to a wide variety of Englishes at school, they can become aware of the importance of the diversity and free from the sense of inferior to native speakers. This awareness would foster the understanding and respect to other versions of English, as well as their own English. (Student Y of Sociolinguistics Class, Foreign Language Major, 2014)

And yet another student in the class said

> English has spread all over the world through the political powers of Britain and the USA, and although in some cases English as a lingua franca has greatly benefitted people, it has caused several problems concerning diversity within the language. In order to solve these problems, Standard English should be established and spread. (Student Z of Sociolinguistics Class, Foreign Language Major, 2014)

It is very interesting to note just how closely these students' essays and responses to the theme of World Englishes reflect the Quirk–Kachru debate of the 1980s. It seems that, although Kachru is more widely cited than Quirk on the subject of World Englishes, the debate has not been fully settled, at least not as far as my learners are concerned. The implications this has for authenticity are both obvious and unclear. With all of this going on in the wider world, is it possible to make sense of it by looking more closely at how authenticity relates directly to language teaching?

Conclusion

English's position as a hyper-centralised, global language means that it is something of an abstract and yet ominous presence throughout globalised contexts. It is abstract because it is disembodied, not just because various diverse groups have equal claim to its ownership, but also because of the social pressure that learners will experience simultaneously with the already formidable challenge of learning a foreign language. Learners of English know that this is a global language, they know that they 'should' learn it or 'will need it' and they know also that doing so will empower them somehow. And yet, for many people learning English, the reality is that it is just a subject taught at school, a gatekeeper of opportunity and not so much something experienced or lived as a language. On the other hand, there are millions of people who have just as much claim to English as anyone who speaks English as their only and first language. These people may be bilinguals with an English-speaking parent (as my son is) or they may be people who grew up in countries where English has some official status, although it is not their first language *per se*. To talk about authenticity when there is such complexity is to talk about something that is inherently contextual and dynamic. However, although some discussions in the field of applied linguistics and SLA have attempted to problematise the notion of 'native speakers' and yet others have directly connected the issue of authenticity to these discussions, there remains an ingrained culturism in the way authenticity is defined in English language education. One of the reasons for this is that authentic materials are often defined according to their source of origin. Even though for decades the problems associated with the 'native speaker' have been discussed, it is still implicit in the definition of authenticity in language teaching. I will examine this in more detail in the next chapter.

4 Authenticity in Language Teaching

Introduction

It might appear strange to the reader that this section, which would appear to be one of the most important discussions of the book, has been relegated to the fourth chapter. It seems likely that many readers will pick up the book, look at the contents and choose to start at this page. However, the previous sections are important precursors to this chapter, as they greatly undermine many of the established notions of authenticity as it relates to second language instruction. Although I have tried to make each chapter of this volume able to stand alone as a self-contained unit, I would still advise that readers be familiar with the concepts that I established in the previous chapters; namely that authenticity is a term with philosophical implications, deeply related to Self, identity and an individuals' position in society; and that the society in which learners of the English language will find themselves is no longer recognisably the product or possession of countries where English is the first language. Rather, English now belongs to a global movement of people who wish to communicate across cultures and borders. In the previous sections I argued that chaos/complexity theory is perhaps one of the best ways of making sense (or at least attempting to conceptualise the complexities) of the process of learning a foreign language, as well as the multiple and interdisciplinary strands that contribute to the study of second language acquisition. In the light of these developments in SLA, I feel authenticity is in need of an updated examination.

The use of authentic materials has for almost a hundred years been a relatively common place occurrence in the language classroom (Gilmore, 2007a: 98), although Mishan (2005) states that using authentic materials for language instruction is as old as the learning of other languages itself. Authenticity is used often in and around the language classroom, and it can describe either the learning materials used for input, the tasks employed by the teacher or the actual language produced by a speaker. A widely accepted definition, which still holds today, is that authentic language is something which was produced in a context where the language was meant for a 'real' purpose, and that this text or sample has not been modified in any way in order to aid language instruction. Used in this way, authenticity is being applied in much the way it would be to a work of art, a historical document, a Swiss watch or an archaeological find. Golomb states that this version of the word 'authenticity', 'presupposes the existence of a genuine and original product, to be contrasted with potential forgeries' (Golomb, 1995: 5). I have an expensive watch at home and with it there came a certificate of authenticity, which is basically proof that it passed the test of authenticity; that an expert in jewellery has looked at the item and is satisfied that it is not a copy. However, when applied to anything but an inanimate object, this notion becomes highly questionable. Golomb goes on to ask:

> But is it wise to adopt a model from art and apply it to human life and human selves? Who is the legitimate prototype, the paradigm of authenticity? (Golomb, 1995: 5)

Authenticity in language teaching is referred to both in practical terms as a methodologically sound component of learning materials and also frequently mentioned in the research literature, usually in terms of its desirability and the way it can affect motivation and add value to what is being taught. In this section I will attempt to briefly examine the most important developments in authenticity as it relates to language teaching. I will first provide a brief historical overview, tracing how authenticity has been defined and put into practice in language teaching and acquisition. I will examine just how important the concept seems to be by looking at academic journals and publications, while attempting to provide some kind of synthesis of what is a very long and rich history. I will start by examining the meaning of the word and how it relates to another important concept in language teaching; autonomy. I will then look into what I have termed the 'classic' definition of authenticity, which seems to be the most pervasive definition in practice. I will then attempt to demonstrate why this 'classic' definition is so problematic. Following on from this I will examine the numerous definitions of authenticity, which will lead into a discussion of authenticity as an approach, predominantly based on the work of Freda Mishan. At the end I will discuss the problems of researching authenticity, having identified what I refer to as a dearth of empirical research. Given the importance of the concept of authenticity in SLA, it is frankly astonishing that so few studies have attempted to examine authenticity, and those that did have often fallen rather short. Despite authenticity being at the heart of language teaching, it remains elusive, perhaps because most of the discussions about authenticity have tended to originate from sources that inadvertently prioritise culture, or perhaps because of the overall culturism inherent in the ELT industry (Canagarajah, 1999b; Holliday, 1994a, 1994b, 2005; Jenkins, 2014; Pennycook, 1994; Phillipson, 1992, 2009). In the previous sections I argued that chaos/complexity theory is perhaps one of the best ways of approaching the process of learning a foreign language and the multiple and interdisciplinary strands that contribute to second language acquisition. In the light of these developments in SLA, I feel authenticity is in need of an updated examination.

Historical Overview and Development

The less-popular sibling

The word *authenticity* derives from the Greek words *auto,* meaning self, and *hentes,* meaning doer or being. In the mid-14th century, the word came to mean that something had the property of being factual, and since the 18th century *authenticity* has contained the modern implication that the item being described is factual (not fictitious), real or genuine (Harper, 2013). Right down to its etymological roots then, authenticity is closely related to autonomy. Autonomy is made of the same Greek root, *auto-* and *nomos,* meaning custom or law. Both words are of great relevance to language teaching and neither is likely to be unfamiliar to teachers. But the two words seem very different and are not usually directly associated with one another in language teaching, rather like estranged siblings, although some scholars such as Little *et al.* (1988), van Lier (1996), Widdowson (1996) and Holliday (2005) Little *et al.* (1988) have made the connection. Both autonomy and authenticity are part of the language teacher's everyday vocabulary. Autonomy is something we try to foster, it is something teachers cannot just enforce within their learners; it has to come from the learners' own volition. Autonomy is the 'capacity to take control' (Benson, 2013b: 61) or 'the ability to take charge of one's own learning' (Holec, 1981: 3) and it is a complex psychological construct, somewhat abstract but definitely vital to practice. Authenticity, its etymological sibling, is viewed entirely differently among much of the language teaching community. Authenticity is something generally attached to one of four distinct domains: it refers either to the tasks being used by the teacher to facilitate learning, the linguistic output or production arising from the classroom, or authenticity could refer to the actual language in use, generally taken to mean real communication between speakers outside of a classroom context. And finally, of course, authenticity can refer to the materials being used in the classroom as input. It is partly thanks to these different domains that there is still a lot of confusion over the definition of authenticity, as they tend to overlap.

Neither authenticity nor autonomy are simple concepts, but both play a vital role in language learning and teaching, and both are concepts that are at least familiar to most teachers. However, whereas autonomy has special interest groups (SIGs) and newsletters devoted to it, authenticity is less prevalent in the mainstream of language teaching. Authenticity is quite often just something people talk about in the staff-room. For those interested in autonomy, there is the AILA Research Network on Learner Autonomy, the IATEFL Learner Autonomy SIG, the Independent Learning Association, the International Society of Self-Directed Learning, the Japan Association of Language Teaching (JALT) also has a Learner Development national SIG and there are numerous dedicated journals and newsletters, on top of which are the European grant-funded research that occurred in the 80s and 90s (see Benson, 2013b: 243–249 for an overview). Whereas autonomy is the subject of a number of monographs and edited books, the word 'authenticity' generally receives less attention. As I mentioned in the introduction to this book, in a State-of-the-Art paper for *Language Teaching,* Alex Gilmore (2007a) cites 240 works, but of these only 29 specifically mention authenticity in the title. As I showed in Chapter 2, books that do specifically list authenticity in their titles and limit their focus to the theme of authenticity have tended to take either an existential approach that focuses on the theory or a practical approach in which ideas for lessons or descriptions of methodology are presented. Some of the most important work on authenticity arises as part of a discussion on other topics, like many of Widdowson's books in which he discusses authenticity in the light of the communicative approach.

Another example of authenticity being neglected comes in passages such as the following:

> The issue of authenticity has been proved to be somewhat controversial, and there is no space here to go into the complexities of the argument. (McDonough *et al.,* 2012: 27)

Straight after this sentence the authors refer the reader back to Mishan (2005). I do not mean to criticise this book on ELT materials, but I find it notable that the book (which is over 300 pages) clearly does not have the space to go into the issue of authenticity, and I think in some ways the authors are suggesting that delving into the issue would not be constructive. Despite this, I have found another 37 instances of the word 'authentic' in this book, used in a variety of ways. The book I just cited from is primarily a *practical* book, and for that matter so is Freda Mishan's, although she does attempt to bridge theory and practice by covering both in some detail, as well as explicitly stating on page ix that she is trying to break away from the practical/theoretical genre division. Books that deal solely with authenticity from a *theoretical* perspective are still fairly unusual in the literature on second language acquisition. However, as Gilmore's citation list proves, many works in applied linguistics and SLA deal with authenticity, albeit somewhat indirectly.

In establishing that autonomy is the more popular sibling of authenticity I am attempting to address what could be one of the causes for the confusion surrounding authenticity. Whereas autonomy has been defined in much the same way for several decades, enjoying a body of research which has been able to make explicit connections with motivation (Gao & Lamb, 2011; Ushioda, 2007, 2011c) and language acquisition (Benson, 2013b; Little, 2004), authenticity still seems to evade definition. Indeed, in some ways authenticity is indefinable by definition, or it at least 'resists definition' (Golomb, 1995: 7). So, it is hardly surprising that there is no Authenticity SIG or a dedicated journal about it. I feel the problem may be that authenticity does not exist as a standalone concept, but rather it is part of a set of inter-related dynamic components, which all play an important role in the acquisition of a foreign language. This misunderstanding of the nature of authenticity manifests itself in definitions which are untenable, especially in today's environment of superdiversity and cross-cultural interaction (Blommaert & Rampton, 2012; Blommaert & Varis, 2011). I think in many ways that the main culprit in this misconception is the 'classic' definition of authenticity.

The 'classic' definition

> Some teachers assume that they can achieve the purposes of communicative teaching simply by giving learners an authentic text, or engaging them in authentic discourse. They seem unaware that authentic materials can appear 'unauthentic' to learners, just as unauthentic materials can appear 'authentic'. In practice, the extent to which materials appear authentic to learners seems to depend very much on how they are presented to them. (Lee, 1995: 323)

Authenticity in language teaching has become something of a paradox. Teachers and textbook writers seek authentic content to build lessons and materials around, despite the 'classic' definition of authenticity being tied to the 'real world' or basically 'not the classroom'. I have mentioned the 'classic' definition several times in this volume, and now I will attempt to justify it now and establish how *established* this classic definition is. First of all, in the Longman *Dictionary of Language Teaching and Applied Linguistics*, now in its fourth edition, 'authentic materials' are defined as something 'not originally developed for pedagogical purposes' (Richards & Schmidt, 2013: 43). 'Authenticity' is then defined as having been taken from 'real-world sources' and then the example of a newspaper is given. Furthermore, this definition seems to be, at least in my own experience, the one favoured by language teachers. Two recent observations from my personal experience come to mind, both of which are reliably documented in my teaching journals and in other texts. The first is the fact that I was asked to write some materials for a new course being offered by our department from next academic year. The departmental memo which contained the brief for the materials specifically stated that we should use 'authentic' texts, and examples of possible sources were listed, including: advertisements, brochures, newspaper articles and magazine articles. The second recent example from my own experience is a recorded discussion for the podcast *TEFLology*. The regular hosts of the show invited me to do a guest section all about authenticity. At the start of the section I asked the hosts 'what do you understand by the word "authenticity"?' to which they replied 'things that reflect the real world', 'train time tables' and 'basically something that's not designed for students'. The criterion that seems to be most widely accepted then for something to be labelled as authentic material is that it be from the 'real world', which by implication seems to suggest that the classroom is not part of the 'real world' and also that the material is something not designed to be used in the classroom, which would therefore imply that its purpose was something 'more authentic' than language teaching.

Jeremy Harmer's highly practical book *The Practice of English Language Teaching* is now also in its fourth edition (the first one having coming out in 1983). Having won the 2007 HRH Duke of Edinburgh English Speaking Union Award this volume is very familiar as a resource book for both in-service and pre-service language teachers. Harmer defines authenticity as 'real' language and he defines authentic material as:

> [L]anguage where no concessions are made to foreign speakers. It is normal, natural language used by native or competent speakers of a language. This is what our students encounter (or will encounter) in real life if they come into contact with target-language speakers, and, precisely because it is authentic, it is unlikely to be simplified or spoken slowly. Authentic materials which have been carelessly chosen can be extremely demotivating for students since they will not understand it. (Harmer, 2008: 273)

It seems evident from this that the 'classic' definition is widespread and within it there is an embedded culturism and implied (or possibly even explicit) mention of the native speaker. Even though L2 models of English have long been recognised as valid (Bolton, 2008), even to the point of being used to sell textbooks (as I have established in Chapter 3 with the quote from Macmillan's *Global* series), when it comes to the idea of authenticity, the native speaker definition is hard to get away from (Holliday, 2005, 2006; A. Matsuda, 2003; Pinner, 2014b, 2015; Suzuki, 2011). Teachers generally view L2 varieties as non-standard and thus confusing or irrelevant, having a lower social status. This is not a view put forward only by those for whom English is a first language, but also by students and teachers who are L2 speakers themselves. If people hold the view that 'standard' English is the best model, it follows that such people would also view authentic English as being the product of native speakers too. This is still the case, despite the strength of English as an International Language and the associated movements within applied linguistics, such as ELF, World Englishes and so on. As I stated in the previous chapter, it seems that 'All Englishes are equal, but some varieties are more equal than others'. However, now I would like to examine how to change this, and more importantly, why we should want to.

Getting back to the 'classic' definition of authenticity, I would like to add that Harmer, even in a relatively brief description of authenticity, still feels the need to explain that 'deciding what is or is not authentic is not easy' (2008: 274) and provides examples which clearly show that he feels learner speech is authentic and that some things, such as a play, can be both authentic and inauthentic at the same time. By touching on the complexities even in his concise and practical definition, I think he highlights again the need for synthesis, and shows that even the most practical definition is fraught with complexities. At the crux of the reconceptualisation of authenticity is the central tenet that authenticity is a dynamic component with both social and individual properties, which belongs to a complex dynamic system that permeates through every stage of the second language acquisition process. Therefore, the concept of authenticity will necessarily support numerous definitions.

The Numerous Definitions of Authenticity

Alex Gilmore's (2007a) article provides an in-depth overview of the complicated and rich history of authenticity, which has been a useful reference point for my own inquiries into authenticity. Although his paper deals with many other issues surrounding authenticity (including the issue of World Englishes and motivation), here I will only briefly outline a small aspect of his paper, in which he identifies the numerous definitions of authenticity that have arisen over time from the research literature. Gilmore identifies eight inter-related meanings, which are:

(1) the language produced by native speakers for native speakers in a particular language community (Little *et al.*, 1988; Porter & Roberts, 1981);
(2) the language produced by a real speaker/writer for a real audience, conveying a real message (Benson & Voller, 1997; Morrow, 1977; Nunan, 1989; Porter & Roberts, 1981; Swaffar, 1985);
(3) the qualities bestowed on a text by the receiver, in that it is not seen as something inherent in a text itself, but is imparted on it by the reader/listener (Breen, 1985; Widdowson, 1978, 1979);
(4) the interaction between students and teachers which is a 'personal process of engagement' (van Lier, 1996: 128);
(5) the types of task chosen (Bachman, 1991; Benson & Voller, 1997; Breen, 1985; Guariento & Morley, 2001; Lewkowicz, 2000; van Lier, 1996);

(6) the social situation of the classroom (Arnold, 1991; Breen, 1985; Guariento & Morley, 2001; Lee, 1995; Rost, 2002);
(7) authenticity as it relates to assessment and the target language use domain (Bachman, 1991; Bachman & Palmer, 1996; Lewkowicz, 2000);
(8) culture, and the ability to behave or think like a target language group in order to be recognised and validated by them (Kramsch, 1998).

(adapted from Gilmore, 2007a: 98)

I have developed a simplified diagrammatic version in order to help summarise these definitions, and to show how they contribute to and contradict one and other (see Figure 4.1).

Notice how the very first of Gilmore's collected definitions frames authenticity as deriving from the L1 or 'native speaker' realm. For a long time, this definition was accepted as the unchallenged norm. Perhaps this is because it is only relatively recently, say in the past 20 years or so, that more precedence has been given to the voices of the international community who speak and use English daily as their second language. As I have already established, previously the 'classic' example of authentic materials was to obtain a newspaper from the target-language culture and to use that in class in some way, either for linguistic analysis or for a debate of some kind around current affairs. While newspapers certainly can be authentic, they are not necessarily the archetype of authenticity. Furthermore, newspapers force us to question the concept which for a long time was the bedrock of authenticity; the idea of the target language culture. In framing authenticity from the realm of the 'native speaker' we automatically presume that there exists some kind

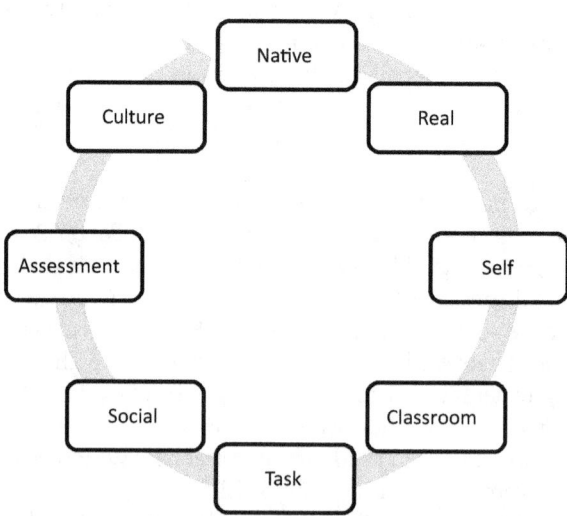

Figure 4.1 Summary of Gilmore's eight inter-related definitions of authenticity

of target culture from which examples of 'authentic' language can be extracted and then presented, preserved and still with their authenticity intact, to our learners. This falls under the definition of what Hung and Victor Chen refer to as extrapolation approaches. They point out that such an approach assumes 'similarity between abstracted concepts and the actual phenomena' (2007: 149). This is something that Widdowson (1978), Breen (1985) and van Lier (1996) have also commented on; the idea that authenticity cannot be absolute, and must therefore be seen as something relative to the learner's individual nature. Authenticity is a product of the learners' interaction with the text. The cultural foundation for the definition of authenticity has proved to be unstable now, because we no longer, or indeed never did, reside in a world where culture is clear-cut and where samples of language can simply be picked like fruit from the single tree of the target culture. Pavlenko notes that cultures are increasingly homogenous in certain respects because they 'continually influence each other' (2002: 280), and therefore it can be difficult to draw distinctions between one culture and another using such binary notions.

Classroom vs 'reality'

It is clear from Gilmore's definitions that ideas of authenticity have been evolving as the world took English more and more as its second language. Important developments such as ELF, Global Englishes and the empowerment of L2 speakers, have clearly had an influence on the concept, which was for a very long time grounded on assumptions about the nature of culture and especially believed to be the sole domain of the native speaker. Many of these shifts are indeed particular to the English language as it became 'hyper-centralised' (de Swaan, 2001). Gilmore's definitions offer a useful opportunity to take stock of what exactly is meant by the term 'authentic', which is so often used in and around language learning. Authenticity is seen as important; however, I think it seems to either become over-simplified and distorted (as with the 'classic' definition) or discussed into a dead end where the validity of the entire act of teaching comes under fire (see van Lier, 1988; Widdowson, 1978). Gilmore provides a glimpse of the frustrations involved in trying to gain a firm theoretical footing with the concept when he asks whether the term has become 'too elusive to be useful' (2007a: 98). Gilmore overcomes this difficulty by choosing to ground his inquiry based on Morrow's definition, that authenticity is 'real language produced by a real speaker or writer for a real audience and designed to convey a real message' (1977: 13). Here Morrow uses the word 'real' as oppose to what he calls 'imaginary', meaning made-up or fabricated for teaching or 'illustrating [...]specific language points' (Mishan, 2005: 12). Gilmore, thus following Morrow, decides that this allows the criteria to be limited to something objectifiable, therefore becoming more conceptually manageable. Although it is certainly useful to keep the definition grounded in tenable concepts, the definition of authenticity becomes untenable again when examining the use of the word 'real'. It seems to me that, although certainly useful, as a term 'reality' is still rather elusive. Distinctions have been drawn already between 'real' language that takes place outside the classroom and 'genuine' language that is brought in from outside and possibly adapted to suit the learning environment. Henry Widdowson (1978) famously makes the distinction between *authentic* materials and *genuine* materials. Here, genuineness relates to an absolute property of the text, whereas authenticity is relative to the way the learner engages with the material and their relationship to it.

> We read what is relevant to our affairs or what appeals to our interests; and what is remote from our particular world we do not bother to read at all. To present someone with a set of extracts and to require him [or her] to read them not in order to learn something interesting and relevant about the world but in order to learn something about the language being used is to misrepresent normal language use to some degree. The extracts are, by definition, genuine instances of language use, but if the learner is required to deal with them in a way which does not correspond to his [or her] normal communicative activities, then they cannot be said to be authentic instances of use. Genuineness is a characteristic of the passage itself and is an absolute quality. Authenticity is a characteristic of the relationship between the passage and the reader and it has to do with appropriate response. (Widdowson, 1978: 80)

Under this view, it might in fact be impossible to bring any degree of authenticity into the classroom, since the very act of bringing into the classroom samples of language for input isolates them from the essence of reality that made them authentic in the first place (see Hung & Victor Chen, 2007 on extrapolation approaches). Personally, I find this an undesirable way of talking about authenticity, although I agree with the principle. The issue of whether the classroom can be seen as 'reality' was another of the many aspects of authenticity that has been debated over time, and the reason for the aforementioned 'dead end' to the discussion. Talking about authenticity to the point where it ceases to become useful as going any further with the discussion would seem to undermine the work those involved in the debate. Widdowson (1978), in a characteristically pragmatic sentence, took the discussion into dangerous territory and then returned swiftly to safety when talked of 'pedagogic contrivance' and went on to explain, however, that 'the purpose of pedagogy is not to deny reality but to develop a heightened awareness of it' (Widdowson, 1978: 81). Although there is no exclamation mark in Widdowson's original sentence, I think one might certainly be implied. Mishan notes that the classroom is no less real than a post office or bank (2005: 16) and other scholars have also argued the same point

(Badger & MacDonald, 2010; Taylor, 1994; van Lier, 1988; Widdowson, 2001). However, this distinction is a persistent one and I myself have fallen into the trap of discussing reality on the one hand and the classroom situation on the other, as if the two are separate. The reader will have also noted that the aforementioned 'classic' definition of authenticity is a clear culprit in the way it implicitly frames the learning context as 'not real'. In the 'classic' definition, authenticity is not only defined according to the origin of the source material, it is also often referred to through the nature of the language, in that it should not be scripted or invented. This is another dangerous aspect of the definition, which often calls upon the notion of 'natural language'.

Natural language

> Authenticity concerns the reality of native speaker language use: in our case, the communication in English which is realized by an English-speaking community. But the language which is real for native speakers is not likely to be real for learners [...] They belong to another community and do not have the necessary knowledge of the contextual conditions which would enable them to authenticate English in native speaker terms. Their reality is quite different. (Widdowson, 1996: 68)

As I have already mentioned several times, definitions of authenticity quite often fall back on the term 'natural language', which is meant to mean language as it would be encountered in the target language community, in actual use or in 'reality'. This was the topic of some heated discussions, with scholars such as Widdowson, van Lier, Breen and Mishan arguing that reality and classroom should not be seen as mutually exclusive. To avoid the use of the word 'reality' I prefer to adopt Bachman and Palmer's (1996) term 'language use domain'. This refers to the fact that language tests are supposed to simulate and assess a certain domain of use, into which the test takers intend to integrate. However, the word 'reality' does come easier to the mind and therefore I think we can excuse people for contrasting 'reality' with the classroom, as long as in doing so they are not denying the validity of the classroom as a place where meaningful interactions can take place. Another criticism often levelled against the use of authentic language for language learning is that it is too difficult, potentially being too lexically dense, too full of cultural references which assume a certain amount of collective schematic knowledge. Below are some interesting examples of newspapers (most of them probably apocryphal) that use so-called 'natural language' and would be very confusing to learners.

(i) Statistics show that teen pregnancy drops off significantly after age 25
(ii) Federal agents raid gun shop, find weapons

(iii) Homicide victims rarely talk to police
(iv) Missippi's [sic] literacy program shows improvement
(v) Diana was still alive hours before she died
(Buzzfeed Community Member, 2012)

These headlines are, however, perhaps to be taken with some scepticism. For example, v) is attributed to a 'stupid' newspaper headline but it is in fact from a 2007 edition of satirical British magazine *Private Eye*, who themselves were making fun of the media hysteria surrounding Princess Diana even 10 years after her unfortunate death. Regardless of the *authenticity* of the source (something I discuss in more detail in Chapter 7), I think it would be unwise to unleash any of these examples on our learners. For a more trustworthy example I searched the headlines myself and found a confusing example from *The Metro* newspaper:

Luis Suarez memes flood Twitter after Barcelona striker bags first-half brace against Manchester City. (Bhardwaj, 2015)

Clearly, in order to understand this headline one needs to know who Luis Suarez is, one needs to know what a 'meme' is and the word's relationship to social networking site Twitter. We also need to know that Barcelona and Manchester City are football teams in this context, not the actual cities. Explaining all the cultural schemata and specialised word use in a simple headline like this could take an entire lesson, and leave learners feeling as though they may never get a grasp of the language. I could elaborate further with other examples from my experience of learning Japanese, but the central point is that this type of language use is very common, not only in newspapers but also more broadly in the way that particular discourse communities mark belonging through coded schemes of specialised discourse, which will use a particular jargon or argot that forms an important aspect of ingroup identification(Fromkin *et al.*, 2001). When people read a newspaper in a foreign language, it is common to think that this has been written for an entire nation of speakers, and therefore the language use is broadly representative. However, most newspapers are divided into specialised sections, furthermore different types of people read different types of newspapers, and as such they are often quite far from being representative of a 'standard' type of language. In order to understand an utterance we need a great deal of cultural schemata and other information in order to make sense of the words as they fit into sentence. Therefore, rather than teaching the meaning of lots of individual vocabulary items, it might be best to teach strategies for dealing with unknown words and phrases.

Another example of confusing 'natural language' is pointed out by the literary critic Terry Eagleton, who discussed a sign on the London Underground, which reads 'Dogs must be carried on the escalator' (2008: 6).

The sign means that if you have a dog, you must carry it when riding the escalator (presumably for safety reasons). However, Eagleton points out that it could also mean that you are not allowed to ride an escalator unless you are carrying a dog. There are many technical terms for this kind of phenomenon, but what we are basically talking about is pragmatics – the fact that meanings are dependent on context and understanding an utterance or sentence requires more than just knowing the coded semantic meanings of each word. Going even further, deixis is another linguistic term that refers to words such as people, places and times, which cannot be understood at all outside of the context. For example, if we imagine that we are walking down a street and find a note on the floor which says 'I will meet you there in five minutes', clearly this note is a complete mystery to us. This is because of the deictic nature of the word 'you' 'me' 'here' and the fact that 'in five minutes' requires the reader to know exactly when the note was written. The semantic shifting of words can add another layer of complication, for example the word 'nice' derived from the Latin word *nescius* which meant ignorant, yet somehow around the 16th and 17th century its meaning changed completely to mean something agreeable or pleasant (Harper, 2013). A more recent example of the broadening of a semantic reference is 'troll', which used to be just a rather unintelligent monster with a tendency for lurking under bridges, but they have been all over the recent news as the word 'troll' has now become a verb which means to purposefully goad or abuse someone online. Also, entirely new coinages such as the deliberately misspelled 'pwned' and anagrams like, 'lol', 'lmao', 'rotflmao' and even acronym derived new words such as 'roflcopter' are difficult for parents of teenagers to understand in their L1, let alone for learners of the language. I will discuss these issues further in Chapter 7.

Further issues such as polysemic words with more than one meaning, metaphors, expressions and the issue of cultural schemata make understanding authentic texts based on 'natural language' a potential mine-field. From this perspective, rather than being a desirable thing, authenticity seems to become something we might wish to actively avoid. This is what Widdowson perhaps meant when he suggested that 'Inauthentic language-using behaviour might well be effective language-learning behaviour' (Widdowson, 1990: 46–47). In other words, perhaps the best learning materials are ones that are actually designed for learning; a theme G. Cook (1997, 2000, 2001) has expanded on in some detail.

The opposite side of this argument, then, is to create invented sentences that demonstrate certain grammatical or lexical features. This is familiar territory to language teachers, and could just as well be referred to as 'textbook language'. And now I am breaching an age-old argument, and one which is very persistent. Henry Sweet, the pioneering philologist and grammarian, argued against contrived sentences back in 1899 when he recalled his Greek teacher 'evolving' a sentence that went 'the philosopher pulled the lower jaw of the hen' (cited in G. Cook, 2001: 367). I have seen similar, although less elaborate, contrived sentences in a recent Japanese university entrance exam, which read:

> Young as I was, I did not know that a police detective was questioning my mother as to where my father had gone, still less did I know that the police were gathering evidence against him.

But are these contrived sentences just as bad as the confounding 'natural language'? Or are they worse since they exist only in a fantasy reality created for textbooks whose sole aim is to teach 'declarative knowledge'? These issues affect all languages, not just English. It is for this reason that decontextualised language is certainly not authentic. A sentence such as 'I will have been waiting for you for 12 hours by the time your plane arrives' contains a stub of invented context, but there is almost no way for a learner to attach any personal or social significance to it. Further expanding on this argument, Cook (1997) argues that not only is the use of so-called 'authentic' texts based on false assumptions about the nature of language learning, but also a lot of the 'real' communication that takes place in the world is not actually for 'a real purpose'. He argues that much of the way individuals use language is playful and that it does not always serve a communicative function in that strict sense of trying to achieve something or construct meaning. His argument is that what we perceive as inauthentic is actually based on a narrow view of communication in the 'real world'. Although he seems to be arguing *against* the use of authentic materials, I have to say that I completely agree with him. However, the crucial point he is making is *for* authenticity in language learning, but a reconceptualised version, which is not polarised by debates for and against 'natural language' or 'natural learning' behaviour.

Owing to these complications, I find Tomlinson and Masuhara's definition very persuasive, which states that authentic materials are 'designed not to transmit declarative knowledge about the target language but rather to provide an experience of the language in use' (2010: 400). In this definition, a clearer concept is provided by explaining what is *not* authentic – i.e. language teaching which prioritises description over actual use. Tomlinson and Masuhara's description also adds a new term into the mix, the use of the word 'experience'. An experience is almost as hard to define as what is real; however, the definition clearly places the emphasis on language as it is used and casts aside the notion of breaking language down into compartmentalised rules which can be explained as 'declarative knowledge' but which do not necessarily provide any context or present the language as it would be in its natural state. In this way, Tomlinson and Masuhara's definition places authenticity within a sociocultural context, prioritising the use of language as a 'tool' through which some other function is achieved. So, in the Vygotskyian (1964) sense that language is a psychological tool through which other forms of learning are mediated, authentic language should arise as a natural by-product of meaningful interaction, or 'experience of the language in use' (Tomlinson & Masuhara, 2010: 400). To put it simply, authentic language is language where something other than language for its own sake is being discussed. Grammar drills and repetitive explanations of the rules for forming correct sentences in the target language are not authentic, whereas discussions about environmental issues or exchanges of other information such as personal beliefs and opinions are authentic.

Of course, in illustrating the argument about contrived sentences vs natural language I have presented two polar extremes, and what we generally find in the language classroom is a more balanced approach, something nearer the middle of each argument. For example, some contrived or invented sentences can poses their own degree of authenticity. 'An [invented sentence] thought up by the teacher for his or her students has the inbuilt benefit of being something specifically made for them, belonging to that particular classroom – with consequent positive effects' (G. Cook, 2001: 380). However, even a textbook, full of invented sentences and contrivances, can still read in quite a natural way, in just the same way that we might find ourselves immersed in the dialogue from a good play or film despite the fact that it is the scripted and unnatural product of a text that was contrived. However, contriving a convincing and natural script is a skill, and different people will have different interpretations or reactions of course. This is what Harmer hinted at when he said a play could be both authentic and inauthentic at the same time. So, basically natural language is part of the authenticity debate, and it is part of a wider debate about teaching approaches and methods which has gone on for well over a century. But, the point is that it need not be a binary issue of either using extremely complicated, lexically dense and culturally encoded texts out of context vs using nonsensical, invented, surreal gibberish structured around a grammatical point. A graded reader, for example, can be very authentic and so too can a photograph with no words at all. An authentic text might well be a newspaper headline or a script written specifically for the classroom, but its authenticity is not an inherent feature, what makes it authentic is the interaction with the learner in the context of the classroom and the broader social environment in which it takes place. As scholars have long been arguing, we cannot simply extrapolate texts from one context to another and expect them to remain authentic. So, what does an authentic approach to language learning look like? And, most importantly, why should we strive for one?

Authenticity as an Approach

If someone interested in authenticity asked me to summarise Freda Mishan's book *Designing Authenticity into Language Learning Materials* (2005),

I would simply have to say that it is essential reading. I would dearly like to summarise the entire work better, but I feel it would not be possible to do it justice. In her work, Mishan overviews the issue of authenticity in language learning with reliable examples that date as far back as 2700 BC (2005: 2, although most are from the last 30 years), with a very up-do-date and accessible coverage of the recent debates. It was thanks to reading her book that I was able to find many of the sources that have led me to this point in my own quest for authenticity. She also offers a very practical rationale for designing authenticity into learning materials, as well as a workable criterion for doing so. First, she covers research into SLA that provides a solid empirical justification for using authentic materials, touching on input, affect (motivation and engagement), learning style, autonomous learning, consciousness raising and language processing. She ties research into each of these areas within SLA to the idea of designing for authenticity through the use of 'cultural products' in the classroom. One of Mishan's most useful discussions is her own original contribution to 'the authenticity debate' in which she proposes that the research in SLA can be 'encapsulated' by a pedagogic rationale which she bases around the 3Cs of authenticity. These are – culture, currency (as in time) and challenge (2005: 44–64).

Culture

Basically, Mishan argues that culture is inseparable from language, and that language is both a product of and a prerequisite for culture. Therefore, to successfully teach a foreign language, one needs to also learn about the foreign culture. This is certainly true from my own experience as a learner of Japanese, where certain words are simply un-learnable without some knowledge of the culture that produced the concept which the word describes. However, Mishan also acknowledges what she terms as 'the spanner in the works' because for learners of English (and other global languages) 'one language does not mean one culture' (2005: 44). Her solution is to embed an aspect of locality within the concept of culture as it relates to authenticity. In other words, the notion of culture should encompass the culture where the target language is spoken *and* connect with the place where it is being learned. She connects the ideas of schema theory with the teaching of culture, which provides the SLA justification for an approach that uses authentic materials based on 'cultural products'. She also uses this argument to launch an attack on the 'neutralised' or 'Anglo-centric' focus of many commercially produced ELT textbooks. She explains that cultures generally have different culturally conditioned behaviours, such as work ethos, eating habits and of course attitudes to learning (2005: 53). Thus, too much diversity is detrimental, and the notion of 'culture' needs to be approached from a perspective we might these days label as glocalised, meaning a local approach to global issues. Glocalisation is as much a marketing term as anything else, and in this case I think it is appropriate, since part of the process of getting learners to engage with or 'buy into' the English language is to ask them to imagine themselves as consumers of that language, despite what I previously labelled as its disembodied status as a language. Globalisation, the democratisation of culture and the digitalisation of cultural products has resulted in a paradox of authenticity, not just in language teaching but as a phenomena that affects all disciplines (Cobb, 2014). I would argue that this paradox of authenticity is something that can only be negotiated or overcome at an individual level, and it requires that authenticity be viewed as a contextually situated process of negotiation between self and society.

Currency

Mishan defines 'currency' as the temporal dimension to authenticity, which she particularly elaborates with respect to the changing nature of language use, although she does also associate it with topical issues and current affairs. The idea of currency might not just refer to things that are recent, but also to things that are relevant. For example, I could talk to my students about The Beatles or Nirvana, both bands which I love but which are also quite old now. Kurt Cobain, the lead singer of Nirvana, took his own life on 20 February 1994, which is over 20 years ago now. Most of my students were not born when he died. As for The Beatles, I wasn't even born when John Lennon was murdered on the 8 December 1980. Should I really expect my students here in Japan to know anything about these bands? Their age in time though, is not so much the point here. If I do a lesson about John Lennon in December, it would have more currency than doing the lesson in, for example May, because I could use the opportunity to mark the anniversary of his death. I could also ask students to talk about their own favourite musicians, and the dangers and stresses that fame brings. Currency not only refers to the 'up-to-date-ness' of the materials but also their topicality and relevance. Language teachers frequently choose to create a lesson around something happening in current affairs, but a teacher could just as well use a sample from *The Epic of Gilgamesh*, the oldest surviving work of human literature, and that can also contain an element of currency because it retains relevance, partly by virtue of its age. Certain things age better than others – which is why a speech from a historical figure like Abraham Lincoln can still have currency, whereas using one of, say, George Bush's speeches will be much less likely to carry much currency. In this way, currency is tied to what Eagleton (2008) calls 'value judgements', which he argues are part of a society's collective process for elevating the cultural status of certain texts. This is why textbooks and materials are constantly in need of updating, as time moves on certain topics lose their contemporary appeal, a process that a colleague of mine rather poetically described as 'the living textbook'.

Challenge

The final of Mishan's 3Cs is challenge. In this third part of her pedagogical rationale for authentic materials, Mishan defines the process of cognitively engaging learners with interesting materials as challenge, and she makes a distinction between difficulty and challenge. She explains that 'the very feature of authentic texts that is often perceived as an impediment to their use with language learners, *difficulty*, is in fact an advantage' (2005: 45). Her SLA justification for this rests somewhat on Krashen's Input Hypothesis (1985), an idea commonly represented as $i + 1$, where i refers to input and +1 means the next structure that should be learned. There is a further obvious parallel with this and what Vygotsky (1978) called the zone of proximal development (ZPD). The fundamental idea behind both concepts is that learning happens best when it is just slightly beyond the current level of ability. Vygotsky's concept relates more broadly to education, but Krashen's idea is specific to language acquisition. Mishan argues that the suitability of a text needs to be factored into the choice of material, again making the concept of authenticity contextually and socially specific. Mishan also uses the concept of challenge to criticise the practice of giving low-level learners boring or over-simplified materials, or patronising them by assuming their lack of language also implies a lack of experience or knowledge (see also Amor, 2002). She effectively turns the argument against authenticity, that it is too linguistically dense and relies too much on cultural schemata, on its head. Her central justification for doing so is basically that the authentic content, being more challenging, is therefore more engaging. In other words, challenge connects authenticity to motivation and language acquisition.

The domains of authenticity: Texts, tasks and language in use

In Tomlinson and Masuhara's definition cited previously, in which 'experience' is a central element, authenticity is being used to refer mainly to the materials (texts) being presented to the students. As I stated at the start of this chapter, authenticity can refer to different aspects of the language classroom, besides just the materials being used. Michael Breen (1985) identified that language teachers are 'continually concerned with four types of authenticity', which he summarise as:

(1) Authenticity of the texts which we may use as input data for our learners.
(2) Authenticity of the learners' own interpretations of such texts.
(3) Authenticity of tasks conducive to language learning.
(4) Authenticity of the actual social situation of the language classroom.

(Breen, 1985: 61)

A further way of assessing authenticity might be to separate it into the various components that interact and overlap in the learning and teaching process. Authenticity could relate to the type of materials or the text being used to present the language, the tasks the teacher uses to interact with the text, or it could also relate to the language produced by the students as output. Authentic refers not just to the learning context, but also what Morrow (1977) and Gilmore (2007) refer to as the 'real' aspect of the language, in other words the language in use domain. These various aspects of authentic language all have a close connection and may not always exist in isolation (see Figure 4.2).

Throughout this book I have been talking about authenticity as a single concept, which is represented by the central circle of Figure 4.2, showing the domains of authenticity. I find it useful to distinguish the different areas of the classroom that the word 'authenticity' can apply to, but I still feel that the central concept should be definable in a way which relates to all domains, and in a format that can be communicated easily to others. For my own part, I have tried to read widely on the subject of authenticity, and I have also spent even longer pondering the subject, wrestling with it in my mind. Although by compartmentalising authenticity we can break it into distinct segments which may seem on the surface to be more manageable, what we may actually be doing is avoiding the central concept. Despite the different domains of authenticity, surely at the core of each domain is a shared nucleus of meaning, although this is somewhat unclear in its current state.

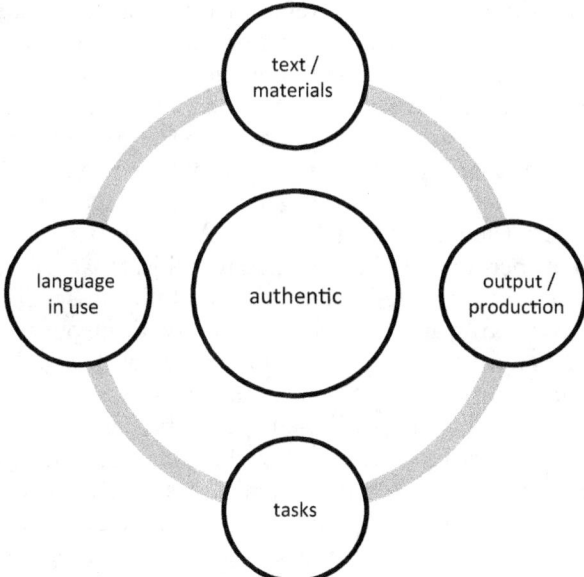

Figure 4.2 The domains of authenticity

In overviewing the positions of authenticity in language teaching, I have found myself back in a maze of confusion. Language teaching seems to often use its own special meaning for the word 'authenticity', which is quite distinct from the use of the word in general. As I have shown in this chapter, several scholars have defined and problematised the usage of the word 'authenticity', and there is an established strand of existentialist discussion which makes a clear case for what authenticity is or is not (Amor, 2002). However, as I have already shown in previous chapters and through establishing the prevalence of the 'classic' definition, these discussions seem to have gone unheeded by the general language teaching community. Authenticity is side-lined as a concept for discussion and analysis when compared to words which closely connect with it, words such as autonomy and motivation. And still, authenticity is a word all language teachers know and use regularly. Even when the word 'authenticity' is not being used, discussions seem to revolve around it, as the following quote demonstrates:

> It is through the dialogic construction of rhetorical roles through the written and spoken medium that students experience themselves as both private, individual, and public, social sign makers, and that they appreciate the fluidity of meanings they can attribute to themselves and others. (Kramsch, 2000: 151)

Kramsch here is not talking directly about authenticity, but she *is* talking about it as we have approached it so far in this book; basically, as a social and contextual dimension to the relationships between individuals and societies, and how they engage in meaning making through language use. In summing up the confusing list of compartmentalised authenticities as they relate to different chunks of what teachers and learners do in and out of the language classroom I have brought us to the current state of authenticity in language teaching. However, this is more like a mechanical watch that has been disassembled. It no longer works, and we cannot easily step back and see how the parts all fit together. After identifying the different definitions of authenticity, Gilmore called for 'objectifiable criteria' (2007a: 98) to assess authenticity. Well-meaning and intelligent scholars have done the hard work of taking apart the concept and working out what each part is. However, it is now time to put all those pieces back together and try to understand authenticity not as a *thing* made of parts but as a *process* which relies on dynamic interactions. These types of processes cannot be understood in a purely objective way; however, they must be re-assessed continually for each context and each individual. This is why chaos/complexity theory is the best approach for a reconceptualised view of authenticity as it relates to the superdiversity of English as a global language and its myriad of complexities which surround the acquisition of English as a second language.

Authenticity and the Dearth of Empirical Research

In this section I will provide an overview of empirical research into authenticity. Of course, many of these studies are based on the reductionist definition of authenticity, and as such I believe they are not actually able to explain the complexity of the term as it is reconceptualised for the global era, particularly in relation to English. Despite Mishan's convincing review of SLA literature which supports the use of authentic materials for learning foreign languages, it is worth noting that few of the studies she cites actually deal explicitly with the theme of authenticity. The bibliography to Mishan's (2005) book contains 415 entries, but the word 'authentic' is only mentioned 35 times in the titles of the works she cites. This does not prove *per se* that there is a lack of empirical studies in authenticity, but it does indicate that even in Mishan's in-depth survey, the number of articles which specifically mention authenticity in the title is only 8% of the total number of references (see Figure 4.3).

Similarly (and as mentioned previously), Gilmore (2007a) cites 240 items, of which only 29 make specific reference to authenticity (a total of 12%, see Figure 4.4).

Of course, this is not meant as a criticism of either of these scholars' works, but purely as a very simple way of demonstrating that works dealing with authenticity directly (or at least that mention it in their title) are in the minority, whereas other works clearly still have significance and relevance to the topic, although they may not deal with it directly. In the interests of fairness, although at the time of writing this book is still in progress (obviously), I do have a references section for the entire volume, which at present stands at 420 entries, of which 68 mention authenticity (14%, see Figure 4.5) – two of which are my own publications. Of course this is still rather inaccurate, since for example Taylor (1994) mentions the word 'authentic' five times in the title to his entry.

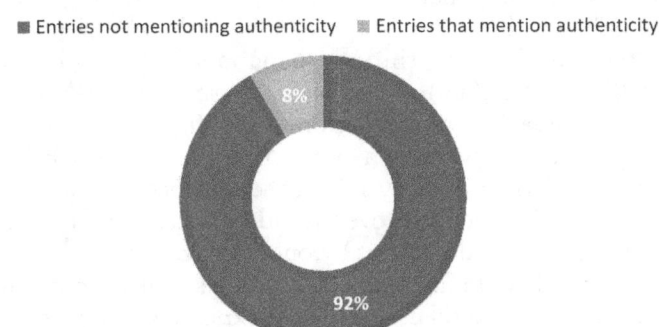

Figure 4.3 Overview of Mishan's (2005) citations

84 Reconceptualising Authenticity for English as a Global Language

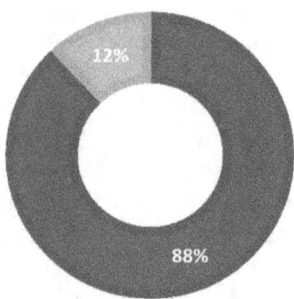

Figure 4.4 Overview of Gilmore's (2007a) citations

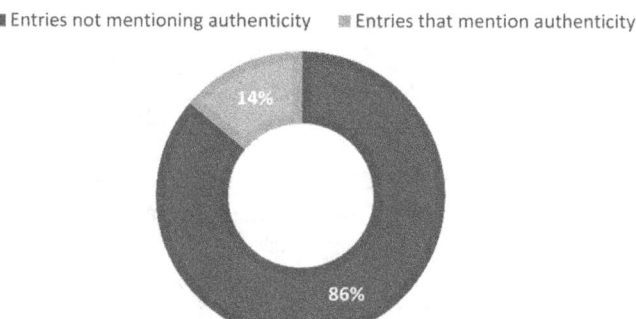

Figure 4.5 Overview of Pinner's (current volume) citations

The key point is that authenticity is a centrally important concept in language learning and teaching. It has been for a long time. Furthermore, it often connects directly with motivation, which is regularly cited as the most fundamental component in ensuring success in language learning (Dörnyei & Ushioda, 2009, 2011). The issue is dealt with in both long and short chapters all the way through handbooks of language teaching (Harmer, 2008; Hedge, 2000), and it is used to sell textbooks and promote the validity of language courses (Macmillan, 2010). It is even a vital aspect of language programme evaluation and testing (Bachman & Palmer, 1996; Lewkowicz, 2000; Lynch, 1996). And yet the evidence from actual research studies specifically designed to prove that authenticity is more effective and more motivating is marked by what I would call a dearth in empirical studies. In this section I will outline the few studies that I am aware of and, sadly, explain the flaws in them. I will then explain why I believe there is a dearth in studies and I will propose how this might be addressed in future research agendas.

Authenticity and motivation

Studies that do exist which have authenticity at the heart of an empirical inquiry are scarce, but one of the most well-known was written by Matthew Peacock (1997b), which was also the subject of his PhD research (1996) and the data were also presumably used in at least one other article (1998). (This is presumed from the way Peacock refers back to his 1997b paper as a way of glossing the research methodology for the 1998 study. From this it would seem to follow that they are different write-ups of the same study.) His study looked at the use of authentic materials with low-level learners and tried to empirically prove the long-established belief that authentic materials are more motivating for students. First of all, I would like to say that this study is of great importance and, despite the criticisms I am about to level at it, I do not wish to imply that the study was not useful. It was one of the only studies, to my knowledge, that attempted to establish a link between two essential and yet unwieldy subjects – authenticity and motivation. Peacock is one of the main inspirations behind my own empirical work, as I am currently engaged in a research agenda to connect authenticity to motivation. However, a key criticism I have of this study is that at no point in the article does Peacock actually define what authenticity is. He does explain other concepts, such as 'motivation' and 'materials' but at no point does he define what he means by the term 'authenticity'. Reading between the lines, I think his definition is actually what I have established as the 'classic' definition. At the time the study was published in the *ELT Journal*, Keith Morrow was the editor and his 1977 definition of authenticity based on 'real' language for a real purpose (as oppose to invented) was probably implicit to the informed readers who would take an interest in such a study. However, this is only conjecture. In Peacock (1998), authentic materials are explained through examples:

> Among the authentic materials were two short poems, used in a listening and discussion exercise; television listings for that day from the local English-language newspaper, used for a short roleplay of choosing what to watch; three topical newspaper articles and the problem page, used for small group discussion and a related writing exercise; and a song on tape with a tapescript, for listening comprehension and as a stimulus for writing a dialog. (Peacock, 1998: np)

Another issue with Peacock's (1997b) study is the fact that, although he reported that students found authentic materials more motivating (drawing on Ushioda's (1993) practitioner validated view of motivation), this was somewhat problematic as he also reports that learners found the authentic materials to be less interesting. In my own understanding of the word 'motivation', I think that might be something of an oxymoron. It would seem contradictory to find something more motivating if it is less interesting. In his detailed summary, Gilmore (2007a: 106–108) also points out this flaw in Peacock's study, but he also explains that Peacock's is to date the most convincing empirical study in the connection between authenticity and motivation. I should also point out that Gilmore ranks Peacock's study as the most convincing out of three that he is aware of – the other two (González, 1990; Kienbaum *et al.*, 1986) were also cited in Peacock's paper, which suggests that nothing had been done on the subject in the 10 years between Peacock's study and Gilmore's state-of-the-art review. In fact, González (1990) refers to an unpublished EdD thesis from West Virginia University, which is not available online from the awarding institution, and therefore rather obscure. It is quite astonishing that there is such a paucity of empirical studies into the link between authenticity and motivation when the two are such common collocates.

Gilmore states that not only is the belief that authentic materials are more motivating widespread throughout the literature on authenticity, but it also seems to be held by the language teaching community at large, as well as being a common selling point for text book producers (2007a: 106). Why this vacuum of research? This is especially incongruous given the rich body of literature which deals with motivation (Dörnyei & Ushioda, 2011). And yet, the fact that authentic materials are more motivating seems to be widely accepted by the research and teaching communities. However, there are also those who warn against the belief that authentic materials are intrinsically more motivating, citing the linguistic density of such texts and the fact that the excessive difficulty could negatively impact motivation (Harmer, 2008; see Rebuck, 2008 for an empirical study). In a study by Gilmore (which I will discuss in the next section) one of his participants noted that, after completing a listening activity which used a video of 'a NS English couple, Mark and Alison, performing exactly the same role-play' (2007b: 246) which the students had just performed themselves. Gilmore's participant, ES, notes:

> ES: I didn't understand the conversation of Weekend Away between Mark and Alison well. I couldn't catch the phrases or vocabularies when I listened to the conversation. Therefore I was surprised to look at the tapescript that was composed of well-known vocabularies. (Gilmore, 2007b: 246)

Gilmore explains the reasons why ES probably felt confused by the listening, although he does not elaborate on the possible consequences of the student's realisation that she already knew much of the vocabulary and yet was unable to comprehend it as used in the dialogue.

In order to study the link between authenticity and motivation, qualitative and mixed-methods studies would be essential. One of the strengths in Peacock's study was the presence of qualitative data, an essential part of the design of any study hoping to gain real insights into what are essentially two highly contextual and personal constructs. The act of reducing individuals into numbers on a chart 'depersonalises learners' (Ushioda, 2009: 216), especially in purely quantitative studies looking into highly individual affective factors such as motivation. In fact, the very idea that we might ever be able to fully understand such a complex and dynamic system is probably rather optimistic. However, Ushioda and others (D. Atkinson, 2011; Bandura, 2001; Larsen-Freeman & Cameron, 2008a) advocate a more qualitative approach to SLA research, and certainly current trends in L2 motivational research are moving towards an understanding based more on complex dynamic systems (Dörnyei et al., 2015; Muir & Dörnyei, 2013; Ushioda, 2013a), which require an understanding of people as individuals within contextualised social settings.

Authenticity and second language acquisition

In order to truly justify the use of 'authentic' materials, it needs to be shown that there are learning gains in doing so. Again, Mishan (2005) has addressed this by overviewing SLA theories which support the use of authentic materials, discussing learning style, autonomy, consciousness raising, language processing, and even instructed SLA, She also goes into detail about motivation, affect and empathy. However, actual studies into the use of authentic texts and the benefits they have for learners are not common, and Mishan is connecting the research to authenticity rather than discussing actual research into authenticity. She is unable to present much research that deals directly with authenticity because there is a dearth in empirical studies.

Despite this apparent poverty, there are some studies that exist which look into authenticity and attempt to measure its effectiveness for language acquisition. Not surprisingly, Alex Gilmore is probably the leading researcher into authenticity as it relates to learning gains. He conducted a study for his Doctorate in which he taught groups of Japanese second year university students (n = 62) using authentic materials and compared them against control groups who received 'textbook input' from the same teacher (Gilmore, 2005, 2007b, 2011). The main focus of his study was on communicative competence, operationalised against a model 'broadly accepted by experts in the field [consisting] of five interrelated components' (2011: 787):

(a) Linguistic competence
(b) Pragmalinguistic competence
(c) Sociopragmatic competence
(d) Strategic competence
    (i) avoidance or reduction strategies
    (ii) compensatory strategies
    (iii) stalling strategies
    (iv) interactional strategies
(e) Discourse competence

He utilised a battery of eight different language assessments (both pre- and post- instruction) in order to gauge the students' progress in each area. The various tests ranged from receptive vocabulary tests to role-plays and oral interviews (which were also tested for interrater reliability). This was an extremely thorough and no-doubt quite demanding study, both for the teacher/researcher and for the students. Gilmore was able to report statistically significant differences between the experimental (authentic) groups and the control (textbook) groups, although not for all areas of communicative competence, most notably pragmalinguistic competence and particularly on the grammar tests. Gilmore also notes that a replication study would be 'unlikely [to observe] statistically significant differences in sociopragmatic measures [...] in European students, for which behavioral norms are closer to those of NSs of English' (2011: 811). Gilmore's study provides hard, empirical evidence that authentic materials were better than the two textbooks he used in developing a range of communicative competencies. This was because of the richer input of authentic materials and the carefully designed consciousness raising tasks which he utilised to negotiate meaning from the authentic input. The experimental group received input from authentic materials, which Gilmore defined based on the 'real' definition put forward by Morrow (1977), described in the study as having been 'taken from films, documentaries, reality shows, TV comedies, web-based sources, home-produced video of native speakers, songs, novels, and newspaper articles' (Gilmore, 2011: 794). Gilmore's study is very convincing in this way, and provides support for Mishan's (2005) assertions that authentic materials provide richer input and, if used correctly, this can influence gains in acquisition. This is made manifest by the tasks the teacher employs, which should focus on strategies for making sense of the authentic input (see also Siegel, 2013 for further support of the explicit teaching of strategies in listening). However, readers of the present volume may have already noticed that Gilmore's authentic materials could be labelled according to the 'classic' definition, and furthermore he makes specific reference to English native speakers as a measure for sociopragmatic communicative competence. Although I know for a fact that Gilmore does not ascribe to the 'native' definition of authenticity, the design of his study has led him to fall into the trap of making native-speakerist assumptions about what his learners should be able to do and the 'correct' forms that they should emulate. His oral interview was based on IELTS; one of the gate-keeping tests, along with TOEFL, which paradoxically prevents universities from being truly international even as it seeks to allow international universities to accept students from abroad (Jenkins, 2014).

A further issue with Gilmore's (2011) study is the lack of qualitative data, although in fairness to Gilmore, his PhD research is based on mixed-methods research, and he collected a good deal of qualitative data, which 'was collected at regular intervals during the trial using a variety of techniques: learner diaries, case study interviews and transcripts of classroom interaction' (Gilmore, 2007b: 137). Furthermore, he expands in detail about the shortcomings of purely one-sided data, even providing a continuum of qualitative and quantitative data (Gilmore, 2007b: 107), see Figure 4.6.

However, when it came to writing up the study for journal publication, Gilmore chose to divide the qualitative and quantitative aspects of his study and present first only the quantitative results and analysis. He provides a note explaining that 'The qualitative results from this study will be reported on in a later publication' (2011: 814). However, the data he presents in his PhD thesis are certainly very convincing that learners found the authentic materials more enjoyable (and presumably motivating), although he is careful to note that:

> Some of the qualitative data in the study from student feedback and instructors' logs did indicate a positive reaction towards the authentic supplements but to what extent this is due to the materials themselves and not just a desire to do something other than the assigned textbook is impossible to determine. (Gilmore, 2007b: 86)

Mostly the research I have discussed so far concerns itself with materials development, which is already marred by a lack of empirical evidence (Gilmore, 2012; Mishan, 2005; Tomlinson, 2008), so a dearth in research is not particularly surprising. Furthermore I would like to add that several recent edited volumes, such as Mishan and Chambers (2010); Tomlinson (2013);

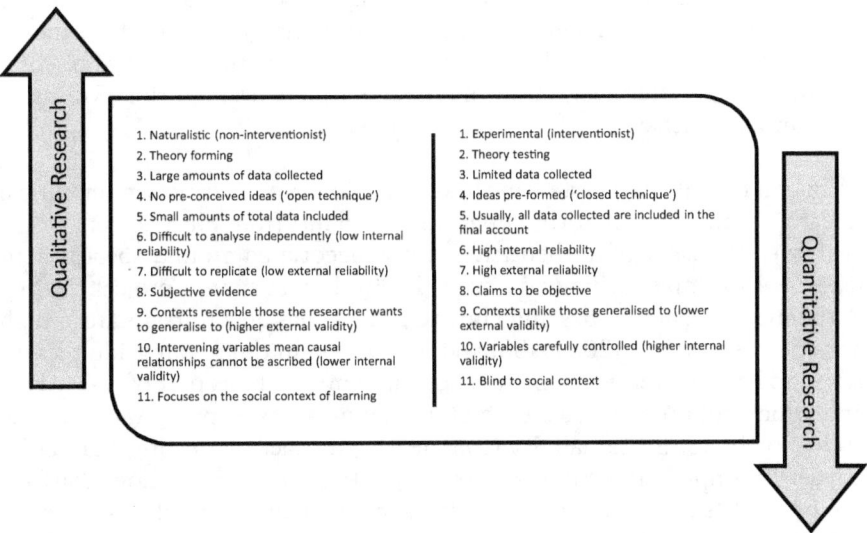

Figure 4.6 Gilmore's (2007b) qual-quant continuum, adapted

Tomlinson and Masuhara (2010) as well as the *Folio* journal of the Materials Development Association (MATSDA) (of which Freda Mishan is currently the editor) represent good attempts to address this imbalance. However, more qualitative research is needed in order to understand more about the complexities of authenticity as a dynamic process. There is also a need for more investigation into the links between affective factors that could potentially influence not just materials design, but also best practices in language teaching and therefore language teacher education and training. The lack of qualitative research into the nature of authenticity seems reminiscent somehow to the differences in research between motivation and autonomy. As Ushioda points out, research in motivation tends to come from the positivist tradition, but generally work in autonomy is done in the constructivist paradigm (Ushioda, 2011b). The trend is now more towards mixed-methods, or rather the applied linguistics community as a whole seems to be trying to move away from the dichotomy of the 'paradigm war' (Dörnyei, 2007: 9) and attempting to seek methods of inquiry which focus on quality. To this end, the edited volumes by Dantas-Whitney and Rilling (2010) and Rilling and Dantas-Whitney (2009b) represent two ventures into practitioner research and reflexive narrative description of classroom activities.

> All chapters in this volume demonstrate that authenticity is more than just the materials we use. Authenticity also means using language for real purposes. It means engaging students in collaborative learning, involving discussions, negotiations, and decision making. Authenticity is creating real uses for English, not just holding native-speaker language and culture as the sole model. With English increasingly being used as a lingua franca to connect second language speakers, authenticity takes on new meanings as we seek to develop learners who can face the challenge of communicating effectively in an increasingly globalised world. (Rilling & Dantas-Whitney, 2009a: 8)

Although not all the chapters in these two edited volumes present empirical research, many of them do offer narrative accounts from practitioners which deal with the issue of authenticity as it is negotiated around specific contexts. For example, Stipe and Yasen (2009) discuss how a project dealing with environmental issues and climate change was able to facilitate 'a high degree of ownership' (2009: 138) and motivation in their young adult learners, who had to interview a member of the community as part of the project and which culminated with each group giving a poster presentation at the 2006 Northwest Sustainability Conference. Another interesting chapter by Snyder-Parampil and Hensley (2009), presents a reflection on how YouTube can be used as a 'private' video sharing site which allows students to record their own presentations in class, add comments, provide peer-review and in doing so build up a virtual portfolio of their learning. Exploratory practice and practitioner research offer the most 'authentic' type of research methodology for investigating the dynamics of authenticity in language learning, because these methods are not *third-party research*, as Allwright and Hanks (2009: 109–115) pejoratively refer to it. They criticise other classroom-based research methods (including action research) because they neglect 'the agency of *learners* as potential researchers' (Allwright & Hanks, 2009: 108 original emphasis). In exploratory practice, the emphasis is not just on collecting the data, but on collecting *ethical* and descriptive data which arisee naturally from the process of teaching. The research should involve all the participants, rather than treating them as subjects. The learners (and not just the small and isolated research community) should be the ones to benefit from the insights gained by conducting the research. For Allwright, exploratory practice is about improving the 'quality of classroom life' (Allwright, 2003, 2005), and therefore it seems to be a truly authentic form of inquiry for researching this type of phenomenon.

The problem of authenticity when teaching English for international business is the subject of Trabelsi's (2010) case-study in Tunisia. The definition of authenticity remains rather elusive to his participants, and he reports instances where both learners and teachers might actually reject 'authentic' materials for being too Western, or for being unsuitable for their learners or context. This contrasts rather sharply with the way English *is* an international business (indeed an entire industry) in Japan, where English is sold as a shrink-wrapped and pre-packaged version of culture, what Seargeant (2005) calls a 'simulation of authenticity'. In Seargeant's article, he sketches out some of the inherent contradictions of the 'authentic' foreign-language theme parks in Japan, such as British Hills in Fukushima, New Zealand Village in Hiroshima, and the Maruyama Shakespeare Country Park in Chiba. He points out the apparent contradictions in these parks. For example, Canadians and Australians working at British Hills, and the fact that the parks claim to be 'more English than England itself' (Seargeant, 2005: 340) because they are cleaner and are not marred by crime, overpopulation and other modern concerns:

> Indeed, the cultural meaning the language as promoted through these schools would seem to pre-empt or prejudice any attempts by TESOL theory to further a workable model of English as a neutral lingua franca. (Seargeant, 2005: 342)

Seargeant's fears are justified, as I showed in Chapter 3, because many learners and L2 speakers (at least in Japan where my research was carried out) still hold the mistaken belief that the 'native speaker' is somehow at the top of the 'authenticity hierarchy' (Myhill, 2003). Seargeant also highlights the deep-set Native-speakerism that utterly obscures the reality of English as an international language. For me there is something truly terrifying about this, although elsewhere Seargeant (2009) does provide a slightly more optimistic view of English in Japan. This phenomenon is not isolated to Japan either, there is also a Korean version called Gyeonggi English Villages, and a self-proclaimed English only immersion school called Gateway Language Village in China. There is also a US version in Minnesota, the Concordia Language Villages, which are actually a series of villages each offering an 'authentic' experience of another culture, mainly Spanish, German and French speaking mainland cultures. The fact that businesses and advertising seem to think that potential language learners *want* the 'native speaker' versions of authentic language experiences is further promulgated by international textbook publishers, as I will discuss in the next section.

Authenticity vs textbooks

In a particularly thorough study, Siegel (2014) looked at the difference between textbook presentations of dialogue and dialogues that occur in the student's lives when English is used as an international language or lingua franca. She looked at Japanese and non-Japanese university students' discourse in a dormitory of a Japanese university. Her study involved hundreds of hours of transcription, and the size of the undertaking is certainly impressive. She found that the topics which students actually discuss outside the classroom when using English as an international language were under-represented in EFL textbooks, leading her to conclude that such materials were not authentic in that they were neither relevant nor representative of the actual communication that students engage in. She states that textbooks should incorporate 'more topics that are authentic to the specific interests and contexts of the L2 users, I believe the EFL classroom can provide a more suitable context to better prepare students for the "world out there"' (2014: 13). Ten years earlier, Gilmore (2004) came to a similar conclusion when he compared dialogues from textbooks with 'authentic equivalents', finding that the scripted dialogues of textbooks were inaccurate representations of the way people actually speak, lacking many of the discourse features such as overlapping and turn-taking patterns which would be necessary for students to know about in order to perform well in communicative settings. Matsuda (2002), in analysing the Japanese Ministry of Education's approved EFL textbooks, found that they tended to emphasise the inner-circle varieties of English. Canagarajah (1993) conducted a critical ethnographic examination to understand his students' lack of engagement with their textbook in Sri Lanka, because they quite frankly had nothing in common with the lifestyle which their US textbooks presented, so instead many of them adorned the books with crude graffiti, in an act of what Canagarajah termed 'resistance'. He notes that because 'students had written these during class time, this activity suggested that topics other than English grammar had preoccupied them while teaching was going on' (1993: 612–613). For them, English truly was a disembodied language, so they had drawn the body parts themselves.

Authenticity and corpora

Interestingly, one of the main strengths for advocates of corpus linguistics and the use of corpora for language learning, is that a corpus helps to describe the way people really speak – they provide authentic examples of language (Mukherjee, 2004; O'Keeffe et al, 2007: 25–26). However, Mishan argues that this is not the case, because corpora 'forfeit a crucial criterion for authenticity, namely context' (2004: 219). Tan (2005) also attacks the practice of corpus builders and corpus linguists for the way they base their definition of authenticity directly on the problematic notion of 'native speakers'. She argues that they make claims about 'correctness' and 'language errors', which 'unintentionally convey a misguided impression among teachers and researchers that learner language is indeed flawed – in the sense that it is unnatural and does not exhibit native-like language behaviour' (2005: 127). Allan (2009) suggests using Graded Readers to build a corpus to use for data-driven learning. She examines to what extent 'authenticity' is compromised by incorporating texts which have been graded for language learning, to which she concludes that a graded corpus can still be authentic in that it adequately reflects the way language is actually used, but in a balanced way more appropriate for language teaching. There are other corpora too, which are designed to reflect not the way L1 speakers of a language talk but a broader spectrum of varieties. Of course, one of the most famous being the work done by Jenkins (2000, 2002) on the lingua franca core. Other examples are the Vienna-Oxford International Corpus of English (VOICE), the English as a lingua franca in Academic settings (ELFA) corpus, the Asian Corpus of English (ACE) and the Online Corpus of Academic Lectures (OnCAL) (see Seidlhofer, 2005 for a summary).

Authenticity in research literature

So far I have presented a small handful of studies which have dealt directly with the issue of authenticity, and I have also examined the shortcomings in many of them. Despite this, there have been some very interesting findings which represent avenues for further inquiry. However, in order to justify my claim that there is in fact a dearth in studies I wanted to examine how much the issue of authenticity is referred to in research journals. I selected five major journals from the field of applied linguistics and language teaching. The journals I chose (see Table 4.1) were selected based on an attempt to reflect a broad spectrum within the discipline; in other words I selected highly respected journals, some dealing mainly with empirical studies and some with more of a practical focus. This was based on my own familiarity with these journals. The results are based on a search conducted on the 28 March 2015. I simply searched across all issues of each journal for the keyword 'authentic' (including titles, abstracts and body of the articles). Table 4.1 presents the number of hits, the number of issues of each journal and the ratio of mentions of the term 'authentic' per issue. Impact factor is also reported for each journal as reported by the journals' own homepages, which I provide merely for reference.

Table 4.1 below shows that the term 'authentic' is mentioned frequently in each journal, especially in the ELTJ which claims to be more practitioner-oriented. However, even more research-oriented journals such *Applied Linguistics* and the *Modern Language Journal* seem to mention authenticity about one and a half times per issue. However, a modified search looking only for mentions of the term 'authentic' in the titles of articles revealed a very different picture (see Table 4.2 and Figure 4.7).

Of course, I cannot say with any certainty that this method has narrowed down the articles to only those that present original research into authenticity. This is an extremely crude and quick method of searching over the literature from a very narrow selection. However, it does allow us a very rudimentary insight into how the concept of authenticity orbits many of the discussions about language learning and teaching without ever really being looked at in-depth. The lack of titles dealing with authenticity would suggest that very few of these studies are actually dealing with empirical research into the topic, as it would be unlikely for a study that does deal directly with authenticity to leave the key word out of the title of the paper.

Table 4.1 Journals surveyed for authenticity articles

Journal	Journal start	Hits	Over X years	Over X issues	Ratio	Impact factor
Modern Language Journal	1916	1090	99	641	1.70	1.181
ELTJ	1946	692	69	285	2.43	0.759
Language Learning	1948	175	67	226	0.77	1.433
Applied Linguistics	1980	198	35	129	1.53	1.833
Language Teaching Research	1997	110	18	59	1.86	1.022

Table 4.2 Journals surveyed for mention of authenticity in the title of articles

Journal	Whole text hits	Title hits	Whole text ratio	Title only ratio
Modern Language Journal	1090	0	1.70	0.00
ELTJ	692	10	2.43	0.04
Language Learning	175	3	0.77	0.01
Applied Linguistics	198	2	1.53	0.02
Language Teaching Research	110	0	1.86	0.00

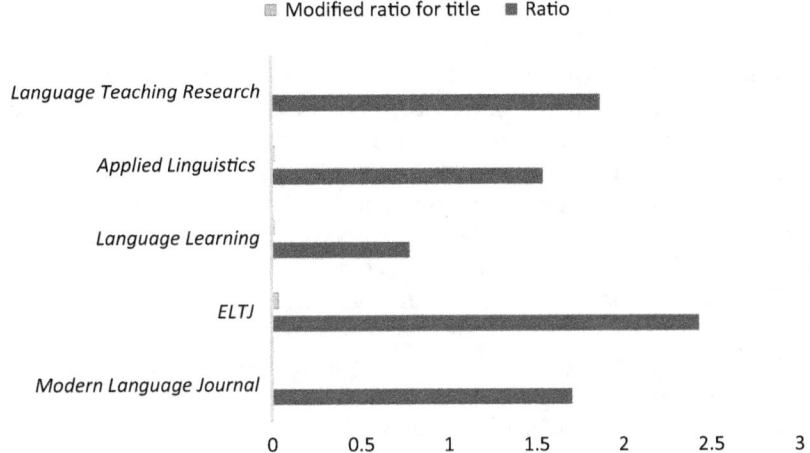

Figure 4.7 Ratio of hits for search term 'authentic' in whole text vs title

Although the evidence I provide in this section is by no means a comprehensive survey of the research literature into authenticity, it is designed merely to demonstrate that authenticity is a word which is commonly used in research literature but very rarely the subject of research in itself.

Complementary to my own brief survey, in a comprehensive study Amor (2002) used a qualitative, interpretive design to look at the scholarly discussions that form the 'authenticity debate' and to examine 'the incompleteness of the previous research' (2002: 15). Amor not only surveys the literature on second language acquisition and applied linguistics, but also the literature on the nature of language and how authenticity manifests itself differently in these areas. He also pays particular attention to what he calls genuine language use (following Widdowson, 1978), and uses discourse analysis with detailed commentaries on transcripts from a variety of spoken, written and even visual language samples. Amor's genuine samples are eclectic, drawing from sources as diverse as advertising, service encounters, poetry and news media, and in doing so he often compares scripted or pedagogically contrived versions with the 'genuine' article. His study delves into certain controversial aspects of authentic or genuine language use, such as word-play and unpredictable spelling. He criticises the notion that such discourse is inaccessible, and he states that stressing genuine material 'is only for "natives" merely deepens the rift between so-called "natives" and "non-natives"' (2002: 14). Amor discusses the way teachers and learners move together across a continuum during the process of authentication, which draws heavily on the work of Widdowson and van Lier, whose work in turn is a reflection of the existentialist conception of authenticity. I will also expand upon this idea in the next chapter.

Amor's work also examines how authentication is written into certain types of discourse, such as the method of addressing the reader directly, as in the famous 1914 war-time poster by Alfred Leete which reads 'your country needs YOU' (Amor, 2002: 274). He also, albeit briefly, examines international varieties of English from countries such as Singapore and Pakistan, alongside a contextual tendency to reference Germanic countries, where Amor conducted his studies. In an interesting section he presents a sample from Singaporean poet Edwin Thumboo. The poem 'May 1954' was published in *Ulysses by the Merlion* and can now be accessed on Thumboo's personal website (Thumboo, 2005). In the commentary, Amor states:

> Here the English language is used as a weapon against the British colonial masters. The language is absolutely British. The anger is absolutely Singaporean and Anti-British. (2002: 78)

This extract again highlights the complex nature of authenticity when the construct is applied to language. Although Amor's study provides an additional reference for those who are interested in the study of authenticity in second language acquisition and applied linguistics, the fact that it has not been more widely mentioned in other studies is perhaps an indication that the more prestigious journal articles (such as Gilmore's) or well-known scholars (such as Widdowson and van Lier) tend to dominate these discussions, but there are a number of scholars working on the topic whose contributions are equally valuable, such as Römer (2004) Trabelsi (2010) Lai-kun (2014) and others yet unknown to the present author. Therefore, when I discuss the dearth of empirical studies, perhaps it would be more appropriate to speak of a small body of empirical work which seems to hold a monopoly over much of the discussion, and certainly a need for more comprehensive reviews of the literature.

Finally, although this is more of an anecdotal observation, it is worth noting that many of the people who have made major contributions to the small body of research that does exists have often done so as part of their PhD research. For example, Matthew Peacock's (1997b) study is based on his PhD (1996), and then presumably used again for two articles (1997a, 1998). Alex Gilmore's review (2007a) is based on the literature review for his PhD (2007b), and the research presented in his paper for *Language Learning* (2011) is also based on the PhD data. Freda Mishan completed her PhD at the University of Limerick, entitled *Authenticity in language learning materials design* (2000). Although it is safe to assume that her PhD was just the starting point for her long interest in authenticity, and that much of what she put into her book *Designing Authenticity into Language Learning Materials* (2005) had moved on and developed a lot in the time since she completed her doctoral degree, it would also seem important to note that her PhD was on the same topic and therefore she must have put a great deal of work into the initial stages of her own quest for authenticity. Readers may not be surprised to learn that authenticity and motivation is the subject of my own PhD research. In some ways, this demonstrates that interest in authenticity at the level of empirical research is something rather specialist. It is not a subject to be taken up lightly, by any means. And yet, it is suffering greatly from a lack of empirical evidence that directly examines authenticity as a concept and how it influences motivation, acquisition and other affective factors in the process of learning a foreign language. In particular (as is often the case) there is very little research into language teachers on the subject of authenticity (although see Külekçi, 2015).

Conclusion

Authenticity is a complex issue, and even a limited understanding of it requires an understanding of other inter-connected concepts as well. This is not surprising, since the entire field of SLA is itself an interdisciplinary one. In order to study SLA one needs to have more than a good understanding of ideas that originate in as diverse fields as linguistics, psychology, sociology and education, to name a few. Rod Ellis mentions that even back in 1993 when he wrote the first edition to his comprehensive overview of SLA, the field was 'a rather amorphous field of study with elastic boundaries' (2008: x). He then went on to explain that he had worried whether SLA would even be able to survive as a 'coherent field of study' but that 'today, I am more prepared to acknowledge that this may not be important and that diversity of approach and controversy constitute signs of the field's vigour and an inevitable consequence of the attempt to understand a complex phenomenon' (R. Ellis, 2008: xxii–xxiii).

Here, Ellis seems to be echoing the complexity which I discussed in Chapter 2, and which has recently started to emerge as an essential aspect in our understanding of the language acquisition process. Tudor (2003) says that complexity theory and ecological perspectives seem to be an obvious and natural fit for second language acquisition, and these theories are now causing what Dörnyei and Ushioda (2011) refer to as the fourth distinct (and emergent) phase in L2 motivational theory which they label the sociodynamic period. Since motivation is a vital component in successful language acquisition, this is a key piece of evidence that complexity theory is being influential in reshaping ideas which are central to language learning and teaching. It is no coincidence that authenticity and motivation are often mentioned in the same sentence, and have what I would even call a symbiotic relationship in SLA. Authenticity and motivation are common collocates in both literature and staff-room discourse. It was due to my reading on the developments in motivation that led me to question how such influences would be relevant to authenticity. Much as the field of L2 motivation is adapting to the complications that globalisation brings to important issues such as culture and integration, using dynamic systems approaches as a way of seeking a fuller understanding, I feel authenticity is also in need of an updated examination.

As I mentioned in the previous section, authenticity is something of a paradox. There are some contradictions inherent in the various definitions, and as Gilmore (2007a) points out there is also a deal of overlap. One definition which is most unfavourable is the one based on native speakers. As I explained in Chapter 2 when I looked at native-speakerism, this definition can potentially harm teachers' self-efficacy by excluding them from being able to feel like an authentic speaker, and the prejudice against non-native speaker models is as much the product of non-native speakers as it is of native speakers. And learners too, will be affected by this, as their own prejudices are more and more deeply ingrained by institutional practices and by potentially detrimental teaching practices. Of course I am not saying that all bad teaching or all teacher self-efficacy issues can be attributed to authenticity, but it is certainly an important and yet under-examined aspect of teacher cognition. I completely agree with Illés (2009: 145) when she notes that 'it is not necessary for a piece to be written by native speakers for native speakers in order to be authentic in the classroom context'. It would be easy to dismiss this 'native speaker' definition as being out of date and no longer in use, but the reality is that this is a persistent definition. Much like a Trojan virus, we don't always see it in the open, it is not always overtly stated, but the native definition is implied by all kinds of long established gate keepers which are not likely to change overnight, and not without a firm reconceptualising of the idea of authenticity. To this we also need to add serious and meticulous empirical inquiry in order to understand fully what the relationship is and how authenticity plays a role in contemporary teaching practices around the world. As I have already established, authenticity is an important concept within existential philosophy; Henri Rousseau defined authenticity as coming from one's own volition or natural self, and by contrast inauthenticity came from external influences. Martin Heidegger also spoke about authenticity as being part of one's true identity (Yacobi, 2012). Interestingly, these philosophical concepts highlight the actual difficulty of being an authentic person or living your life in a 100% authentic way. We are constantly struggling with both internal and, especially, external forces that prevent us from being our natural selves and, therefore, being authentic. I provide this information simply to once again highlight the close etymological links between authenticity and autonomy, and the philosophical connections between authenticity and self-volition, which ties it to motivation. Autonomy is also vital in motivation, as I shall discuss later, and I believe that these three concepts – authenticity, autonomy and motivation – are all vital ingredients for setting up successful language learning scenarios.

5 The Authenticity Continuum

Introduction

In the previous four chapters I have gone over the discussions about authenticity from various positions, and explained how it stands in our current super-diverse, multilingual society where a hyper-centralised and yet disembodied version of the English language floats around the globalised world, changing shape and colour depending on who you are, where you are and how you look at it. This could be what Fairclough (2001) refers to as the globalisation of discourse. It has been something of a personal quest for me to get to this stage. Most of this chapter is in fact a synthesis of the ideas put forward by scholars as part of the 'authenticity debate' (Mishan, 2005). Having dissected the concept of authenticity as much as possible, it is now my intention to reassemble the main points in a way which attempts to highlight the relevance of these discussions to the present environment of English as a global language. In this chapter I will explain how authenticity can be viewed as a continuum, and how this continuum can be used to evaluate the appropriateness of learning materials selected for language teaching classes. The continuum is also envisioned as a way of empowering learners and allowing them to get a better understanding of English, which is for many of them merely a subject to be taught and learned rather than a living language. The global position of English also makes it more abstract, and although many learners know English is important in the world, many of them will find it hard to see how it relates to them directly. In some cases, English and the institutional pressure that surrounds it can become a disadvantage, especially for those wanting to pursue careers in other languages (Piller, 2015; Zhang, 2011). On the other hand, for many others, English is a language that frees them from a prescriptive identity imposed upon them by their own society, and conversely they are able to express themselves more freely and authentically in English, despite it being their second language.

A Pivotal Period in the Evolution of Authenticity

The more we drill down into the concept of authenticity, the more it begins to break up and separate. Although these reductions and compartmentalisations may seem to complicate the matter rather than to simplify it, I believe that having identified some of the main components of authenticity we are in a good position to actually step back from it and try once again to view the central idea that authenticity is a process, dependent of various other components. Seeing authenticity in this way may help reflect the interactions of authenticity in the no longer clear-cut domains in which English is used throughout the world as a tool for international communication. For this reason, I would like to once and for all do away with the idea that authenticity can be defined in terms of a single target culture or in relation to the origin of the text used. Authenticity needs to be conceptualised in a way that takes into account the degrees of involvement and levels of personal engagement that will result from the interactions taking place in which the language is being used, which preferably will also feature some form of local contextualisation. Authenticity also needs to take account of the context of the learners, particularly in order to gauge the relevance of learning materials to them and thus facilitate a higher level of engagement. However, all this complexity in the definition could make the notion of authenticity very difficult to convey to other practitioners, and therefore this subjective concept needs to be packaged in a way which can be presented simply and effectively. Indeed, as I said at the start of this book, these ideas are not new. Amor (2002) argues that 'authenticity in its various manifestations should completely replace an emphasis on form and accuracy in [language] teaching' (2002: 20). Although conceding that learners need to be able to acquire an understanding of both form and meaning (which he sees as inseparable), Amor also argues that a process of negotiation (with the teacher) is also required in order to choose topics which are personally meaningful.

> These two necessities form the ends of a continuum along which teachers and learners should be moving throughout the process of teaching and learning a foreign language. (Amor, 2002: 20)

In this way, Amor closely follows the existential strand of the authenticity debate, with particular focus on the process of authentication that happens when a learner encounters a text or piece of language.

The idea that authenticity is a process, that it is not culturally specific and should incorporate social and contextual aspects has been a feature in the literature on authenticity for decades, as I have demonstrated many times in this book. However, these discussions do not seem to have made much impact in the language teaching classroom, where the definition of authenticity is still often essentialised and reduced into something that could disadvantage the majority of English speakers around the globe. In order to make a more complex, dynamic and realistic version of authenticity accessible to language teaching practitioners, I feel there is a need for a conveyable and easily communicated explanation of authenticity that takes into account all of its complexities and shifts the centre of gravity away from culturist notions. In order to take into account all these complex factors, I have developed an authenticity continuum which tries to depict the interactions of authenticity and includes social and contextual axes.

The Authenticity Continuum

In order to incorporate the majority of speakers of English into the concept of authenticity, while also allowing for such important factors as motivation, autonomy and identity, I believe that authenticity might best be considered not as a binary set of absolutes, or even as a grey area with two extremes on either side, but as a continuum with both social and contextual axes. The horizontal axis represents the social dimension of authenticity, at one end the learner or *individual* and their needs, linguistic ability and personal motivation to learn, at the other the target language use *community*. This might a community within an L1 country such as the USA or UK, or it might be the international community where English is used as a tool for communication in multilingual contexts, or it could even be a workplace community where English will be needed in order to interact with colleagues. This community is very likely to be manifested as an *imagined community*, as proposed by Benedict B. Anderson (2006) and developed as an aspect of language learner identity by Bonny Norton and others (see for example Kanno & Norton, 2003; Norton, 2013). In this way, the community is not so much a physical reality as a social extension of the individuals' identity, albeit one based on a real group of people or an actual discourse community. The vertical dimension of the continuum is meant to represent the context of language use. The continuum presents the two contexts which are likely to be most relevant to language learning; the *classroom* and the *use domain* where the communication takes place. The term use domain borrows from the concept of target language use (TLU) domain as described by Bachman and Palmer (1996) as a dimension for evaluating the usefulness and authenticity of language assessments. They define the TLU domain as the 'situation or context in which the test taker will be using the language outside of the test itself' (1996: 18), in other words in situations other than those being assessed where the language is being used, presumably for a 'real' communicative purpose. For Bachman and Palmer, the TLU is also an essential aspect of their definition of test authenticity 'as the degree of correspondence of a given language test task to the features of a TLU task' (1996: 23). For the purposes of the authenticity continuum, I am expanding on Bachman and Palmer's TLU domain concept and applying it to mean communicative interactions where the foreign language is used beyond instructional settings. In other renderings of the continuum I have used the word 'reality' in place of the use domain (Pinner, 2014a, 2014b), but I have now altered the continuum in an attempt to avoid polarising the classroom context as 'not-real', for reasons discussed in the previous chapter (see also Mishan, 2005; Taylor, 1994; van Lier, 1988; Widdowson, 1978; Widdowson, 2001). In essence I have no problem with the use of the term 'reality', as it is used by Morrow (1977) and Gilmore (2007a, 2007b), just as long as this does not exclude the classroom as being a situation where language can be described as being used for a genuine communicative purpose. Community and context are similar in some respects, although the context is supposed to represent situations where language is used, whereas the community refers specifically to persons and social groups. The continuum is presented as a vertical contextual axis and a horizontal social axis; however, the continuum should not be seen as linear, although it is presented as such because of the two-dimensional nature of the diagram. In order to represent how the various components may overlap and influence each other I have presented them as circulating arrows, rather like currents which affect dynamic changes in the nature of authenticity, since authenticity is understood more as a process than a state (see Figure 5.1).

It is my hope that the diagram offers a communicable version of authenticity that can encourage a more open dialogue about the nature of authenticity as a process, dependent and multiple dynamic variables. The continuum attempts to visualise some of the interactions that contribute to authenticity as conceptualised from a chaos/complexity theory perspective. In this way, the diagram is an attempt at presenting the complexities of authenticity as simply as possible. By doing so, I am attempting to provide a kind of 'packaged' definition which can be more widely disseminated than the hundreds of articles and books that have gone previously into making up the 'authenticity debate'. In other words, I have spent many hours reading up on authenticity and struggling with the conflicting arguments and overlapping definitions, and it might be unrealistic to expect others (even those with a deep interest in authenticity) to do the same. Of course, many scholars will no-doubt be well aware of these discussions and there are many eminent applied linguists and SLA researchers who understand the issue of authenticity much better than myself. However, it is certainly not practical to expect the majority of language teachers to be aware of such theoretical discussions, or to have the time and energy to do so much background reading. Language teachers are not ignorant to the educational theories that surround them, by any means. In fact, many practitioners benefit from and contribute to theoretical discussions in education all the time (Williams & Burden, 1997). However, from my own research and experience I have come to the conclusion that for the majority of practicing language teachers (both L1 and L2 speakers of the language

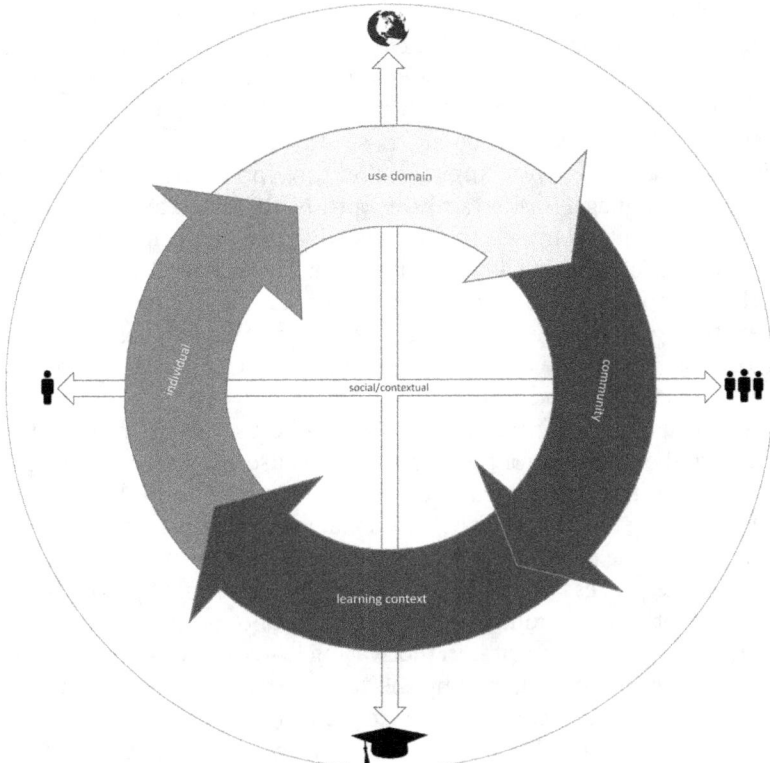

Figure 5.1 The authenticity continuum

they teach) the issue of authenticity is thorny and vague, and generally people tend to default back to the 'classic' definition of authenticity as being some piece of realia, usually one generated by the target language culture. Although this is not necessarily always problematic, it does invite the dangerous association with culturism and linguistic imperialism. As discussions on these issues continually assert, culturist assumptions and ideologies that disadvantage and segregate people tend to happen on an almost subconscious level. For example, people who contribute to the native-speakerist 'othering' of individuals based on the status of their first language and the culture of their origin do not often do so intentionally or out of malice. Native-speakerism is something that arises from ingrained assumptions that have become part of the ordinary way of things. By returning to the 'classic' and persistent definition of authenticity time and again, the concept of authenticity has come to a pivotal stage in its evolution because it is no longer tenable in the context of English as an international language. This is because of the incredible diversity of English varieties, the globalising hyper-diversity of cultures and the dissemination of information facilitated by modern forms of digital communication. Therefore, although the ideas within the authenticity continuum are not particularly new, there is an urgent need to reconceptualise authenticity from the perspective of English as an international language, and to communicate this in a way which can reach the main stakeholders in the 'authenticity debate'. In particular, these stakeholders are those for whom English is a learned foreign language, and for whom English is becoming a disembodied language. It is certainly an optimistic vision I am presenting, and in truth I am sceptical myself that a single diagram can help to empower the billions of English learners around the world. But, hopefully by compressing all of that complexity into a single diagram I am making it easier for language teachers to begin critically evaluating the content that they use for teaching, and to question its contextual relevance and social implications in relation to their own students as individuals.

The authenticity continuum might also be useful when materials are being selected or adapted for the classroom because it invites both the teacher and the learner to question their relationship to the content being used and how it will relate to them and their personal learning aims (see Pinner, 2014a for examples). One purpose of the continuum is to allow for the importance of self and the process of engagement with the materials and the language. In this way, the continuum incorporates autonomy and identity, which Ushioda (2011b) notes are vital in motivating learners. For Ushioda, a person cannot be adequately explained by the sum of their parts or by categorising them according to individual differences or learning styles. She advocates a *person in context relational* view of motivation in her paper (Ushioda, 2009), and in many ways the continuum tries to encompass both the individual and multiple identities of the learner and bridge that with the often distant realties of the target language use domains. This view of motivation is also compatible with Dörnyei's L2 motivational self system (2009), which has been widely adopted as a way of conceptualising motivation. The notions of context and self are especially important in EFL contexts, where learners may not know much about the culture and they may be learning in compulsory language classes. In this respect, motivation and authenticity are closely related, and hence through experiencing the materials and language in a process of personal engagement, the students would hopefully find authentic materials more motivating if they can relate to them personally and as individuals. This also strongly ties in the concept of autonomy, which is an essential ingredient in motivation (Deci & Ryan, 1985; Dörnyei & Ushioda, 2011) and, as I stated earlier, autonomy is twinned with the concept of authenticity back down to its most basic etymological origin.

The continuum was devised as a way of guiding teachers and materials writers to consider things from other dimensions and contexts, and as a way of validating those contexts. I saw it as a way to get away from the cultural and linguistic imperialism embedded within the 'classic' definition of authenticity and to give more credibility to materials that focus on local contexts closer to the individual learner. A way of showing that there is no *best* material or type of material or even *best* model to learn English. It was also my intention that this idea should be communicated back to the learners, as quite often learners themselves view authenticity as something belonging to the realm of the target language community. By informing the students that their language is valid and authentic, I hope that they will find this empowering and enable them to engage more with the learning process. In Chapter 3 I briefly touched upon a research project which I carried out with Japanese High School teachers of English as part of a training workshop which is accredited by the Japanese Ministry of Education (MEXT). The workshop was entitled *Using and Adapting Authentic Materials to Help Motivate Students*. During the day-long workshop I spent a good deal of time discussing the practical points of authenticity, but for the first of the four 90 minute sessions I go over the theory of authenticity. The purpose of this is to first gain an understanding of what my participants understand by the term 'authenticity', and then to help realign their ideas to those that I have presented in this book (although admittedly somewhat more concisely). In 2013 I was just beginning to flesh out the idea of authenticity as a continuum, and so I took the opportunity to collect research from my participants about their reaction to the proposed continuum (see Pinner, 2014a for a more detailed outline of the study). Basically at the end of the session, we are required by MEXT to set some kind of assessment, since the session counts toward the renewal of the participants' teaching licence, which they must do every ten years by attending professional development sessions like the one I was holding.

As one purpose of conducting this research was to gain a better understanding of teachers' perceptions of the authenticity continuum, I asked specifically what the teachers thought about it. This study collected data from two groups of teachers during an INSET training activity, which was part of a MEXT accredited training course. I made audio recordings of the sessions, as well as keeping field-notes as the session took place, which were then used to create a detailed research journal entry. In addition, participants completed questionnaires before the session (designed by the awarding institution, not by me), which I had access to beforehand so that I could design my session around the participants' requests. Many of the comments made in these questionnaires were also useful for analysis. After the course, participants were asked to write a reflective paper, which could be done either in English or Japanese, and this is where the majority of my data came from and the source for most of the analysis. Three out of 33 wrote in Japanese, which was then translated by myself with the aid of a Japanese colleague. I then typed up the responses into a Microsoft Word document, which was then imported into NVivo 10 qualitative analysis software for coding and analysis. Figure 5.2 is a word-frequency cloud generated by NVivo 10 using the participant's collected responses.

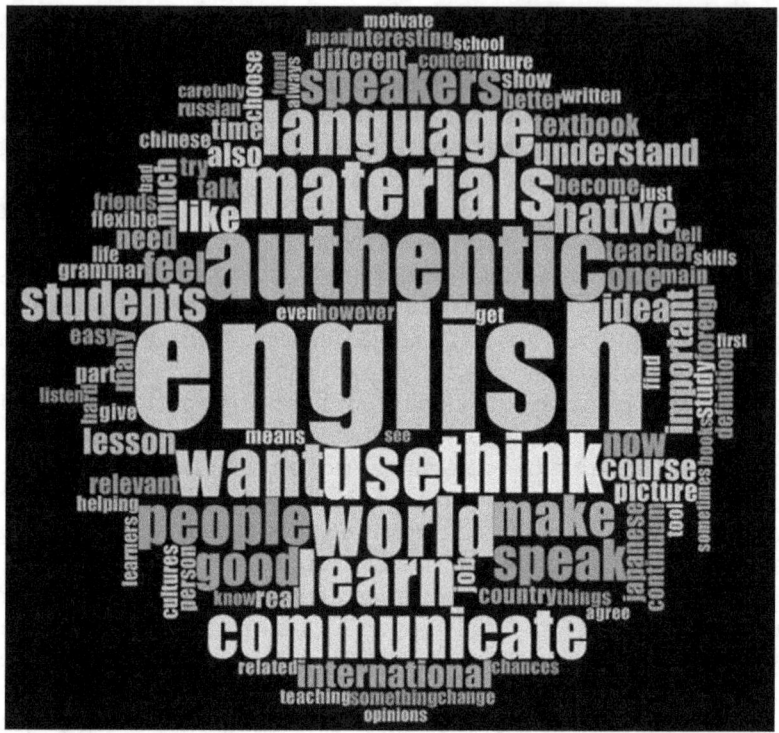

Figure 5.2 Holistic word frequencies from authenticity continuum study

In the final assessment the report question provided a written summary of the continuum as well as the diagram, and then participants had 40 minutes to write a response to the following prompt:

- What is your opinion about the authenticity continuum? Has your idea about authenticity changed by participating in this workshop? In what way (if any)?

However, I did not mention to the participants that the continuum was of my own invention. When I put it on the screen, I left out any citation or attribution. However, I cannot be sure that participants did not 'read between the lines' and guess that the continuum was part of my own research, so the responses I present below should be taken with that in mind. All the responses come from two sessions of the workshop, which I held in Osaka and Tokyo in August 2013. The fact that the data I collected were from pedagogical sources, natural products of what happened in the training course anyway, means that the study's methodology falls under the framework of exploratory practice (Allwright & Hanks, 2009) because 'exploratory research embeds data collection into the actual practice of teaching' (R. Ellis, 2012: 31). There were ten in-service teacher participants at Osaka and 25 at Tokyo. I included a tick-box at the bottom of the sheet to ask if teachers consented to my using their responses in the study to ensure the data collection was in-line with ethical guidelines. Not all of the participants opted in; two out of 35 chose to opt out, so their data were omitted from the coding and analysis, so the total number of participants in the study was $n = 33$. Names have also been altered. One participant commented that she felt the continuum was useful as a way of analysing the learning materials she chose to use in class:

> I think the authenticity continuum is very useful to evaluate the materials from several aspects. Also, it is important to know whether the materials are authentic or not before giving them in class. [...] Evaluating the materials will lead us to improve our lessons. It's also possible to say that even the students can assess the materials after the class by using the authenticity continuum to improve the lessons more. I think the authenticity continuum [can be used] to improve the lessons more. (Mari, Tokyo, 2013)

Here, Mari thinks the continuum is not only useful to teachers in assessing materials but also for students. Explaining to students the relevance of the materials being used in class is certainly an admirable strategy to encourage autonomy and engagement. Quite often I think it helps to directly explain the value of the materials being used in the class, and even localised textbooks possess a degree of authenticity on the continuum if they are well designed or the teacher makes the most of them using appropriate tasks. There is certainly an argument for explaining the authentic value of the materials to learners, as Clarke (1989) advocates, because involving the learners in assessing the materials leads to greater involvement and thus motivation. Tomlinson (2011a: 11) also highlights the importance of making learners aware of the pedagogic value of the materials, citing empirical evidence that has connected improved learning and recall when students perceived a direct personal significance to the learning materials. This way such materials and lessons can be authenticated and their learning value made clearer.

> In my opinion, as authenticity includes some complicated elements such as materials, language in use, tasks, productions, classrooms, culture or community, authenticity continuum helps us understanding what are the important things for both of English teachers and learners as a second language. Living in the modern international world, it is very important for the English teachers and learners to communicate with people [who] speak different languages. (Shiori, Osaka, 2013)

Again, Shiori's comments show that she could see the value in involving her learners with the materials and encourage them to engage and evaluate them. However, at the end of her report she wrote:

> Authenticity continuum could shows and give us some clues for making communication easier, helping us further understanding each other in our world and helping us to live our life better and more meaningful. (Shiori, Osaka, 2013)

In my coding of this comment I made a note that I was worried that Shiori had possibly guessed that the continuum was my own design, and that she was purposefully trying to overstate the importance of the continuum in order to say what she thought I wanted to hear. In other words, I was dubious that her comments were genuine, as she basically seemed to be generalising the continuum to the extent that it could be used to make the world a better place. Perhaps it was cynical of me to think this, but then on the other-hand, perhaps Shiori was genuinely empowered and optimistic about the effect of broadening the concept of authenticity. After all, authenticity is a central component to the Self, and a person's professional identity can often be a defining feature of who they are, and how they are seen by society.

> According to this continuum, the definition of 'authenticity' is very wide and flexible. I was surprised at this definition and will try to deal with authentic materials in more flexible ways in future. First, as a language teacher, my first goal is to have students acquire good skills of using English as a communication tool. Therefore, I want to choose authentic material in real settings, which are in lower half of the continuum. I didn't intend to use the whole part of the authentic material, but I want to let students get the general idea of the materials. If they grasp the outline of the authentic materials, they will gain more confidence than when they learn text books. Second, I will choose more materials from World Englishes, which are in the right half of the continuum. Before this class, I sometimes hesitated to use that kind of materials, because it may not be accepted as 'authentic' one. Now, I will choose world English material more flexibly if the content it is appropriate for my class. I also need to be carefully about the task because the task also need to be real. To sum up, this continuum gave me wider and more flexible ideas about 'authenticity'. I will try to use more various 'authentic' materials and be more careful about planning 'authentic' tasks. (Takako, Osaka, 2013)

One of the few male participants (from a total of only 5 out of 33), made a comment reminiscent of Widdowson's (1990) means/ends equation of authenticity. Writing in Japanese, he explained that:

> I think authenticity is necessary to learners. My idea [of] authenticity hasn't changed, before or after this class. I have been using authentic materials before this workshop. First of all, students want to learn living English, I use textbooks and other activities and try not to bore the students, but when I use authentic materials in the class, compared to using textbooks, students react very differently to authentic materials. When I use authentic materials, students enjoy it more and seem to engage with the class more. (Tada, Osaka, 2013)

The perceived authenticity of the materials here seems to generate a reciprocal feedback loop of positive motivation in Tada and his students. It has been commented that teacher and student motivation is deeply connected, and may even be 'either positively or negatively synergistic' (Deci *et al.*, 1997: 68) and so it follows that teachers who are motivated by what they teach will be more motivating for their students in the way they teach. Tada's belief that what he is teaching will be useful to the students through its authentic achievement of being *a means to an ends* probably means that these classes are the ones which both he and the students get most of out of. This also connects with some of the comments that a number of teacher-participants made about using authentic materials as a kind of a 'treat' or motivational 'carrot' (as oppose to 'the stick' which is preparing for assessments). This is something I detailed in my research journal, noting that several of the teacher-participants had approached me between sessions or commented during the session that they felt authentic materials were the language teaching equivalent of a reward for students after having completed difficult tasks, which were also implied to be both boring and inauthentic. One of the teacher-participants detailed this in her report:

> I knew the word 'authentic material' in Japanese and I sometimes use newspapers, websites or DVDs in my lesson to motivate students. But I thought authentic materials were optional, just for fun and use them after term exams to kill time. After term exams, student don't want to prepare for lessons and it is difficult to have them concentrate on lessons using textbooks. That's why I use them after exams before vacation. However, I learned that authentic materials have much more possibilities. If I can choose an appropriate material, giving careful consideration to age of learners, their levels of language ability, relevance of materials, they can be the main materials and I can greatly motivate my students. Also, I learned the authenticity has some grey part and the definition is not strict. But I didn't notice first point is that there is a strong connection between students' motivation and teachers' one. From now, I try to choose materials interesting to both my students and me. Second, I should have thought about 'autonomy' when choosing materials. Teachers should control lessons to come extend, but 'autonomy' is very

important in education. There are still some questions to solve, but I'd like to adapt authentic materials to my lesson and I'll enjoy myself learning English with my students. (Hiromi, Tokyo, 2013)

Hiromi here highlights the process of interaction and enjoyment, making it seem that she needs to use authentic materials in order to reward and maintain a bond with her students, especially after putting them through their paces studying toward exams. However, she is unable to make the connection between what she wants to teach and what she has to teach. This is somehow at odds with Mishan's concept of challenge (see above section 'Challenge'), in which she explained that authentic materials are actually good for learning because they force learners to work hard in order to understand and acquire new structures. Interestingly, Tada also added to this discussion when he noted that:

What students want is not just fun but a little bit difficult so they feel they have gone over a hurdle to reach a slightly more difficult point. <L + 1> because of that, I think sometimes it's time consuming to choose the right materials, but I pay attention to the visual and audio so that students can learn 'living English'. (Tada, Osaka, 2013)

Here, Tada seems to question the instructional validity of enjoyable lessons – something which is quite a common belief that the more serious learning (non-fun) type of learning is a necessary evil, and fun learning is a reward for having got through the drudgery of preparing for exams and doing dull, probably very inauthentic, language work which is designed only to improve declarative knowledge rather than providing an *experience* of the language in use (Tomlinson & Masuhara, 2010: 400). This is something which goes against certain educational principles, such as flow theory (Csikszentmihalyi, 1997, 2013) and gamification (Lazzaro, 2009). I would like to say that I think that all learning should be meaningful and enjoyable, but I am also aware that many teachers are forced to teach from Government Issue textbooks or have responsibilities to prepare students for high-stakes exams, and they are not in positions of power to be able to do much to alter the situation. In such cases, it is still possible to maintain authenticity in the language classroom, by facilitating the moments of interaction and personal meaning making that make up the process of authenticating learning at the personal level (Külekçi, 2015). This is something that Mai touched on when she described the process of personalising lessons by considering contextual relevance and attempting to predict both her own and her students' level of engagement.

Before taking this class I was thinking that authentic materials are newspapers, magazines, movies and so on. Now I know that more and more things can be authentic materials if I use them in an authentic way. The biggest reason I thought so is that I learned there are four keywords to be authentic; text/materials, language in use, tasks and output/production. I thought only about 'materials' and didn't really think that 'tasks' can be authentic. I learned that even a school textbook can be authentic when I make student think about their own ideas about the topic. So from now on, I will think about how the students can think that the material is relevant to them. Secondly, the authenticity continuum was new to me. When I choose a material, I thought only 'is this good to teach a certain grammar?' and 'Are my students interested in that?'. Now I know there are more aspects. I think community is a very interesting way of rating materials. [...] I should think about to whom (or what community) I'm teaching. I learned that authenticity is not simple, so I can try to think about MY authentic materials (Mai, Tokyo, 2013).

Mai seems to agree that the continuum is a useful tool for evaluating materials before choosing what to use in class, although she seems to simultaneously hold the view of authentic materials as being something interesting, while at the same time evaluating that materials pedagogic applications in terms of grammar. In this way, she highlights the paradox of authenticity by selecting authentic in order to both provide an interesting experience and yet also supply examples for grammar; inauthentic and authentic seem rolled into one as she makes her decision considering grammar and linguistic focus but also the students' level of personal engagement. Although she does not mention motivation, it is clear when she talks about materials that are authentic to her, she will be drawing on the discussions that took place around the workshop, in which I made it clear that content that is motivating for the teacher will probably also be more motivating for the students. The connection between teacher and student motivation, and how this is facilitated through the use of 'authentically engaging' (Holliday, 2005) learning content is something which I think could be looked into more deeply, and would certainly be an interesting avenue for further inquiry. Research of this kind would be difficult to measure or ascertain statistics on, however, so I would recommend qualitative forms of inquiry that view motivation and authenticity as dynamic components (N. Cowie & Sakui, 2011; Dörnyei et al., 2015; Ushioda, 2015). Momoko, in comments which reflected those made by Mai, also mentioned the continuum as being useful in helping her to select appropriate and potentially useful materials.

I think the authenticity continuum is a relatively new idea for Japanese teachers, but really important. When I make a lesson plan, I always focus on its purpose and its goal. 'Why do you use these contents?' 'what ability can my students foster?' These questions are sometimes really hard to answer for me and other Japanese English teachers, even if we teach English every day. The authenticity continuum is one of the best clues to make English lessons practical. Since then, in Japanese education only teacher and students have been mainly involved. I mean it's like classrooms are the world and it's real. However, the authenticity continuum shows classroom is the part of it in learning and show our connections to reality. I think it will surely be able to have teachers and students use English in practical ways. Before this workshop I just thought that 'authentic' means 'native'; using a newspaper in English class is better than using a textbook. But now, at the end of the workshop, I can talk more about authenticity, giving my today's experiences as an example. I have felt negative about myself as a non-native English speaker but teach English. Now, I don't. Authenticity connects me to not only English but also learning. I think my students also are a little afraid of English in a different way but authentic materials, authentic tasks etc. will surely help them to learn. This is not because the contents are filled with English but with authenticity. (Momoko, Tokyo, 2013)

I have already partially cited Momoko's comments about feeling negatively about being a 'non-native' speaker of English, but I chose to include the entire comment in all its context because it is such an important piece of discourse. This also echoes findings by Kimura (2014), who conducted a seven-year longitudinal study to create an ethnographic narrative of one Chinese teacher of English. When interviewing his subject, his participant talked about her 'shame' in being an L2 Chinese teacher of English, even though this person was clearly fluent in English and taught it for a living. For Momoko, acknowledging the reality of the classroom situation is essential for her in being able to authenticate both her own and her students' use of English. I imagine this is particularly because in Momoko's school (like thousands of schools across the expanding circle of English where the language has no official status except as a foreign language) the classroom is most likely to be the only place where students use and encounter English. It may even be, for many of them, the only place they *ever will* use English. And yet, they are still faced with high-stakes tests and social pressure to learn English as if their economic future rests on their language ability. In such cases, English can be an oppressive force (Piller, 2015; Zhang, 2011) and therefore, I would argue that being able to authenticate the language being used in and around the language classroom is an essential component in motivating Momoko's students and in helping her to feel that her work as an English teacher is valid. However, not all the participants felt so strongly about this, and there were even two people who said that they were unable to get away from the 'native speaker' definition of authenticity, despite the way I forcefully rejected that definition as an integral part of the workshop.

I have to confess that I have not really comprehended the concept of the authenticity continuum. I still have the idea that the languages use by so-called 'native speakers' in L1 countries are authentic. It is hard for me to eliminate the conventional ideas about authenticity after classroom English by non-native speakers was considered only for test and exam for long time. I partially agree with the concept of continuum in terms of context. Languages are used 'classrooms' are not opposite 'real world' or 'reality'. Classrooms are also part of reality and the English used in the classroom can be authentic. When I tell my students to open their textbook at page 10, my direction can be authentic because it is related to the real world. Context of language include the classroom situation and classroom English can be contextual. The concept of the authenticity continuum explains why classroom English can be authentic in some cases. (Mayumi, Tokyo, 2013)

Mayumi's comments are somewhat puzzling and the logic is sometimes hard to follow. For example, she seems to say that non-native English speakers are only able to teach test preparation and that real communication requires a native speaker. She then goes on to say that even a textbook can be authentic, but without fully elaborating on how she came to that realisation. She seems to be paraphrasing from the description of the continuum without having accepted it for herself. Indeed, she clearly states that she could not understand the continuum, and I fear that much of the discussion of authenticity may have gone over her head. It seems that Mayumi's difficulty could potentially stem from English proficiency issues, or at least from her own perceived lack of proficiency, which would result in a compounded lack of teaching self-efficacy. This is something I have not really touched upon much in this book, and therefore I think it would be a very useful avenue for further inquiry. To what extent is authenticity and proficiency related in foreign language teacher self-efficacy? Could it be another form of 'self-discrimination' as I mentioned in Chapter 3? More research into this area would be useful, especially looking at L2 teachers in regions where English is a foreign language; contexts that now make up a large majority of where English is spoken and learned around the world (Graddol, 1997, 2006).

Not only did teachers feel that the authenticity continuum would be helpful in their planning of lessons and involvement of learners in the evaluation process, but also they commented on how it had helped them to expand their own ideas about authenticity, which for many was a motivating or empowering experience. In addition to the comments I have already cited above from Momoko and Nanako about being motivated to use more authentic materials in class, I would draw the reader's attention to the following comments:

My idea about authenticity has changed dramatically by participating in this workshop. Before I joined this workshop, my definition of authenticity was the language material source from native speakers. Now, I have

> learned what really makes material, lesson to be authentic is how we teacher use it. I live in Hong Kong teaching language at an international school students from grade 1 to 8. I understand easily that English is used as a tool for communication in multilingual context. The authenticity continuum has well described what I have been doing in my classroom and makes a clear direction to where I aim at when school I work is going to be a cyber-school more and more ICT equipped. As a language teacher, I wish to motivated students. Each student has his/her own interest. When the materials and task is relevant to one's interested student will be more focused. While language is in use for community, we teacher incite each student to use language in community. That is shown as the horizontal axis. I have learned many teaching ideas to have students choose topic, discus on their interest while sharing in community, scaffolding their language proficiency with teachers help. The vertical dimension of the continuum present the context of language use. I have learned many tasks to connect language used in reality to classroom topic, sentence structure and grammar. And scaffolding language to more advanced and useable one. ICT tools makes class more accessible to the real situation of the language use. I feel more outgoing for ICT. (Takako, Tokyo, 2013)

As I stated earlier, the intention behind the workshop was to gain some kind of praxis and to be able to convert theories of authenticity into something practical. Momoko stated that '[t]he authenticity continuum is one of the best clues to make English lessons practical'. She stated that she believed using the continuum to assess the authenticity of the materials she was using could make her lessons more practical because it forces her to assess her students' needs. Again, this demonstrates the strong conceptual links between authenticity and motivation.

> The authenticity continuum tells me how to evaluate the authenticity of materials, and it's interesting. Before I participated in this workshop, I believed that authentic materials were the English statements used in countries like the UK or USA, English native countries. However, when we evaluated the authenticity of the Wall Street Journal according to the continuum, its authenticity was not high. Also, by comparing three examples of tasks, I realised that I chose A [see Figure 5.3], the task using an English language newspaper, as the least authentic. I was surprised at the result myself, and it was interesting to know that most of the teachers here had the same choice. This experience made me think it is important to have several points of view, or factors, to assess the authenticity of materials, and of course how to use them. (Aya, Tokyo, 2013)

Although widening the concept of authenticity may endanger it by making it 'too elusive to be useful' (Gilmore, 2007a: 98), what Aya has observed here is that because of the complexity of authenticity, it is helpful to view it as being composed of various dimensions because it *is* a multifaceted concept. Rather like the six blind men all touching a different part of the elephant and coming to a different conclusion about its nature, having just one definition for authenticity makes it hard to build a true understanding of the concept. Therefore, by presenting authenticity as a continuum we are inviting more engagement with the concept, rather than taking it at face value. In doing so, people bring their own critical applications to the concept of authenticity, and begin to analyse it subjectively while hopefully leaving behind the harmful culturist associations of the 'classic' definition of authenticity.

Practical examples

In order to show some examples of how the authenticity continuum might be used to evaluate the authenticity of learning materials, tasks or content, I will provide three examples and plot them onto the continuum. In a previous article and in the workshops described from which the above data were collected, I plotted authenticity directly onto the continuum like a radar chart (see Pinner, 2014a for two examples). Perhaps an even simpler representation of the authenticity continuum could utilise a radial Venn diagram, with the greatest authenticity being achieved where there is greater overlap between each component. For example, a balanced depiction would look like this (see Figure 5.3).

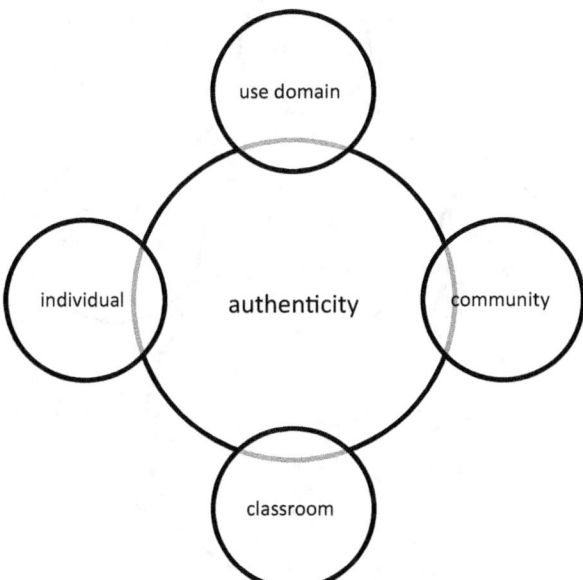

Figure 5.3 Plotting authenticity onto the continuum

116 Reconceptualising Authenticity for English as a Global Language

This simplified version will be used later in this section to illustrate how practical examples can be mapped onto the continuum in order to evaluate the authenticity of learning content or tasks. I think this is a better way of representing authenticity than the previously used radar chart method, because radar charts are typically used to display very accurate and precise measurements of multivariate data. However, using a radial Venn diagram as above, the inherent lack of measurability seems more apparent, and therefore I think there is less temptation to be led into thinking that authenticity can be measured accurately and objectively in the positivist tradition.

First I will illustrate the general principle with the example of a textbook being used in a general English class for a group of learners in a Korean high school. In the example I will imagine a textbook which was chosen by the teacher and written for an international (as oppose to local) audience. This example can be considered as one of the 'anodyne' examples much maligned by many materials writers and advocates of authenticity (Meddings & Thornbury, 2003; Mishan, 2011b; Tomlinson, 2008). In such a situation, authenticity might be plotted onto the continuum in a way that looks like this (see Figure 5.4).

In the above rendering, the classroom situation is foregrounded, and the relevance of the work done will mainly be concerned with the topics dictated by the textbook. The use domain is, of course, referenced in most foreign language textbooks, but it is not easy to connect the predominantly Anglo-global

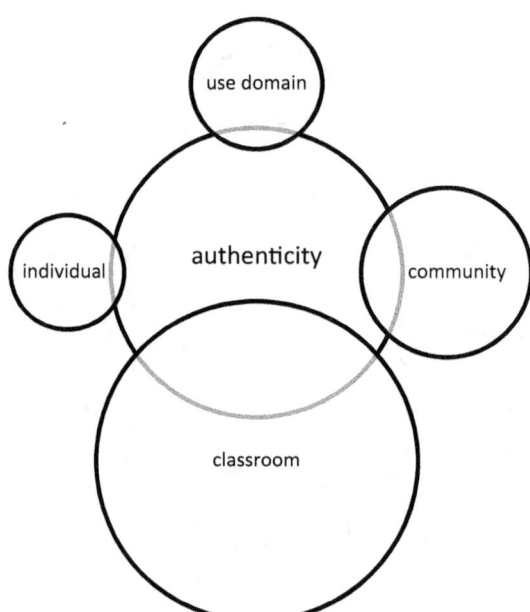

Figure 5.4 Plotting the authenticity of an international textbook

representations with the imagined community of English as an international language to which the student or teacher may ascribe. It may also be the case that the students do not have a very well fleshed out vision of the imagined community, which could lead to motivational inertia. This will also be connected to the student's image of their L2 Self (Ryan & Irie, 2014), which again would lead to problems with engagement. However, I would like to point out that even if the imagined community of language use and the individual's image of L2 Self are under-developed, they are always in existence and there is always a connection. Good teaching should be about facilitating and exploiting this connection as a way of capitalising on the link between authenticity and motivation.

By reconceptualising authenticity as a continuum, almost any classroom material or interaction can be evaluated to see how it relates to the different areas of authenticity. For example, a Graded Reader which has been abridged for a particular level might not be seen as authentic under the 'classic' definition of authenticity, in that it exists specifically for language learning purposes. However, Graded Readers would certainly count as authentic in that they provide an experience of the language and do not focus specifically on declarative knowledge. If a student has selected the Graded Reader themselves or it is relevant or of interest to them, Graded Readers would score highly on the Individual section of the spectrum, although they might fare less well on Community and Use Domain because they have been abridged and may bear only a slight resemblance to the original text (see Figure 5.5).

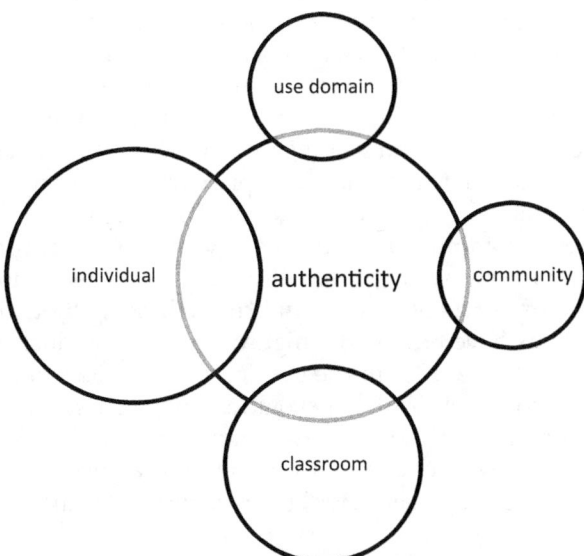

Figure 5.5 A Graded Reader chosen by the student for self-study

For my final illustration I would like to draw on an example from my own classroom practice that I have referred back to several times in this book, from a class I taught in 2012 called *Discussions on Contemporary Topics*. Previously, I mentioned that this was in many ways one of the authentic highpoints of my teaching career, in which I set a video project as the final assessment for this class, one that could be uploaded to YouTube or other public video sharing sites. As a class, we negotiated the marking criteria together, but one of my stipulations was that the project should feature relevance beyond the classroom. One of the most impressive projects featured a group having badges printed which they sold on campus and then donated the money they raised to a world hunger charity. After learning that 1.4 billion people live on less than $1.25 a day, as part of their video project the students attempted to live on $1.25 for a whole day, and they recorded what they ate in order to prove the point that it was not enough. Clearly, this group was highly motivated, and they went above and beyond what was required of them for class. I believe one reason for this was the shared belief that what they were doing was highly authentic. If I was to plot this activity on the authenticity continuum, it would score highly on all four dimensions of authenticity, being highly relevant to the real world (donating money to charity) but also having been assessed as part of the class. It also had a strong connection with the target language community (being uploaded onto YouTube for others to watch and comment on) but also having been decided on by the students themselves and chosen because of their own interests and passions (students had a lot of autonomy in terms of choice of topic and formed groups based around these choices – see Figure 5.6).

The above diagram shows that each domain is flourishing, and the task and content have relevance to the both learner and community, and in fact the task involved the individual making direct contact with the target language using community, and the wider social community as a whole. Raising money for charity and sending a donation is a very positive example of community work. The task also took place in an environment in which the 'real world' outside the classroom is actually brought into the classroom by making use of communicative technology that makes the work done in class connect directly with people outside of the institutional setting. Because autonomy was encouraged and through being motivated to work hard, the students have produced a highly authentic product which has as much (if not more) relevance in the use domain as it does in the classroom (cf. Hung & Victor Chen, 2007 co-evolution approaches to authenticity). I would like to stress that although these diagrams plot authenticity according to their relevance to extremes on a continuum, the purpose of the continuum is not to measure authenticity but to validate the various and equally important dimensions of authenticity. These measurements are indications only and of course as a result they are rather general. In fact when I say that authenticity can be measured, I am not talking about a scientific measure

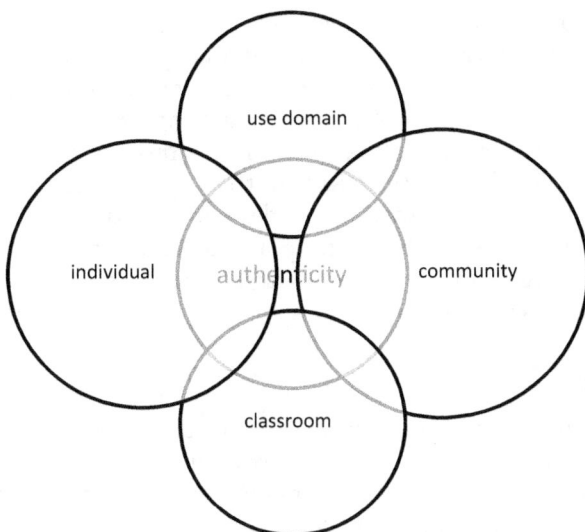

Figure 5.6 Video project – awareness campaign and raising money for charity

that can be universally applied, but rather a way of evaluating authenticity as it applied to each context. Therefore, I would advise that the above diagrams not be taken literally, but merely as practical examples about how the continuum can be utilised to encourage critical evaluation of materials or learning content.

Of course, these representations are based in hypothetical and generalised scenarios, something I would discourage overall. They are merely visual representations and not to be taken as accurate measures of authenticity. However, the above illustrations are attempts to show how one might utilise the continuum in evaluating the authenticity of resources, tasks and content for language learning purposes. Such an evaluation is useful as a way of conceptualising the complex dynamics of authenticity in language learning, and the organic nature of authenticated interaction. This evaluation will be more accurate if it is subjective and specific to each context and each class – or even each individual learner if possible. However, even at a personal level, contextualised to an individual and single task, the continuum can only really present a view of authenticity that can be shaped and mapped to a wide range of different settings. For a view of authenticity that emphasises materials, highlighting the interactions between teacher, learners, text and task, the continuum is not so useful. Taking again the example of the textbook, each page and task within the textbook will dictate a different dynamic of authenticity, and as such the levels of authenticity will be in constant flux as the learner moves through the content and reacts differently, invoking different aspects of their identity and also responding to classmates and teachers in a social process of interaction. At such a micro level of interaction, I believe Külekçi's model is more useful in evaluating and understanding the interactions of individuals, allowing us to focus on the process of authentication as interactions between the different dimensions of authenticity. This is because '[i]ndividuals, as social beings, are in the very centre of the process of meaning-making and of the process of authentication' (Külekçi, 2015: 63). In this way, I think that the continuum and Külekçi's dynamic model can work together in describing authentic interactions at different levels and from both the point of view of social interactions between indivuduals in context and also as a process of engagement with learning materials (see Figure 5.7).

Empowerment

The continuum is also an empowerment device, specifically aimed at those for whom English is a learned second language rather than a mother tongue. I realise that in trying to empower people, I also run the risk of patronising them. In conversation with a friend and colleague from my own PhD, I was very interested to hear about how she viewed English as something that already empowered her. She did not have trouble trying to express herself in English, whereas her native language of Urdu led her to adopt an identity which she felt did not reflect her status as a member of an international community, something other people (and particularly women) may also have experience of (Takahashi, 2013). Of course, my friend was not disowning her native language, but she was able to express herself better in

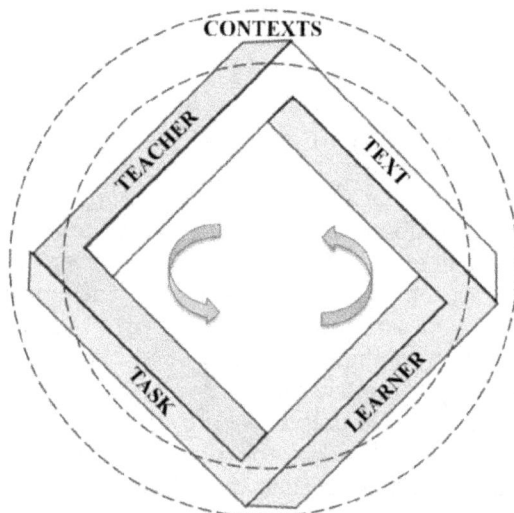

Figure 5.7 Külekçi's (2015) dynamic model for conceptualisation of the process of authentication in the language classroom

English, and she said that because she had been using English for so long and reading and working in English academically, she never had any comprehension problems or felt disadvantaged or marginalised as an L2 speaker of English. This was rather eye-opening for me, as my experience of learning my own L2 (Japanese) has been a series of minor successes that are peppered with thousands of debilitating failures. My experience of being a teacher and observations of my students also led me to feel that language learning was something of a battle. Furthermore, some scholars such as Medgyes and László (2001) and Torikai (2011) have argued that highly proficient speakers of English (especially those for whom it is a first language) have a natural advantage over those who have had to learn it as a foreign language. This disadvantage does not only affect those working with languages directly but also other fields such as general education, (Nunan, 2003; Ramanathan, 2005) the sciences (Ammon, 2001), international business (Rogers, 1998) and a wide range of other domains (Kachru, 1986). There have even been studies that show that people who speak English have a better advantage in the digital world as well, by having more access to computers (Ono & Zavodny, 2008). But, my colleague was here telling me that she felt the exact opposite, and to attempt to 'empower' someone who already feels empowered is to patronise or belittle them, which is certainly not my intention. A person who is reading this book probably does not need to be 'empowered' by a redefined concept of authenticity. However, it is naïve to assume that such empowered people are in any way a majority. My empowered friend and colleague was someone who had just completed both an MA and PhD at a university in England. She had won various awards already for her work, and received competitive grants and funding to conduct her research. She is a member of an elite of speakers, and she works in an environment of similarly successful people, many of whom would share her view of English. However, the people she has gone on to teach, those who are learning English, *they* are likely in-need of the redefined concept of authenticity in order to open their eyes to a visualisation of an empowered self. Language teachers who wish their learners to be successful must somehow tap into this and help their learners to visualise that authentic self, and to position the image in an imagined community of connected, multilingual people who work as part of a global community. Telling people that English is important and that they must be a member of this disembodied language's speech community is not likely to be conducive to helping our learners see their authentic self and understand how it connects to these distant communities.

As I stated in the introduction to this book, the authenticity continuum is not in itself a particularly original or novel idea within the literature on authenticity. Rather, it is an attempt at synthesis. In presenting authenticity as a continuum I am hoping to combine all the most important and dynamic concepts of authenticity under one definition. This continuum builds on the work of eminent scholars such as Widdowson (1978, 1990), van Lier (1996,

1998, 2007), Breen (1985), Mishan (2005, 2011a), Tomlinson and Masuhara (2010) as well as attempting to interject concepts on identity (Block, 2007; G. Murray *et al.*, 2011; Norton, 2013), autonomy (Benson, 2013b; Gao & Lamb, 2011; G. Murray, 2014; Ushioda, 2007), and motivation (Dörnyei, 2009; Dörnyei *et al.*, 2015; Dörnyei & Ushioda, 2011, 2009; Ushioda, 2015, 2013b), and somehow combine them all within a flexible framework that celebrates the process of interactions and acknowledges the complexity and subjectivity of it all (N.C. Ellis & Larsen-Freeman, 2009; Kramsch, 2011; Larsen-Freeman, 1997; Larsen-Freeman & Cameron, 2008a; Menezes, 2013). Furthermore, the continuum is an attempt to do all of that in a visually simple way which can be communicated easily to language teachers and learners in local contexts, who may have been negatively influenced by the culturally embedded definitions of authenticity that continue to be used to represent English as a superior language along with its driving cultural ideology of globalisation (Chun, 2015: 123–126).

On a daily basis I am confronted by images like the following (see Figure 5.8).

In the above picture the white foreign man is the empowered speaker of English, and the woman (who seems to gaze longingly into the man's eye rather than looking at the textbook, which lays open and forgotten on the table) is a learner of English who seeks to gain cultural capital by investing in the English language. However, the English language is personified by a (usually white male) westerner who embodies economic freedom and mobility (K. Bailey, 2007; Seargeant, 2009). As a white, British male in Japan I am

Figure 5.8 Gaba English School's Facebook cover image

afraid to say that I am even complicit with this arrangement, even as I sit here writing about how problematic this notion is. Below is a picture of me which was used as part of the advertising for Nova, a now infamous Japanese English language school for which I used to work (see Figure 5.9).

The picture shows a younger me having fun with the children as I teach them. But, implicitly I am also preparing them to improve their economic chances in an ever more competitive global environment.

Figure 5.10 is taken from the Israeli Hebrew language site of the Wall Street Institute, an international private language school that specialises in

Figure 5.9 Publicity photo of me teaching for Nova English school

Figure 5.10 Wall Street English's Israel Campaign

English instruction. The text offers a traditional rendering of the Hebrew name Rachel and then asks the reader to imagine if they had grown up as Rachel, as written in English. The woman on the right is a simple house-wife, unglamorous and dull-eyed, she lives only in servitude. The woman on the left, in contrast, emits confidence and seductive power. She is clearly more international and has better economic prospects (presumably because she looks like a 1950s glamour model, maybe modelled on someone like Marilyn Monroe). The woman is the same person, but one of them speaks English and in being able to do so she has also bought herself enough cultural capital to escape the drudgery of being ascribed a gendered role as a housewife.

By providing these examples I am trying to demonstrate that the culturally embedded ideals of authenticity belonging to the empowered west have a damaging effect on those who are 'othered' by such discourses. This 'othering' is done through a myriad of subtle and unsubtle means, and it is so embedded within the practice of teaching and learning English that it is often perpetrated by the very people who it simultaneously disadvantages. Although these problems will not go away by simply swapping our notion of authenticity for a continuum, I think that by addressing the concept of authenticity and acknowledging that it is complicit with these damaging, culturist interpretations of English, those of us who are educators may be in a position to start countering such representations with a more balanced depiction of English as an international language. Rather than showing images of English that are entrenched within certain ideologies which may be harmful to or at odds with other cultures or ways of doing things, perhaps English could be depicted in a way which takes into account the local context and realistically examines how English might be beneficial.

The other authenticity continuum

As I have reiterated many times in this book, the ideas that I am presenting in the authenticity continuum are not new. At this point I would like to explain that there is another authenticity continuum, which was originally proposed by Hung and Victor Chen (2007) and applied to education in general, rather than being specific to language teaching. Hung and Victor Chen begin by summarising the predominant approaches to authenticity in education, which they argue can be categorised according to four distinct types of approach: extrapolation, simulation, participation and co-evolution (see Figure 5.11).

As I explained in previous sections of this book, extrapolation approaches are the most problematic, because they assume that something can be taken from one context and brought into another while retaining the authenticity of the original context. For example, just because a newspaper is 'authentic' in the target-language speaking community does not mean it will be authentic to learners in a foreign language learning context. Simulation approaches,

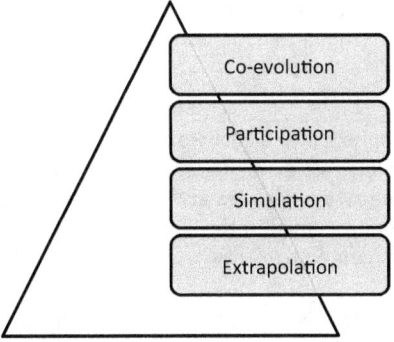

Figure 5.11 Educational approaches to authenticity

as the name suggests attempt to simulate the 'real world' in a classroom setting. This may instantly be recognisable to many language teaching practitioners; practices such as role-play and task-based learning would seem to fit this description. One issue with these approaches is that they require the learners (and teachers) to buy into the make-believe reality of the task or content. This is not a problem in itself, but it is a problem when the necessary 'suspension of disbelief' does not occur. Many of my colleagues have reported great success with role-plays in creating authentic learning situations, but in my own practice I find them difficult to take seriously, something Petraglia (1998b) also discusses in the opening of his book. This is for no reason other than a personal feeling of what is comfortable to me. As Williams and Burden (1997) have noted, teachers are influenced in their practice by their own beliefs about teaching, and the same is true for me in terms of role-play. Hung and Victor Chen note that 3D virtual worlds also fall under the category of simulation approaches, although I believe that virtual worlds also fall under other categories as well, as I will explain shortly. Participation approaches involve taking the learners to the real world, in an attempt to address the issues of simulation approaches which involve the reverse. These approaches draw on concepts found in problem-based learning and connect also with the learner-apprentice model of education. Finally, co-evolution is rooted in ecological approaches to learning, and emphasises 'the in situ emergence of meanings arising in the dynamic relations and interactions between persons and not so much the problem, task, or environment' (Hung & Victor Chen, 2007: 151 following Davis et al., 1996). Each type of approach to authenticity in learning has basic tenets which Hung and Victor Chen go on to explain also have individual problems (see Table 5.1).

For Hung and Victor Chen, the main issue with all of these approaches is that they fail to take sufficient account of context in authenticity, leading them to propose a *context-process authenticity continuum*. The continuum incorporates all four of the predominant approaches to authenticity and attempts

Table 5.1 Summary of approaches to authenticity (adapted from Hung and Victor Chen, 2007: 152)

Approach	Basic tenets	Assumptions/problems
Extrapolation	Decontextualised 'real-world' examples are extrapolated in order to apply abstract theories learned in the classroom into 'reality'	There is little or no contact with context; abstract concepts are assumed to apply to the so-called 'real world'. Little attempt to address the complexity of the 'real world'
Simulation	Brings the reality to the classroom. Makes extensive use of problem solving. Often involves role-playing	Can never be real enough. Assumes stability of professional community. Only recognises professional community authenticity. Does not cover tacit knowledge. Relies on 'suspension of disbelief' in order to validate the simulation
Participation	Brings the classroom to the reality. Emphasises identity formation	Assumes stability of professional communities. Interactions are largely uni-directional. Only recognises professional community authenticity. May remove much of the channels of support which are available in traditional classrooms structures
Co-evolution	Structure learning experiences to occur in situ. Emphasises identity co-formation. Knowledge is an emergent process	Co-determined interactions are bi-directional, but largely observable. Only at the cognitive level. Difficulties exist in researching identity enculturation. Classroom support structures are may be hard to access

to situate them contextually, so that authenticity can be viewed as a process which incorporates identity creation (Wenger, 1998). Hung and Victor Chen present the continuum in a linear sequence (see Figure 5.12), although they stress that it should not be viewed as such, drawing on Wittgenstein (1953) for the metaphor of context-process authenticity taking place in a 'complex landscape of communities and learning for each unique individual is similar yet not equivalent – criss-crossed in different learning paths, where each path could be a different place where the construction of shared meanings could occur' (Hung & Victor Chen, 2007: 160).

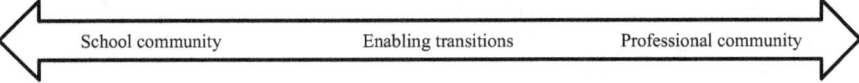
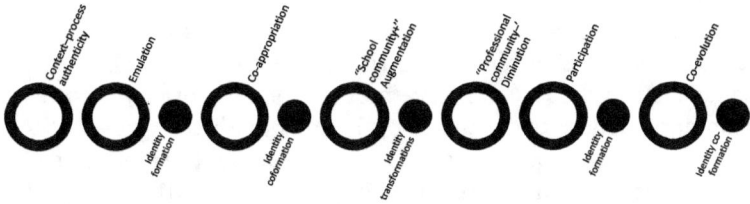

Figure 5.12 The other authenticity continuum (adapted from Hung and Victor Chen, 2007: 158)

Hung and Victor Chen's work is certainly valuable and relevant to language education; however, I still believe that the continuum I presented in the previous section is more suitable for evaluating and conceptualising the authenticity of language teaching and learning. The reason is that Hung and Victor Chen are drawing also on movements in educational philosophy, whereas the continuum which I am proposing tries to act as a bridge between real people in actual contexts and the abstract notion of language which they are trying to engage with. Although Hung and Victor Chen's context-process authenticity continuum is still relevant to the work of language teachers from an educational perspective, I do not think that it would make as much sense to language teachers as the authenticity continuum for language learning, mainly because Hung and Victor Chen's continuum is designed to be descriptive of practices, but does not seem to have been created with the intention of being actually able to influence practice.

The Paradox of Authenticity

There are many paradoxes associated with authenticity. A Shakespeare play could be an authentic example of English literature, for example, but it is no longer (and may never have been) an authentic illustration of how people really talk in English. The play is fiction, it is make-believe, and so it also forfeits one aspect of its authenticity in this way too, as Harmer (2008) noted in his definition of authenticity. For the same reason, the English spoken by people in England, the USA or other L1 English speaking nations may not be authentic either, when approaching English as an international language which is more often than not taking place between interlocutors for whom English is a second language. This creates a problem when we talk about *culture* in authenticity, in that it is all too often used as a taken-for-granted frame of reference, in much the same way that B. Anderson (2006) argues the idea of *nation* is often misunderstood and exploited for political reasons. Of course, learning and teaching does not happen in a 'cultural vacuum', but the role of culture in English language teaching is in need of contextualisation and personalisation – in other words a process of authentication. This paradox is essentially the genuine vs authentic distinction that Widdowson (1978) made between texts from a certain domain and the learner's perception of how authentic something is in relation to themselves. Another paradox, which could be labelled as the make-believe problem of authenticity, is situated in simulation approaches, as discussed by Hung and Victor Chen (2007) and summarised in the previous section. This is essentially the amount to which learners and teachers can 'buy into' or *invest* (Norton, 2013; Norton Peirce, 1995) in the process of learning. These are confusing paradoxes that I have already touched upon to some extent. However, in this summary of authenticity I will focus on the paradox of known vs unknown topics of interest and cultural schemata. Mishan (2005: 49–50, 103–105) highlights the importance of schemata to authenticity, especially in relation to culture. She argues that schemata can be exploited when using literature as an authentic source of input, because certain genres (such as poetry) 'contain schemata which are "trans-cultural". The most obvious ones are universal literary genres, such as fairy tales and legends' (2005: 103 following Kramsch, 1985: 359). This is certainly something supported by the discourses on mythology, most notably by Joseph Campbell, who said 'It would not be too much to say that myth is the secret opening through which the inexhaustible energies of the cosmos pour into human cultural manifestation' (1949: 3). Myths are part of our cultural sub-conscious, and they reflect valuable and universal truths that transcend context and culture and permeate into the fabric of human existence. Mishan refers to such learning content as 'cultural products', which she takes pains to point out should be rooted in the local context of the learning situation. However, if we are to teach language learners about 'cultural products', whose culture are we to choose? Smith explains that:

> '[T]he goal for teaching English… is not to learn about English culture, to broaden the mind, or to learn new patterns of thought. Rather, it is to extend the ability of our students to communicate their ideas and their culture. It is to help them learn about all other cultures, and to be better able to participate in the world community'. (Smith, 1976: 42)

This would then provide the teacher with a very broad (perhaps rather too broad) palette from which to select cultural materials. We can select cultural products from all over the world, and attempt to localise them. If the learners are already somewhat familiar with them, or indeed if they are learning how to express their own culture, all the better. However, the paradox inherent within this view is the distinction between known and unknown topics of interest. The crux of this paradox about what to teach is basically the possible tension that can arise between personal authenticity and social authenticity. Holliday notes that:

> It is indeed culturist to imagine that people can only find meaning within things with which they are familiar within their own community because it implies a bounded culture which cannot dream outside itself. Social authenticity does not therefore only relate to discourses in home society. It can also relate to the interface between home and the world – for example, the Internet, politics, tourism, globalisation, and visions of the Other. (Holliday, 2005: 106)

In this sense also, authenticity and autonomy are very closely entwined, because there is a very clear implication of free-will and personal volition embedded in the definition of authenticity, making it closely dependent on the concept of autonomy. Authenticity is not the only concept discussed here to have a cultural connection and definition issues. Autonomy and culture is also a big issue; quite often being associated as a Western educational ideology (Holliday, 2003, 2005; Palfreyman & Smith, 2003). As these scholars have pointed out, however, the notion of autonomy is not solely the intellectual product of the West. Consider for example the Buddhist religion, which emphasises *Enlightenment*; a state of self-awareness that most certainly cannot be taught or passed from one individual to another. This is an educational ideology originating in eastern philosophy. The idea that an entire group of people (indeed, almost an entire hemisphere) cannot be autonomous because their culture has some historical link to Confucianism is quite frankly an excessive over-generalisation. However, it is also true that people learn differently and are taught differently in the various cultural and political contexts of the globe. Teachers will therefore need to be sensitive to the educational principles which are most prominent where they work, and if they want their learners to be successful communicators in the foreign language, they will also need to educate them about sociocultural standards of discourse and the shared macro-beliefs that influence particular ways of doing things in other contexts. When English is the language being learned though, this is not so straightforward (not that such a thing is ever straightforward). Are language teachers to explain every social nuance and belief system around the world? Perhaps, reversing the strategy would be the best approach; when teaching English the aim should not be to teach these different systems but rather to raise awareness of the differences and to try to prepare a culture of tolerance and understanding. If we can impart an awareness of the incredible spectrum of cultures and an acceptance of the ways of doing things in our learners, then perhaps they can be made ready for a truly international form of communication. Other examples from the real world abound, such as using your right hand to accept money, patting a child's head or showing the soles of your feet in public.

Conclusion

In this chapter I have tried to present a reconceptualised view of authenticity as a continuum, which attempts to take better account of other varieties of English and shift some of the emphasis away from the implied 'native speaker', thus avoiding a Centre/Periphery style dichotomy. The continuum is designed to be a simple representation of the complexities of authenticity. I argued that the complexities of authenticity have either been limited to academic discussions that have hitherto made little impact on the way authenticity is discussed in the classroom, or simplified into an essentialist notion based on source of origin in discussions about materials. The 'classic' definition of authenticity is no-longer tenable in today's diverse contexts of international language exchange. The idea that a material can be 'authentic' because of how it is used or where it is produced in one context does not mean that its authenticity can be transferred intact into another context. Most of the confusion around authenticity, I would argue, stems from that fact that we seem to have one definition that applies mainly to materials and various others which apply to authenticity as a process of personal engagement. For decades, scholars have recognised the issue of authenticity as a complex issue, viewed as a dynamic process, and yet language teachers still tend to define authenticity when discussing materials based on the 'classic' definition, which implies the native speaker. However, with the recent increase in focus on bilingual approaches to language education there has been a shift away from what Phillipson (1992) labelled as the 'monolingual fallacy', i.e. the idea that a foreign language such as English is best taught using only the target language for instruction. This shift in focus has meant that multiple cultures, multilingualism and diversity are given a more central place in the language classroom. These bilingual educational models will be examined in the next chapter.

6 Authenticity in Bilingual Educational Contexts

Introduction

An advert for a washing powder did very poorly in the Middle East (except in Turkey) because the picture showed a dirty shirt on the left, a box of soap in the middle and a clean shirt on the right. Of course, in many Middle Eastern countries where the writing system runs from right to left, this campaign made it seem like the soap actually made the clothes dirty (Valdés, 2000: 273). Similarly with education, adjustments need to be made and sociocultural issues taken into consideration before ideas can be rolled out to other contexts. Education around the world is diverse and often built on culturally specific philosophical principles. I was surprised when I moved to Japan to see that world maps here do not have England at the centre. In the UK, globe icons look like Figure 6.1. But in Japan they look more like Figure 6.2.

Multinational ELT publishers are aware of the potential pitfalls of crossing linguistic and cultural boundaries, and so many of them enforce rules on their writers, often known as PARSNIPS. This is an acronym for no: politics, alcohol, religion, sex, narcotics, isms or pork (Meddings, 2006). But ELT publishers are not the only ones guilty of whitewashing certain topics – indeed history textbooks all over the world present the facts they want their nation to remember. British history textbooks when I was at school presented much of our heroic defeat of the Nazis in World War Two. I learned absolutely nothing of the horrors of the Boer concentration camps or other crimes against humanity that were perpetrated by Britain. I am sure the history books of Yemen do not fail to mention the cruelties of the Aden Emergency, again something I did not learn about at school. On the one hand we have global models of education and multicultural ideals being spread across the developed world, and on the other we have diversification and localisation. Moreover, the spread of English has been vilified as being complicit with the

Figure 6.1 Euro-centric globe icon

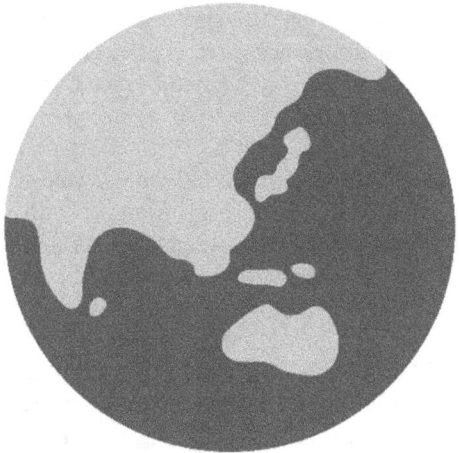

Figure 6.2 Asia-centric globe icon

extinction of local languages (Hale *et al.*, 1992; McWhorter, 2015; although see also Batibo, 2005), while at the same time being hailed as a way of attaining economic power and cultural capital. English is the language of problem solving and it is also the language spoken by the malevolent and faceless powers of consumerism. In this chapter I will not speak any more of the Janus-like two-facedness of English as both the Dr Jekyll and Mr Hyde of globalisation. Instead I will focus exclusively on the theme of bilingual educational models which are becoming more and more widespread around the developed world. The reference to the ancient Greek god Janus is relevant here too, because bilingual educational models often attempt to fuse language learning with content knowledge, and like the god Janus they have links to both the past and the future of education.

The Changing Face of Language Education Programmes

We are in an unprecedented stage of our understanding of the human mind and educational principles, thanks in part to decades of research but also to new technologies and new fields such as cognitive neuroscience and neuropsychology. At the same time, society is transforming itself through interaction and integration with technologies. Even many poor countries have access to computers through charitable schemes such as Lowe's Charitable and Educational Foundation, the Pearson Foundation and even the Bill & Melinda Gates Foundation. Also, more and more universities across the world are selling themselves as *international* institutions in order to attract students from overseas (Jenkins, 2014). According to the Higher Education Statistics Agency's First Statistical Release for 2013–14 (HESA, 2015), the UK had 435,500 international students enrolled, representing 18% of the total student body. In the USA the figure is higher than that of the UK with 819,644 enrolments, but this figure only accounts for just under 4% of the total for both graduate and undergraduate courses in the USA (IIE, 2013). In both the USA and the UK, the largest number of international students comes from China, followed by India in second place. Of course, studying abroad is extremely expensive and therefore available to only a relatively small social elite. In this way, language education becomes embroiled in the arguments about power, capitalism and imperialism. Drawing on Galtung's structural theory of imperialism (1971), a number of scholars have applied his Centre/Periphery distinction to education and, more specifically, language education (Altbach, 1981, 2004; Appadurai, 1990; Pennycook, 1994; Phillipson, 1996). Centre contexts can be anything from a metropolitan city to an entire global network of developed nations. The periphery contexts are the opposite; they are either rural places of simple means or developing nations dependent on the economies of the larger (quite often capitalist) countries that hold political power over them. In the case of the Cold War, the Centre nations did not engage in warfare directly, but many of those in the periphery became entangled in 'spin-off' wars as a result of the USSR/USA stand-off (McMahon, 1994). In university settings, the centre refers to research institutes at the cutting-edge of science, where breakthroughs are made and the field progresses. The periphery university is a place which simply copies or mimics the developments made in the centre contexts (Altbach, 1981, 2004). Usually, there is an overriding geography to this distinction, implying the economically developed countries are where the centre institutions are. It is easy to see how this distinction applies to language teaching too, especially English, with certain varieties enjoying more gravity and esteem. Quite often, people who want to do well in their own countries travel to centre institutions (such as the UK or the USA) in order to gain qualifications, but also in order to gain, through a process of social osmosis, some of the social and cultural capital afforded to the centre variety that they will also come into contact with. An obvious example of this process is the acquisition of Americanised or British sounding pronunciation patterns and other discourse features. For many people, this is something that influences them indirectly, and may happen as a natural part of their acculturation, as they naturally acquire cultural capital in the new foreign language speaking context. Of course, such practices have been criticised because of the way they disadvantage the so-called periphery contexts, making them subordinate and thus denying them access to the same resources (Pennycook, 1994; Phillipson, 1996). The basic argument is that Centre/Periphery structures are lined up in such a way as to ensure those with power gain more and more of it, while systematically impoverishing and denying credibility to those without it. It's a system that exacerbates capitalism into a very unequal state. And, of course, the Centre/Periphery model has itself been attacked for being too much of a dichotomy, too polar in its extremes and therefore un-useful in describing actual phenomena (Appadurai, 1990; Pennycook, 1994).

The global market is placing greater than ever social pressure on people to know more than one language, and of course this has led to the emergence of new educational policies and practices, both for students going abroad and for students who remain in their own counties. Despite the historical roots of such approaches, what we are seeing today is unprecedented in terms of its global scale. Language education is becoming more and more integrated with other types of education and other subjects are being studied in or *through* foreign or second languages. This is having a washback effect on the language classroom, as I will explore in this chapter. Before doing so, I feel that I need to have a cautionary note about such bilingual models of education. The two models that I will examine in this chapter are Content and Language Integrated Learning (CLIL) and English as a Medium of Instruction (EMI). There are a plethora of other acronyms and models that I could discuss, but time and space have forced me to limit the discussion to these two, as they seem the most pervasive and also they overlap well with other models and yet both EMI and CLIL are rather distinct from each other. I would also like to point out from the beginning that these bilingual models are not panaceas for multilingual and multicultural education – teaching content through another language can add additional strain on both teachers and students. Furthermore, these models are not exactly new (Mehisto *et al.*, 2008), and there is a somewhat cyclical nature to educational models, as highlighted by Mishan (2005: 2–3) and Howatt and Widdowson (2004: 6). I am pointing this out simply to draw attention to the fact that, in my view, the only constant is the concept of authenticity as a central requisite to good teaching and learning. Even in the 1970s when Widdowson first began teasing apart the concept of authenticity, he was aware of the potential value of combining subject teaching with foreign language education as a means of achieving greater authenticity, and thus (he hypothesised) motivation. He argued that by combining the teaching of a foreign language with other subjects in the students' school curriculum 'the foreign language is represented as having the same kind of communicative function as his [or her] own language' (Widdowson, 1978: 80–81). However, despite the disproportionate social and cultural capital placed on centre educational contexts, the bilingual models of education on offer at institutions of learning around the world represent a positive way to readdress this imbalance. Of course, certain institutions will always occupy the highest places in university rankings, some schools carry more esteem than others, and the more prestigious places will generally be found in what could traditionally be labelled as centre contexts (such as Harvard and Yale in the US, Oxford and Cambridge in the UK). This is unlikely to change without a shift in the geopolitical landscape of power relations. However, bilingual educational models do make it possible for some learners to acquire some of the cultural capital awarded to immersion and study abroad programmes more affordably and more conveniently from the comfort of their own birth-nations. Furthermore, these programmes also offer a more international appeal and inclusive model of education, not only encouraging international students but also providing more support for immigrant-learners who may not have the same mother-tongue as their country of residence. One central and defining tenet of the bilingual approaches is the amount of authenticity they can offer to learners working in another or foreign language.

Authenticity of Purpose: Bilingual Educational Models

The way languages are taught has undergone some extreme changes over its history (Howatt & Widdowson, 2004). Focusing only on the last century, there have been several distinct approaches such as the Audio-lingual approach, The Silent Way, Situational Approach, Grammar-Translation and Communicative Language Teaching. Listing these all together seems a little incongruous, as some of the approaches were short-lived or even specific to a single institution, whereas others have been more pervasive and spawned other methodologies which compliment them, such as Task-Based Learning and Problem-Based Learning from Communicative Language Teaching. Some of these (such as the Communicative approach) promote the concept of authenticity as an implicit part of their methodology. Others, such as The Silent Way seem to limit the role of authenticity, although I would like to point out that even The Silent Way has some redeeming features, such as the way it highlights the role of learner autonomy. However, the most aspired to and even dominant approach in many contexts, at least from my experience as a teacher, appears to be the Communicative one. Even when it is not adhered to in practice, it is mentioned as an organising principle. For example here, in Japan the ministry of sports, education and culture (MEXT) has issued several documents entitled *The Course of Study*, which explicitly promote the use of communicative methods for language teaching. These are then duly ignored by teachers who have to prepare their learners to pass university entrance exams that do not feature any communicative elements (Tahira, 2012; Yoshida, 2001, 2009). The situation is similar in China, where learners also need to pass tests which are designed to be administered in large numbers at minimal expense. Tests that feature speaking and listening sections are more expensive and less easily operationalised than simple multiple-choice tests. The format of the tests lends itself best to behaviouristic grammar-translation style questions and reading comprehension. This seems to be a situation which affects many contexts, and is not specific only to Asia. However, particularly in Europe, bilingual programmes that specifically teach a foreign language as a subject are being complemented with programmes that simply offer instruction through the target language rather than about the target language. Quite often the target language is English. There are several acronyms for such programmes, and often their definitions overlap. Perhaps the most all-encompassing model of bilingual education is English as a Medium of Instruction (EMI), which means that courses are taught in English and students will learn about subjects by a subject teacher (as opposed to a language teacher) and instruction will be conducted only in English (or the language of instruction). Usually there is no support for language learners or those for whom English is not an L1, and therefore the English requirements of such courses are high because they assume a certain level of proficiency. Examples of such courses are found in universities across the world (Doiz *et al.*, 2012). Naturally, courses in the UK, USA, Canada, Australia, New Zealand and South Africa automatically assume that international students will have the language abilities needed to take part in the instruction, although calling such programmes EMI would be tautological. Needless to say, a multi-million dollar testing industry has sprouted to ensure that universities around the world can assume the students have sufficient proficiency, and therefore millions of people all over the world take TOEFL and IELTS tests each year so that they can study at a 'centre' based institution where English is the first language. This was the original intention of these tests, however they are now also being used by institutions in international settings where English is a second language used for instruction. As I have already mentioned throughout this book, these tests are based on (and thereby propagate) native-speakerist models of English (see also Jenkins, 2014). However, the overall trend seems to me to be a good one. In other words more people can get higher profile degrees either by staying at home or by going abroad (not necessarily to contexts where English is the first language) and receive bilingual education where they will be likely to make gains in both the subject knowledge and foreign language proficiency.

The next type of widespread bilingual educational approaches could be labelled as Content and Language Integrated Learning (CLIL), and these courses have 'dual-focused aims' (Marsh, 2002), meaning that both the content subject and the foreign language are being taught simultaneously, and that learning aims should reflect gains in both areas. Assessment should therefore also reflect gains in both areas, and the literature on CLIL is rich with variants of how content and language can be balanced fairly and in different calibrations. CLIL is a relatively new approach, the term being adopted in 1994 within the European context (Coyle *et al.*, 2010: 3), but Mehisto *et al.* (2008: 9) link the basic bilingual principle of CLIL back 5000 years to the Akkadians and Sumerians. Of course, one example of CLIL under this definition would be the bilingual education programmes developed in Canada in the 1970s and 1980s (see for example Collier, 1992; Swain, 1974). Although the Canadian immersion programmes are generally not referred to as CLIL, they represent some of the modern foundations and justifications for the implementation of CLIL in Europe (Navés, 2009). Dalton-Puffer acknowledges that terms such as Content-Based Instruction, Bilingual Teaching and Dual-Language Programmes all have their own histories, 'contextual roots and accompanying slightly different philosophical implications' (2007: 1); however, these terms are in many respects synonymous with CLIL. Other acronyms for distinct yet overlapping approaches include Integrating Content and Language in Higher Education (Coleman, 2006) and more recently English Medium Education in Multilingual University Settings (Dafouz & Smit, 2014). All these different acronyms show that there is a growing trend towards the combination of content and language disciplines in order to achieve the ever diversifying educational needs of today's global institutions. I could happily try to define each one and explain the differences, but doing so is not necessary to the argument I am presenting in this chapter; an argument which Widdowson (1978) first touched upon when he postulated that teaching subjects from the curriculum would be a way of authenticating the foreign language through what Coyle *et al.* (2010) later called 'authenticity of purpose'. For all intents and purposes I shall lump these acronyms together under the umbrella of either CLIL or EMI. The distinction that I am making between these two is that in CLIL there is some provision for language learning. Although the teachers may not themselves be language teachers (usually they are subject teachers who are using another language to teach their subject in) they understand that the purpose of instruction is supposed to be balanced between content and language. Therefore, in CLIL classes there are concessions made to ensure comprehension, there is scaffolding and there might be overt language instruction at times. In EMI settings, it is assumed that the learners have achieved the language proficiency needed to learn about the subject, so generally no concessions are made for language learners. However, EMI is still conceptualised as being a way for learners to improve their English, and as such it still has relevance as an approach to language learning. I will discuss each in turn in the following section.

Content and language integrated learning

As a language teacher, my first impression of CLIL was that it was something that happened mainly in European secondary schools. It was an interesting concept, but as a language teacher I could not see how it would be particularly relevant to me. However, after moving to Japan I became more involved with CLIL through my involvement with piloting certain content-based courses, which were part of an innovation programme run at Sophia University. I was given the opportunity to teach several CLIL classes and to write about my experiences. Since then there have been a large number of books and articles about CLIL appearing in journals about language teaching. Many of these advocate the methodology not as something relevant only in Europe, but something that could potentially have a profound influence on the way people learn second languages around the world (C.E. Anderson, 2011; Coyle, 2007; Izumi et al., 2012; Navés, 2009; Watanabe et al., 2011). Despite the potential educational gains in two distinct areas (language and content) that CLIL and related bilingual models of education have to offer, they also come with greater challenges to teachers and students alike. Language teachers and content teachers must work together in collaboration and share their skills. It is quite uncommon for a teacher to be qualified and experienced in both language and content teaching, and inevitably the teachers must learn new skills in order to teach in such multilingual environments. Also, for students, the dual-focus of the CLIL class means that the workload might seem very demanding at times. Despite this, CLIL has been found to be extremely successful in achieving its dual aims in programmes around the world (see for example de Zarobe & Catalán, 2009; Ikeda, 2013). It can seem more challenging, but at the same time more motivating and authentic for students and teachers (Doiz et al., 2012; Lasagabaster, 2011; Marsh, 2002: 72).

The rapidly expanding literature on CLIL frequently mentions authenticity. I conducted a review in 2013 and found that in the *International Journal of Bilingual Education and Bilingualism*, since its initial publication in 1998 there had been 78 issues. The search term 'authentic' revealed 119 results, meaning authenticity appeared on average 1.5 times each issue. In four issues of the *International CLIL Research Journal* featuring a total of 29 articles, authenticity was mentioned in 11 of those, a total of 37% of all articles (Pinner, 2013). Authenticity is listed as one of the six core features of CLIL methodology (Mehisto et al., 2008) and Mehisto's *Bilingual Education Continuum* advocates 'authentic materials used in authentic ways and guided communication with

L2 speakers' (2012: 50–51), which he sees as a prerequisite for effective teaching and learning to occur. Authenticity is a central notion to CLIL, although as usual with the term, it is used in the literature to refer to a loose concept of engagement. The eponymous word 'content' in CLIL is basically synonymous with authenticity. Coyle *et al.* specifically define content as 'authentic texts' (2010: 17) and authenticity is also used to define the term communication, where 'language is learned through using it in authentic and unrehearsed yet "scaffolded" situations' (Coyle, 2006: 13–14). Authenticity is referred to frequently as a *defining* aspect of CLIL, and some CLIL practitioners go so far as to claim that it affords a different and fundamentally more authentic type of authenticity than communicative language teaching. Coyle and colleagues have criticised conventional EFL methodologies because they lack the 'authenticity of purpose' (2010: 5) of CLIL classrooms.

> It is challenging for language teachers to achieve appropriate levels of authenticity in the classroom. For example, even if 'authentic' texts are used, and the subject matter is highly relevant to the lives of the learners, the predominant reasons for these texts being in the lesson remains language learning. (Coyle *et al.*, 2010: 11)

Of course, one problem with this is the assumption that language learning is inauthentic because it is being done for pedagogical purposes. So, by the same logic, any subject being learned at school would also be inauthentic. The concept of authenticity is almost as problematic in general education as it is in language learning (Glatthorn, 1999; Hung & Victor Chen, 2007; Petraglia, 1998b). In a slightly less hyperbolic tone, Dalton-Puffer (2007) explains that one of the main advantages of CLIL is that content subjects give rise to 'real communication' by tapping into a great reservoir of ideas, concepts and meanings allowing for natural use of the target language.

> In this sense, CLIL is the ultimate dream of Communicative Language Teaching ... and Task Based Learning ... rolled into one: there is no need to design individual tasks in order to foster goal-directed linguistic activity with a focus on meaning above form, since CLIL itself is one huge task which ensures the use of the foreign language for 'authentic communication'. (Dalton-Puffer, 2007: 3)

Such comments assert that authenticity is not just an important feature of CLIL methodology and practice, but actually a defining aspect of the entire approach and one of its greatest strengths over other foreign language instruction pedagogies such as CLT or TBL.

Having looked at the discourse around authenticity in the literature on CLIL, it seems that the nature of authenticity lies not in the source of the text or in the linguistic complexities and so-called richness of the language.

Authenticity within CLIL is more directly associated with purpose, with reasons for engagement. The authentic texts used in a CLIL classroom are not merely collections of vocabulary and grammar from the target language culture, taken out of one context and placed into another for language learning. Authenticity in CLIL directly relates the student to their immediate learning goals. Students use authentic language in the CLIL classroom not because there is an interesting event in current affairs which might stimulate them to communicate for the duration of a single class. Authenticity is directly related to the purpose for being in the classroom, the learning aims and outcomes for the entire curricula, and more broadly something that will allow learners, hopefully, to take part in the wider discussion as a member of a global, multilingual society, all working together without being hindered by their linguistic diversity. When we talk about authenticity in CLIL we are dealing with something that goes beyond the concept of authenticity in more traditional language classrooms. In this way, although language and culture are not separate, there is much less implied culturism to the process of language learning. Also, because CLIL is a bilingual method of language instruction, often the L1 is allowed in the classroom and utilised by teachers for glossing and scaffolding. When I worked for a language school in London, we were not just told to use only English during instruction, but also we were to enforce a policy of English only upon our students. They were not allowed to use their L1 in the class, even (and especially) if there were others in the class who shared their first language. This is because we would often receive complaints from nationalities which made up the majority of the student body. They had paid a lot of money to come and study away from their countries, only to wind up hearing their first language and hanging out with fellow compatriots. The English only policy is also applied elsewhere in mono-lingual classroom settings, usually as an unspoken rule of the communicative approach. This can actually be demotivating for students as it immediately creates a sense of 'othering' and forces them to leave behind, or even deny, their cultural and linguistic origins. CLIL classrooms and other bilingual models overcome this issue by acknowledging the students' L1 and utilising it in order to aid instruction. This is especially important in CLIL classes where there may be more instances of translanguaging (García, 2009) or code switching as the students deal with the content they are learning and negotiate understanding, which happens naturally in bilingual speakers (see Lorenzo et al., 2010). In summary, CLIL offers a bilingual model of language education that shifts the focus away from culture and onto content. In this way it achieves 'authenticity of purpose' but it could also be argued that this is, in some ways less authentic because culture is almost as neutralised as it is in international ELT publications which leave out PARSNIPS. It would be interesting to know how culture and authenticity interact in CLIL settings, and to investigate how teachers and students understand the concept of authenticity in these contexts.

English as a medium of instruction

More and more universities are under pressure to offer educational programmes that not only compete in the global educational marketplace, but also prepare students to do the same. Internationalisation is a key component in modern educational discourse and planning and many universities are now offering courses and full programmes in English in an attempt to gain more international students while maintaining the interest of home students who wish to prove their English ability while completing a degree or some other form of vocational training. Jenkins (2014) has pointed out that many such programmes are in fact still very much based on native speaker models of English, with the gatekeeper usually being large standardised institutional tests, such as TOEFL or IELTS, which do not account for international varieties of English. That being so, it cannot be denied that offering courses in English is becoming an essential part of many universities' curricula reforms. One example is the *Project for Promotion of Global Human Resource Development* in Japan which offers extra funding to universities to facilitate internationalisation and encourage participation in exchange programmes.

> The Project for Promotion of Global Human Resource Development is a funding project that aims to overcome the Japanese younger generation's 'inward tendency' and to foster human resources who can positively meet the challenges and succeed in the global field, as the basis for improving Japan' s global competitiveness and enhancing the ties between nations. Efforts to promote the internalization of university education in Japan will be given strong, priority support. (MEXT, 2012)

Note the assumption that Japanese young people have an 'inward tendency'. This is something that receives much media coverage here in Japan (Yamagami & Tollefson, 2011), and it is partly linked to the falling figures of Japanese students joining exchange programmes and studying overseas. The blame is turned on the introversion of the young generation, rather than looking at what is more likely to be the main cause which is economic downturn and pressure on young people to find work after leaving university. Job hunting in Japan is competitive and time consuming, and usually taking part in an exchange programme means taking study leave, which therefore discourages many young people. There are two types of funding provided for universities under this scheme, described as follows:

- Type A (University-wide)
  The goal is the internationalisation of the entire university. The universities selected as lead schools are required to contribute to the promotion of the globalisation of other universities.

- Type B (Faculty/school-specific)
  The goal is the internationalisation of the specific faculties/schools. The selected universities are required to promote the globalisation of the specific faculties/schools within the university, as well as to contribute to the internationalisation of the university as a whole. (MEXT, 2012)

It seems quite astonishing to think that an entire university could operate in a foreign language, and yet such is the force of English and globalisation now. English as a medium of instruction is interesting from the point of view of authenticity. Rather than the SLA questions about authenticity being salient, the wider educational view of authenticity comes to the fore. As mentioned previously in Chapter 2, authenticity in the wider field of education tends to concern itself more directly with existentialism and constructivism (Abbott, 2013; Petraglia, 1998a). In this way, authenticity as it relates to EMI is not so much just about the process of authenticating the language, but also it is a question of making the entire subject authentic. This means making sure that the students are learning something that will be useful to them, something that will challenge and engage them, and quite often there is an implication that students will do this if they participate in learning by doing or some form of problem-based learning (Mishan, 2011b). This could be the subject of an entire book in itself, and I would like to highlight the fact that this chapter can only scratch the surface of the complex relationship between language learning and authenticity in bilingual educational models.

Conclusion

English education around the world is now perceived 'as a basic educational skill alongside literacy, numeracy and information and communication technology (ICT) skills' (Ushioda, 2013a: 2, following Graddol, 2006). The requirement of English as a basic skill is further intensified by the powerful educational reforms which are being undertaken as a result of the burgeoning array of bilingual methodologies such as English as a Medium of Instruction (EMI) and Content and Language Integrated Learning (CLIL). CLIL gained prominence in Europe as part of a drive to increase bilingualism and, as bilingual speakers naturally codeswitch in real life, students may be more motivated if they are allowed to bring their L1 identity into the class and integrate it with their L2 self. Such bilingual educational models, implemented often on a national scale in order to represent global trends in language use, could inevitably feel abstract to many students, especially at primary levels where many students have their first encounters with English language education. There are many issues with bilingual educational models, which, along with globalisation, are putting both learners and teachers into unchartered territory.

Of course, one can readily appreciate the motivational benefits of engaging students of English with subject matter content that has real learning vale and curriculum relevance (e.g. Huang, 2011; Lasagabaster, 2011). At the same time, it is clear that integrating content and language presents pedagogical and motivational challenges for teachers who may not be subject specialists or language specialist or who may need to engage in collaborative teaching with language or subject specialist colleagues. Integrating language and content may also present motivational challenges for linguistically weaker students who lack the English skills needed to deal with cognitively demanding subject matter and learning materials (Ushioda, 2013a: 7).

Despite these concerns, both the motivational and educational benefits of bilingual educational methods are convincing (Lasagabaster, 2011; Lorenzo et al., 2010) and the exponential growth in university programmes offering courses in English means that this is how many learners will experience their language education, or at least have that education complemented as another type of instruction on top of more traditional foreign language classes. Elsewhere I have argued that language education which puts content at the top of its learning aims alongside language proficiency will inevitably achieve a higher level of authenticity, or what Coyle et al. (2010) refer to as 'authenticity of purpose'. This is because students need to use language as a tool to understand the content. Thus, following Vygotsky (1964), language acts as a tool through which other aims and objectives are achieved, with knowledge being socially constructed. This also means that CLIL and EMI are deeply situated in a sociocultural framework of learning. In this way, they are approaches which have a great deal of potential in providing authentic ways to learn, in that they bridge the individual and contextually situated learners with the foreign language. Certainly, in the case of English this is a good thing, as the English language becomes ever more abstracted by its use around the world. The overwhelming pressure to learn English coupled with the multifaceted contexts in which it is used likely only serve to distort what it actually means to be a speaker of English for many young language learners. Therefore, bilingual educational models provide a way of making the language tenable to other subjects and other purposes which may be more immediate to the learners' lives. Another thing which makes the English language more directly associable to young people's lives (and people outside of formal institutional learning contexts) is the way technology and communication have become a central part of daily life. This is the topic which I will turn to next.

7 New Media as a Catalyst for Authenticity

Introduction

In their hilarious Fruit Shop sketch, British comedians Ronnie Corbett and Harry Enfield highlight the way technology influences language change; in this case by making fun of the fashion for technology companies to name their products and services after fruit, which has expanded the semantic reference for much natural produce. In the sketch, a man comes into a grocery shop because his blackberry has frozen. We, of course, expect the man to produce a BlackBerry smartphone that has become unresponsive, and the joke is that he produces an actual frozen blackberry. The sketch continues to make puns along the technology-as-fruit motif, with reference to Apple (computers) and Orange (mobile phone provider) and Xbox (eggs box in sketch). This example also highlights another aspect of technology, the fact that it is relentlessly progressive and things age very quickly. For example, the sketch has already lost much of its 'currency' (Mishan, 2005) because BlackBerry smartphones have lost a huge amount of their market share and could be in danger of becoming insolvent (Arthur, 2014). Of course one of the most clichéd examples of language change and new coinages through technology would be the verb to *google*, which entered the Merriam-Webster dictionary in 2006, but other words such as networking, hacking, crashing, uploading, downloading, scanning and surfing have all become a part of everyday life, although their meanings have broadened only in the last two or three decades. But this is only the tip of the iceberg. The word 'computer', for example, originated in the 1640s and referred to people who did calculations until after the 1940s (Harper, 2013). What we refer to now as computers were for years referred to as Turing Machines, after Alan Turing who many people credit as having created the first digital computer in order to decipher German communications in the Second World War. Appadurai (1990) notes that digital communication technology is partly responsible for creating an era of mass literacy, which borrows on Benedict Anderson's notion of 'print-capitalism' (2006) – the notion that political ideas and ways of life can be projected without the need for any face-to-face communication. Before such mass literacy, missionaries and the like were sent to propagate ideas and religions, to convert one way of life to another. This is no longer necessary in today's world, as people are influenced by other cultures and ways of life in ever more subtle ways, through mass media and printed words. This idea is part of Anderson's examination of Imagined Communities; broadly definable as a collective vision of a group in social context as conceptualised by an individual. This also closely equates to what Fairclough (2001) has called the 'globalisation of discourse'. Chatfield (2013b), writing specifically about digital use of language online, also notes that until relatively recently, being able to read and write was an educational privilege unattainable to most people, whereas now people in developed countries all over the world are both consumers and creators of vast amounts of written information. He also discusses that, perhaps counter-intuitively, some people (particularly grammar mavens) may complain that online forms of communication are causing irreparable damage to 'proper' language. Chatfield argues that this is not the case, and makes a convincing point. Languages change constantly, and if the spread of digital communication has accelerated that change it is not necessarily a bad thing.

It seems to be almost a prerequisite of any book dealing with second language acquisition to mention the way that communication has evolved and continues to rapidly change in the face of globalisation. Rather than add another such statement I would like to provide a few examples of how this change affects people in different domains with three stories that illustrate the fact that 'physical geographical boundaries separating communities of language users [have] become dissolved in the world of cyberspace and online communication networks' (Ushioda, 2011a: 199).

Story 1

In 2014 at an informal staff gathering designed to allow teachers a forum to discuss their teaching and research at Sophia University, I was amazed to hear a colleague's story about his research interests and life work dealing with an isolated tribe of people living in the rainforests of Brazil. When my colleague started talking about his work we were all awestruck. At one point I even remarked that it was like Indiana Jones linguistics. The full story of my colleague's work (I will call him G) is not the relevant part of this story though, although some background contextualisation may be necessary. While studying for his MA in linguistics in Brazil in the early 1990s, G was also working at an IT company. One day he received an email from a man wishing to meet regarding both linguistics and computers. The man was an elder in the remote Bachalahi tribe. The man proposed an exchange in which he would teach G his language and in return G would teach him how to use a computer. Thus began a long relationship in which G would return to a remote part of Brazil every year (despite later moving to Japan) in order to learn and document the Bachalahi language and help them with their computer. What is interesting here is the fact that the Bachalahi seldom have contact with people outside their local community; they have no mobile phones, no phone lines, not even televisions. But, once a day for about two hours they have wireless internet access as an overhead satellite passes over them. This way, through email and other tools they are able to communicate with the outside world. Thanks to this connection, they have been able to contact a linguist (my colleague, G) who has created a writing system for their language so that they can keep records and thus preserve their language as their community struggles to remain stable and yet adaptive to their changing environment.

Story 2

One of my wife's friends is a Japanese lady who is married to a Spanish man. She and her husband met each other in the United States while they were both studying. Now they live in Germany because of the husband's job. Although they speak each other's language a little, they mainly communicate with each other in English. They have two children, who are growing up with four languages – Japanese, Spanish, German and English. I present this story because it may seem unusual, however this kind of situation is actually a lot more common than many people realise; as V. Cook (2002) notes, it is actually unusual to find a place in the world where only one language is used. Ushioda, following Pavlenko (2002) and Coetzee-Van Rooy (2006) states that now, 'more than half of the [world's] inhabitants are not only bilingual or multilingual but members of multiple ethnic, social and cultural communities' (Ushioda, 2011a: 200). Needless to say, my wife stays in touch with her friend through social networking sites such as Facebook, and the friend and her husband use Skype to keep in touch with their family, and each other while living on different continents.

Story 3

This is a personal story about myself and how I keep in contact with my family who live over 6000 miles away from me. When I first moved back to Japan in 2011 I was not a father, but when my son was born in 2012 the need for regular updates with my family increased. I didn't want my family to miss out on my son's growing up, so I made sure he regularly saw his grandparents over Skype and also I made short videos of him which I edited and added music to using editing software. Less than 30 years ago (in the space of my own lifetime) this would not have been the simple matter it is today. I would have been writing letters and taking them to the post office, and any videos I sent would have been on VHS. To edit them and add music would have required access to an analogue editing studio and it would have been a lot more time consuming. Although these videos and video-calls are no substitute for real face-to-face contact, I must count myself very lucky that I am able to have even that. Also, thanks to the advances in international travel I am able to fly back to my family in just over 12 hours for a costly yet fairly reasonable fee, and this again is something which we take for granted now. Since 1978, the price of air travel has fallen about 50% (Thompson, 2013) and so if I had been born in my father's generation and my son in mine, I would have seen my dad much less regularly and he would likely have only a few photos of his grandson growing up.

These three stories are designed to exemplify and give context to globalisation, in particular the way communicative technologies have altered not just language but also who we communicate with, how we communicate and the way we communicate. If the force of globalisation has had such a profound influence on communication, it follows that it has had a huge impact on humanity as a whole. If, as I and many others believe, language is an innate and defining part of being human, then such a fundamental evolution in the way we use language now must have dramatic influences across the world, permeating many aspects of people's lives. There are even claims that the average person of today will be exposed to more information in a single day than the average person of a century ago would have been in an entire year. This oft-cited, apocryphal example probably originates from architect and graphic-designer Richard Wurman's (1989) claim that one copy of the daily edition of *The New York Times* probably contains more information than a normal person in 17th-century England would encounter in an entire lifetime. There are even claims stating that more information has been produced since the 1970s than in the last 5000 years combined (Jungwirth & Bruce, 2002). This 'information overload' has been linked to a phenomena called 'peak attention' (Chatfield, 2013a), which is similar to the idea of peak oil or peak water except that it deals with a finite cognitive function rather than a physical geological resource. I see evidence of this quite often, and recently the BBC reported on a phenomena known as 'dumbwalking' (Marshall, 2014) in which people cause congestion or even accidents due to the fact that they are walking while using their smartphones. In Tokyo where I live, safety posters on train platforms include a warning against this, known in Japan as *aruki-nagara* (walking while [on phone]). Being constantly connected has the converse effect of possibly preventing people from being present in their day to day reality. This is something that concerned the existentialists, as I already discussed in Chapter 2, particularly Martin Heidegger, who was very concerned that technology made it all too easy for humans to view the world objectively, thus reducing their presence of *being* in reality (Blitz, 2014). These are long-established concerns that seem to become ever more relevant as advances in technology makes digital communication devices ever more a part of our lives.

Because computers cannot come to us and meet us in our world, we must continue to adjust our world and bring ourselves to them. We will define and regiment our lives, including our social lives and our perceptions of our selves, in ways that are conducive to what a computer can 'understand'. Their dumbness will become ours. (Auerbach, 2012)

In their rather sensationalist book, Enriquez and Gullans (2010) claim that this avalanche of information being delivered daily into our brains is likely to result in the necessary evolution of our brain organ. They claim that this is due to the plasticity of the brain, making it the most likely place for the next evolutionary steps to take place. They cite small differences in DNA as contributing to different species, for example Neanderthal humans share roughly all but 1.5% of our genetic makeup, and Enriquez and Gullans use this to suggest that a new type of human could be produced owing to the increased work our brains are doing processing all this information. Enriquez even has a TED.com talk entitled 'Will our kids be a different species?' A biologist friend of mine told me in no uncertain terms that this was absurd, since his argument seems to be based on a misunderstanding of the word 'species', defined in biology as a group of organisms capable of reproduction, making it impossible by definition for our offspring to be a different species. Also, the closeness of DNA and shared genes is a reductive argument, since by the same logic humans and dogs are closely related since they share 84% of their genes. Even fruit flies share 47% and roundworms 38% of their genes with us. Regardless of how much we choose to believe about human evolution being affected by technology, it is certainly irrefutable that technology and globalisation has had a huge and multi-layered influence on the way the humans in developed contexts use language. In the field of language learning and second language acquisition, these influences are tangible in the classroom practices we employ to learn and teach languages, and they are also heavily impacting on the way we theorise language acquisition too (Canagarajah, 2013). Since the idea of authenticity in language is of central importance to communication and language education, it is now extremely important to reassess the concept of authenticity as it relates to globalisation and the information age. In this chapter I will outline how the internet and advances in ICT are not only increasing our ability to communicate, but also fundamentally changing how we communicate and how we socially construct our digital image of self.

Language Education and Communication Technology

D.E. Murray (2001) provides a very useful example of the way computers influence discourse from the turn of the millennium. An elderly lady calls an airline company to book a flight. Her intention is to get the cheapest fare to visit her daughter in New York. For her the most important information is the cost of the flight and the date is flexible. However, because of the computer booking system used by the operator the date is the first piece of information required in order to perform a search. Because of the computer, the operator requests to know the date the elderly lady is flying. She has not chosen a date because she first needs to know the prices. The agent simply chooses a mid-week flight and continues to ask about the time of the flight, and then proceeds to ask her name. In all of this, the elderly lady's enquiry about cheapest fares is not answered because 'communication gets redefined' (2001: 39) around the computer system. Of course, this experience is not isolated, and of course nowadays most people, even elderly people, would probably bypass the phone call and purchase the tickets online. My own mother uses specialist sites to search for the cheapest deals, and has even set up alerts so she can book tickets when they are at a certain price. She is not elderly, but she is now over 60, and the idea of her calling a plane company to book a ticket seems absurd. An obvious connection between authenticity and globalisation is that the way we achieve certain goals in the real-world is often connected to the way technology dictates the process we go through to achieve the outcome. Technology has changed the way many real-world tasks are done in the developed world. Therefore, an important factor when looking at the question of how information technology relates to teaching is the practical side. Is this relationship available readily or does it depend on having state of the art language labs and computer networks with expensive software? When I was working as the multimedia coordinator for a chain of language schools in London, we replaced our media room's machines with newer computers. The old ones were to be thrown away. I looked into sending our perfectly good machines to Africa, having heard about a charity which does that (computers4africa). However, the machines we had were too old to be accepted by the scheme! I found out that the scheme has been so successful that it can actually afford to be selective about the computers it takes. However, I would still strongly recommend that anyone in a position to donate their computers should sign up to the scheme, which has shipped over 40,000 computers to over 17 countries where otherwise children would not have access to computers for education. This also avoids the problem of refuse computer parts being sent to e-waste sites where chemicals and toxins from the parts have been linked to cancer and other health problems among local inhabitants (Widmer *et al.*, 2005).

Another consideration when utilising computers for language education would relate to the students' and teacher's level of digital literacy. Although low computer skills could be a barrier for some, online and computer-based tasks can of course develop digital literacy, while at the same time working on language proficiency. It is interesting that digital literacy and English proficiency have both come to be termed as 'life skills' (Graddol, 2006; Ushioda, 2011a), and I think it would not be too much to say that both are symbiotic. This is the background to the current educational climate. The implications of language use and of ICT, the pressure on learners to develop

150 Reconceptualising Authenticity for English as a Global Language

these skills in light of economic problems faced by limited resources, the abstract, multifaceted reality of the English language, all these things are influencing the work of language teachers and impacting on the environment in which people acquire second languages. One simple word for all of this is, of course, globalisation.

Authenticity Online

When T.S. Eliot made his comments about television allowing people to laugh at the same joke while remaining in isolation, he clearly was not imagining a world in which social networks (SNS) such as Twitter and Facebook allow people to communicate effortlessly, synchronously and asynchronously, share links, post images and videos and 'follow' each other's activity the way millions of people in developed nations do across much of the globe on a daily basis. The internet is at once a resource for great productivity and collaboration, and also a vacuum for procrastination and a giant haystack in which good information is lost against the avalanche of constant updates. There is a polyphonous and deafening game of Chinese Whispers being played on the internet, and the authenticity (in terms of being true or genuine) of sources can be hard to trace, requiring heightened critical facilities as demonstrated by the following quote (see Figure 7.1). This quote appeared on Cheezburger.com but it has been shared and re-posted virally so the original source is difficult to find. The fact that Abraham Lincoln could not possibly have made the statement because he died before the invention of the internet

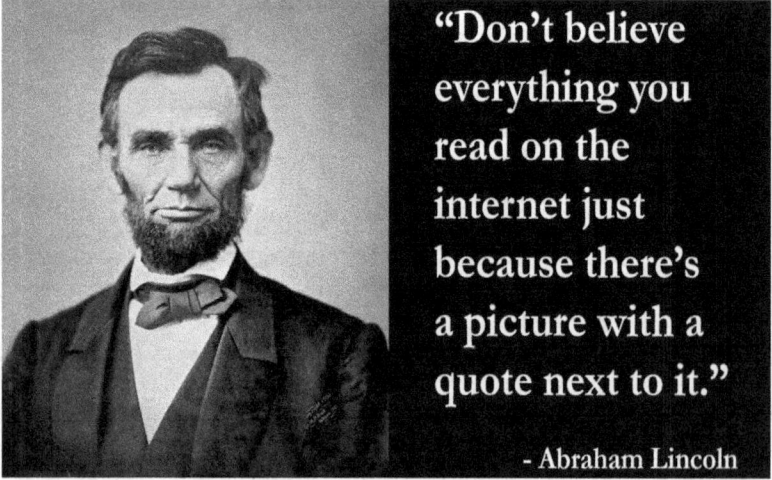

Figure 7.1 Abraham Lincoln's warning about the internet

New Media as a Catalyst for Authenticity 151

is a way of deliberately drawing attention to the dubious nature of some quotes found on the internet. The quote proves its own point in many ways.

Of course the inauthenticity of the quote is supposed to be obvious; however, for some people it is not always clear. For example, an anonymous user posted a question on Yahoo Answers asking how it was possible for Lincoln to have made the comments since he died in 1865 and the internet was not invented until 1957 (Figure 7.2).

Interestingly the author of this post seems to have realised the rather foolish nature of their question and felt the need to add an update explaining that they saw the quote at a public library, which is why they felt it was in fact authentic.

As I explained earlier in this book, authenticity is often defined not by positives but by negatives. Authenticity is not easily defined by positive examples of things that *are* authentic or things that *have* authenticity, but rather authenticity is more often defined by an absence of authenticity. Examples of things which are *not* authentic are better at helping us to define authenticity (Golomb, 1995: 7). The internet is a good example of something which embodies the paradox of authenticity. The Abraham Lincoln quote about the internet is not authentic in the sense that it almost certainly did not come from Abraham Lincoln, but it is authentic in another way. It is an authentic example of how internet memes are made and shared and how they contain implicit messages or warnings to other internet users. Some of these memes are informative while others belong to the category of trolling – using the internet to annoy people by purposefully being abusive or appearing ignorant in order to infuriate (often anonymous) users. The word has been used a lot in recent reports of online bullying and harassment, with several serious and high-profile stories coming out involving suicide and prison sentences. Continuing from the example question posted on Yahoo Answers, the following users replied to the question. Some of them are helpful, some of them trolling, but all of them are authentic examples of language interactions that took place online (Figure 7.3).

Education & Reference > Quotations   Next >

 Lincoln was credited with the quote, "Don't believe everything you read on the internet..."?

...but how is that possible given the fact that the internet was not invented until 1958 and Abraham Lincoln died almost a full century prior, in 1865?

Update: It was on display in a public library. It makes sense now, but I'm just used to libraries hanging posters with factual information.

☆ 1 following   ⁂ 5 answers

Figure 7.2 Yahoo Answers user questions Lincoln quote

152 Reconceptualising Authenticity for English as a Global Language

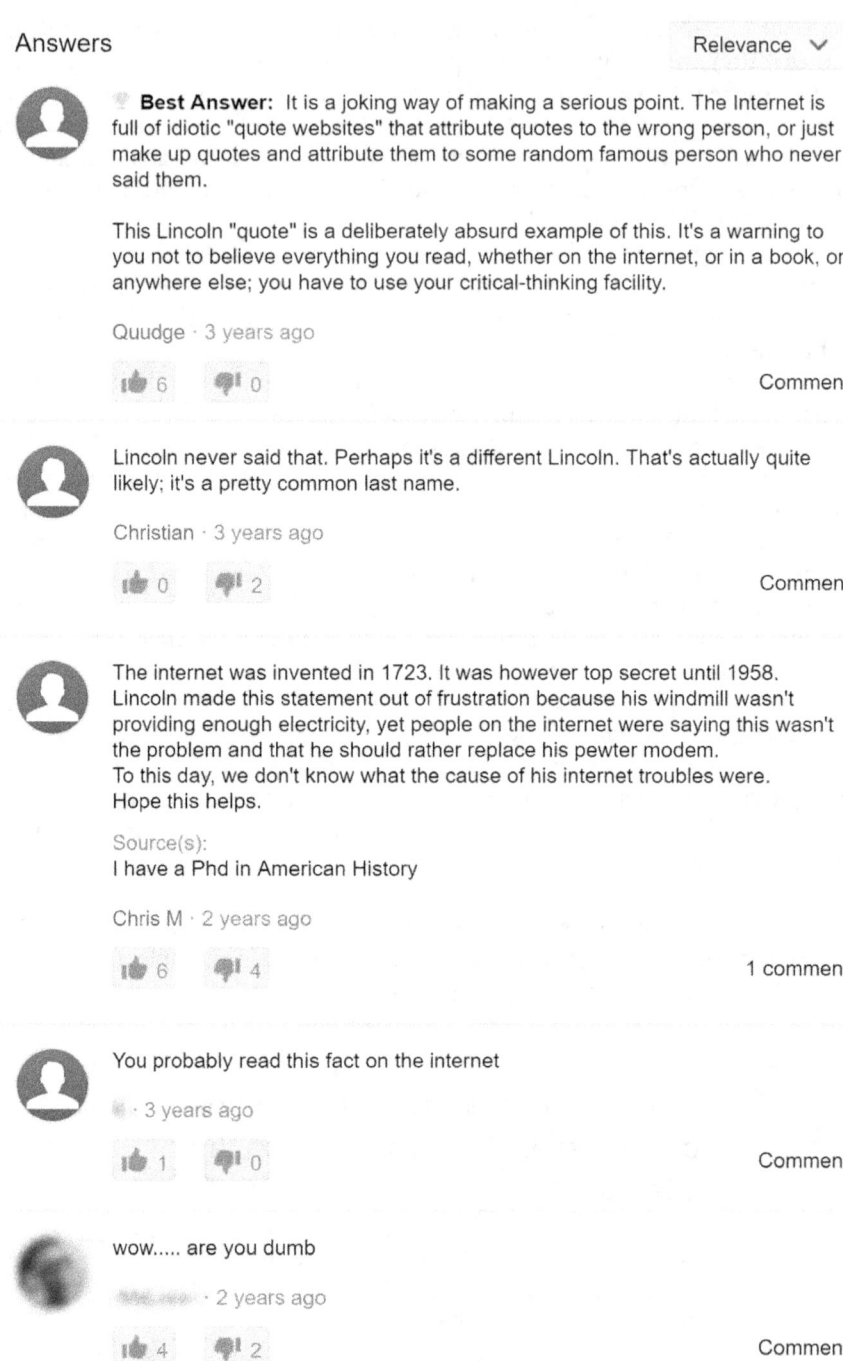

Figure 7.3 Lincoln question replies

It is quite clear that much of the content on the internet, although in one sense 'inauthentic', is in another sense authentic in itself, although in a rather different way. The internet is often cited as a repository for authentic materials. Mishan states that it is due to the internet that authenticity in language teaching has experienced an 'explosion' (2005: x). Mishan also notes that authentic 'cultural products' accessed through the internet are in danger of losing their societal value as they are stripped of their 'cultural interface' and presented merely as a text to be skimmed or scanned. In this way, her argument bears much resemblance to the problem of relying on 'extrapolation techniques' (Hung & Victor Chen, 2007) or presenting decontextualised language samples or content.

> The Internet, in other words, is a great leveller: it absorbs materials and works from different media and re-projects them indiscriminately through the same medium, one that may not, in fact, always be suitable to the material... [T]he Web reproduces cultural products but forfeits their cultural status in the process. (Mishan, 2005: 248)

In terms of authenticity as it relates to the Self, the internet is also having a notable impact on the way people communicate. In a fascinating book entitled *Oversharing: presentations of self in the internet age*, Agger (2012) explains how people are using the internet to be more themselves than they perhaps realise, or to be too honest or make public too much of their own private information. I have seen this phenomena first hand with my own friends, colleagues and even students and former students. One of my students, who I am 'friends' with on Facebook, posted a new profile picture in which she is very provocatively dressed. The picture was quite eye-opening, not just because it left little to the imagination but because it alerted me to the issue of oversharing and the potential ethical problems educators might face if they befriend students on social networks. It is also likely that many students who have befriend me on social networks have learned more about me than I would ordinarily care to divulge. A quick look on my Facebook page and one can learn that I am a father, and see pictures of my child, and from the picture it will be clear that my son is mixed-race and that he is about two years old and that he likes cars. A few more clicks and someone could discover what kind of music I like, what films I like, who my sisters are and where they live, whether or not they are in a relationship. It would also be easy to find embarrassing pictures of me or to read a post of mine that expresses some kind of strongly worded opinion or rudely worded banter. I am not doing this intentionally either, this is just part of the available information. When I accept students as friends on Facebook, I do so knowing that this is unchartered territory, and as such I have taken pains to learn about online security and how to keep track of my so-called digital shadow. I add students to a Restricted list on Facebook, which prevents them from seeing any of my posts or shares unless I choose to make them Public. Luckily for me I am savvy with this technology, having invested the time to work it all out and to remain cautious. A teacher colleague of mine was not so careful, and he was actually fired because of something he published on Twitter. The general public is also well aware of the dangers of posting onions online, due to several widely reported incidents of politicians and celebrities coming under-fire for voicing their opinions before vetting them for a wider audience. The power to publish to the world is carried around in the pockets of people who are quite often ignorant of the potential consequences of their language use in such a plethora of public forums.

Some teachers encourage their students to befriend them on social networking sites, whereas others are understandably wary. SNS can form a very effective way of connecting with students outside the classroom, engaging their real lives and identities. It can also create opportunities for authentic and motivating communication, not just between classmates but also within a web of connections with other learners and speakers around the globe. It could also be a social and ethical minefield. Policy differs from school to school and country to country. For example, in an article for the *Guardian* newspaper in the UK, 16 year old Lizzie Deane criticises her school's policy of discouraging teacher/student fraternisation through social networks. She explains that according to her school's e-safety policy, students and teachers must not be 'friends' and that teachers must 'ensure all online activity, both in and out of school, will not bring their professional role into disrepute' (Deane, 2013). Colleagues and friends of mine working for UK high schools have also informed me that they are not allowed to have any interactions with pupils online, except through the school's own email and virtual learning environment. This could be because the internet is already a well-known danger, where sexual predators engage in complicated grooming programmes that are designed to ensnare vulnerable and sexually naïve young people. In 2011, the General Teaching Council for England found that one in ten teachers accused of misconduct in the UK had used SNS to form inappropriate relationships with students (Vasagar & Williams, 2012). This actually seems lower than I would have expected, perhaps one of the reasons for the low statistic was that many schools still did not have effective policies in place, and there is still no official law for this type of interaction in the UK.

As I discussed in Chapter 2, when people interact in different social contexts, they may invoke different transportable identities (Zimmerman, 1998), which are either latent or explicit within the social context of the discourse. Because SNS communication is both new and subject to rapid changes, the identities which we present online are not as clear or easy to manage as the ones we establish in face-to-face communication. As humans, we spend much of our young and adult lives learning the social rules of interaction; a process made up of hours and hours of observation and trial and error. It is part of the dynamic construction of our identities. Online communication is, of course, part of this identity creation. However, the lack of context can lead people to present different, confusing or even contrasting versions of themselves online. For example, a teacher would not usually speak to a student after having drunk alcohol. However, logging onto Facebook after alcohol is not so unusual. If the teacher has pupils as 'friends' online then he or she may become entangled in a conversation where they are talking one-to-one, without the institutional context and with inhibitions lowered. Vasagar and Williams (2012) reported several cases where teachers had either set-up accounts using pseudonyms or requested that their students do not tell about their online contact. From this point, the conversations invariably slid into areas which fell 'outside the boundaries of the professional teacher/student relationship'. Despite these risks, I have actually had some very positive experiences of befriending students on Facebook. This is because, as I stated earlier, I have invested a lot of time in learning how to monitor and control my online self and how to selectively share the information I post. In the next section I will explain this in more detail, using personal examples.

Increased Social Contact and Awareness

In Chapter 2 I discussed a class I taught in 2012 as an example of how highly authentic classroom content manifested itself as a high level of engagement from students. One of the components which I believe made a large contribution to the success of this class was the fact that the work done in class was published online, which I encouraged through sharing and uploading videos. The publishing aspect to authenticity is something which I feel could be explored in more detail. Publishing online content is, as I have established in the previous section, now a natural part of everyday life for many young people in this era of mass-literacy and interaction (Chatfield, 2013b). The act of publishing students' work from a class is a way of integrating an element of authenticity to the work, by virtue of its availability to a wider community and widened readership. Instead of belonging only to the classroom, the students' work belongs to a virtual community of other people who share the language. Thus, the students are using and producing language for a real purpose (Morrow, 1977) or basically the output is no longer contrived for pedagogical purposes, making such tasks fall under the 'classic' definition of authenticity. In the reconceptualised terms proposed in this book, publishing connects learners more with the social axis of the authenticity continuum whilst simultaneously expanding along the contextual axis as well into the use domain. Publishing is also a way of achieving 'authenticity of purpose' (Coyle *et al.*, 2010); the reason for using the language becomes more than simply *a means to an end* (Widdowson, 1990), and this way, making classwork public aims to provide an actual 'experience of the language in use' (Tomlinson & Masuhara, 2010: 400). Also, by helping the students to integrate into a community of language users, it is likely that they will be able to see themselves as actual members of that otherwise disembodied community of language users. They have been given the vision and experience with which to more fully realise an imagined community to which they wish to belong (Irie & Brewster, 2014; Ryan & Irie, 2014). In my own experience, I have had many successes with publishing student's work as a way of sewing an element of authenticity into the classroom. Of course, the degree to which students authenticate the work depends on each individual and how they engage with the content, but overall I have seen very positive feedback from my own students.

As I established in Chapter 3, one of the problems with authenticity as it relates to the English language is the fact that English is a somewhat disembodied language. Previously, authenticity in language teaching has traditionally been linked to culture and embedded within that definition are the social customs and systems of thought that belong to those cultures (see Mishan, 2005: 51–53 for an overview of this discussion). As I have already explained, these definitions run the risk of inadvertently 'othering' groups of people and becoming culturist, often thereby giving credence to the problematic notion of 'native speakers'. Therefore, despite the myriad of reasons students may have to learn English, the actual reality of English as it is experienced in the classroom is often quite far removed from the idea of English as a global language. By this I mean that students may well want to learn English because they feel it will be instrumental to them in gaining a better job or engaging with the idea of a globalised society. However, when they are actually learning English in the classroom what they encounter are Anglo-global models of English speakers, speaking about culturally castrated concepts which have been whitewashed by international publishers (Bell & Gower, 2011; Meddings & Thornbury, 2009; Tomlinson, 2008). Mishan (2011b) has applied the term 'washback' (usually specific to language testing) to describe the way that ELT publishers rely on previously successful models, basically 'spawning imitations' and perpetuating the cycle of innocuous content. A well-documented alternative is to provide students with a way of breaking out of the classroom via online participation with others.

Increased Opportunities for Exchange

There is now a long and well-established stretch of research into classroom-based online exchanges. This was a natural extension of the 'pen-friend' model which involved writing to someone overseas as a form of cultural exchange. These online exchanges have become more and more developed over the years, with many of them now taking place in 3D virtual environments. One of the first studies of this type was done using email exchanges. Warschauer (1996) did one such study to investigate if computer mediated communication allowed for a more equally balanced level of participation between students than in a face-to-face discussion. His conclusion was that the quietest members of the group increased their participation ratio by a factor of almost ten, whilst the more outspoken class members balanced their participation level out. Although these students did not reduce their participation, the distribution of turns was more balanced than in the face-to-face environment. Warschauer et al. (1996) also looked at how computer networks can lead to student empowerment, and found that if used appropriately they could give students a better means of expressing themselves and are therefore potentially empowering for them. The findings of a further study by Rico García and Vinagre Arias (2000) reports that computers could be used to enhance motivation and lead to more effective learning. Other studies looked at the links between online exchanges, motivation and autonomy (Little & Ushioda, 1998; Ushioda, 2000). These types of study have come under criticism (Levy & Stockwell, 2006; Salaberry, 2001) for the way the results are not indicative of the nature of computer usage as a standalone resource and that the novelty factor was not properly eliminated. However, such studies do suggest that the use of computers has an advantage over traditional methods of instruction which utilise only paper-based materials. This is perhaps because technology-enhanced learning has more options for multi-modal input, with its rich media such as audio, video and other interactive features. One additional factor is that often computers can be used as a resource to encourage autonomy (Beatty, 2013; Benson, 2013b; Benson & Reinders, 2011) and provide increased access to 'authentic' materials as well. Since Warschauer and his colleagues' pioneering work in the 1990s, there have been a huge number of studies which investigate and report on the classroom practices of teachers who have involved their students in some form of online collaborative learning (Cassell & Tversky, 2005; Hanna & De Nooy, 2009; Levy, 2009; O'Dowd, 2007). I have also done online exchanges with students, in which I teamed up with other teachers and their classes in other countries around the world. My own experience is that there are both ups and downs, and sadly in my case more often than not the enthusiasm for the exchange seems to peter out as final assignments and coursework deadlines start to take precedence towards the end of the course. I also got the feeling that the students found it hard to see the exchanges as authentic sometimes – either because they had no real purpose to engage with the other students from another class, or perhaps owing to some factor, which could stem from the fact that the other students were not balanced in terms of proficiency. In one exchange I took part in with a university in Taiwan, the students were all training to be English teachers, but my students were from an intermediate general English class from various faculties, none of them English majors.

Another commonly cited advantage to technology use for language learning is the way it can potentially aid learner autonomy. This is something I touched on slightly in the previous paragraph, and something which is fairly self-evident. Of course, if students are online then they have access to other languages and an inexhaustible repository of online learning materials, both contrived and 'authentic' in the traditional sense of not having been designed for learning. This is something that has already been written about in some detail and both advocated and problematised, so I will only briefly touch on the issues here. One of the issues is the distinction between autonomy and self-access learning. Online self-access centres (OSACs) are potentially very useful, however this is not the same as autonomous learning. Online self-access centres are good in that they often provide focused and vetted materials; materials that have been selected or linked to specifically because of their perceived quality. However, many of these 'purpose-built' online practice materials may be produced by international ELT textbook publishers, and hence potentially lead to the same 'anodyne' (Meddings & Thornbury, 2003) type of content. Having looked at the type of content available on many of the 'interactive' CD-ROMs and DVDs that come with published textbooks, I have come to the conclusion that, although using a wider range of multi-modal input (for example, video and audio content) most of these activities are simply 'drill and kill' activities because, like The Terminator, the computer is basically just 'a mechanical tutor that never grew tired or judgmental and allowed students to work at an individual pace' (Warschauer & Healey, 1998: 57). The reason for this is that most online language questions have to be multiple-choice or simple-answer questions, in order to provide instant feedback to learners. Online language questions and tests must utilise very strict programming syntax in order for the computer to 'know' whether the student has provided a correct answer or not. For example, we had many problems at the OSAC which I set up when I worked as eLearning Coordinator for a private language school in London. Students complained about putting in correct answers but the computer saying the answer was wrong. It turned out that this was all due to a simple issue of apostrophes. There are two types of apostrophe on a computer keyboard, and because our OSAC was looking for a ['] rather than an [`] we ran into some serious problems. In the end, one unlucky person (me) had to go into the system and re-programme all the questions so that they allowed both types of apostrophe. This was just one of many such issues. Furthermore, at the sentence level, a computer is unable to really understand the conventions of language. Anyone who has attempted to use online translation software for sentences with multiple clauses will already know this. Even translating a sentence into one language and then back to the original will often result in some degradation.

Such translation software also causes havoc with students' written assignments, which has been a feature of online plagiarism discussions because it adds an extra layer of difficulty in the detection of plagiarism (J. Bailey, 2011; Selwyn, 2008). Furthermore, an even more troubling variant of translation and plagiarism is known as Rogeting. The neologism refers to Roget's *Thesaurus*, which apparently students are using to hide their plagiarism by changing certain key words. The result is not only hard to trace, but also often the process renders the sentence incomprehensible. In a widely reported case, a Middlesex University lecturer traced one students' sentence to its original source by reverse Rogeting it. The student had written 'common mature musicians [and] recent liturgy providers are looking to satisfy...Herculean personalised liturgies', which had been originally 'the current big players and new service providers are looking to supply more powerful personalised services' (Grove, 2014). I and many of my colleagues have noticed similarly bizarre wordings from students who perhaps wrote their essays themselves in their L1 and then translated the whole thing into L2 with a quick copy and paste from an online translator. This is then basically the rather maligned grammar translation method but without any of the cognitive engagement that might make such an approach to language learning viable. In other words, this is a form of cheating which is not only becoming a more common source of frustration for teachers, but also is more likely to actively impair a learner's understanding of the language and exacerbate any pre-existing negative affect towards the act of learning.

In sum, while potentially providing greater access to various types of rich input and facilitating autonomous learning, computers also provide students with new ways of cheating and plagiarising which are certainly more likely to hinder language acquisition than to supplement it. Furthermore, despite the advances in technology, many computer-based tests and language practice activities still fall under what Warschauer and Healey (1998) labelled as behaviouristic CALL. In this way, technology is little more than an interactive set of grammar-drills and comprehension questions. Although this type of learning can certainly be useful and in many cases leads to increased acquisition for some learners, it falls short of providing the type of authenticity which I have been trying to outline in this book; namely a reconceptualised version of authenticity which links social and individual factors to contexts both inside and outside instruction.

Conversely, there are polar extremes to this type of online language learning. For example, Henry (2013) reports on the situation in Sweden, where learners often use English for online gaming. For these students, the English they learn in classrooms is often too easy, and so they tend to simply coast along enjoying the easy ride. Also in Scandinavian countries, many television programmes are broadcast in English, as well as there being content instruction in English. These countries exhibit an extremely high overall proficiency in English (see the Education First English Proficiency Index, 2014), and in such territories the problem is not getting learners to engage with the English language but finding something sufficiently challenging and engaging for them in the classroom in order to facilitate an investment in the learning. In my own experience teaching in Japan, I have taught advanced classes for English majors where the students' existing proficiency makes a focus on language learning seem rather unnecessary, and I have also taught classes for non-English majors where the majority of students not only struggle to comprehend basic utterances, but also appear to be apathetic or even hostile towards the English language. With such a spectrum of attitudes and aptitudes it is no wonder that both language teachers and SLA literature have a tendency to over-generalise contexts and social groups. The only useful generalisation I can make at this point being that, despite the variety of different settings and individual preferences, technology is able to bring people together more easily and this can create opportunities for meaningful language exchanges.

Increased Exposure to Language and Culture

To say that the internet provides learners and teachers with instant access to authentic materials is like saying that going to a restaurant provides us with access to food. However, what kind of restaurant is it? Can we afford it? Do we have to make a reservation? Are we even hungry? The internet is the same as the good old 'classic' newspaper example of 'authenticity'. Just because something is in English and on the internet does not mean it is authentic or even remotely suitable for our learners. People may be online right now with the intention of learning English and they may be doing nothing of the sort. On the other hand, there may be people logging in with the express intention of doing no learning at all but to play games instead (perhaps when they should be doing some work) and these people may actually inadvertently learn some new language. It would be foolish to dismiss the world of online content and the potential interactions it harbours, and yet it would be equally naïve to assume that just because people are online they are going to be able to access authentic materials and learn from them. Good materials designed for language learning exist, but they are often inauthentic in that they are designed specifically to test isolated grammar structures or provide multiple choice for scripted videos. A hitherto under-explored area of inquiry is into the type of learning that takes place outside of the classroom. Recently Benson and Reinders (2011) have been looking at language learning that takes place outside of institutional settings, using online resources in particular as a medium for input and communication. In other words, what about the millions of people around the world who are no longer at university (where most researchers work and have access) and yet could still be classed as learners? How do these people learn? What resources do they use and how do they engage with them for learning? For instance, in 2014 while watching the trailer for Christopher Nolan's film

Interstellar I found that members of the YouTube community were discussing accents with implicit reference to using films as a way of getting English language practice, although the main focus seems to be purely for enjoyment of the film (Figure 7.4).

It seems rather obvious that language learning takes place outside of the classroom, and it actually seems likely that more learning takes place outside the classroom than inside. However, empirically proving the above statement would be extremely challenging. If we assume that this is the case, surely there is some way for language teachers to utilise this fact in helping learners to maximise on their out of class learning, perhaps with training activities which allow them to develop critical frameworks for analysing online content's usefulness.

The internet could also be a cultural repository, a way of exposing learners to the target culture or communities which use the target language. However, what culture are we talking about here? Are we talking about a culture from the target language? Could this be, for example, the *Guardian* newspaper's website, with all its visually appealing layout, videos and audio content? The issue here is that we are right back to the 'classic' definition of authenticity, a definition which has a tendency to gravitate towards 'standard English' and inner-circle, centre culture. Furthermore, there is another type of culture on the internet – the culture of mass-literacy and interaction, the culture of Hacktivism and trolling and everything dark and beautiful in-between. Furthermore, for many teachers who work with young people, it seems that we are the ones who do not understand the internet in the way they do. Prensky (2001) makes the distinction between digital natives and digital immigrants to refer to an older generation of people who had to learn how to use the internet vs the young generation who grew up with it. Although some people may find an element of truth in this binary view, it falls short of being accurate on many points. For one, he seems not to have

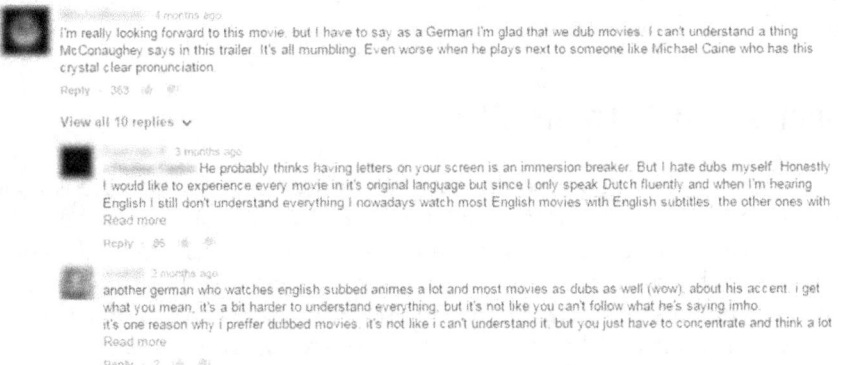

Figure 7.4 YouTube users discuss accents and comprehensibility in comments

taken into account that the technology to which his distinction refers was created by the so-called digital immigrants, and therefore overlooks the fact that the so-called digital natives are actually consumers of a product designed for them by the previous generation. Furthermore, if I were to adopt Prensky's terminology I would probably label myself as a digital-native, since I grew up with technology. But, the games I played as a young teenager were Street Fighter 2 and Treasure Island Dizzy. I owned a PlayStation back when there was no need to put a number after it. Before that I had a Sega Mega Drive, which I played Sonic the Hedgehog on. When I wrote my undergraduate dissertation in 2003, most of the research I did came from physical books that I took out from the university library. When I started my MA in 2008, part of the induction involved a man from the Information Systems Services coming to show us how to search the online databases. After a very technical presentation, he said rather wryly, 'people like me used to be called librarians'. My son knows how to use an iPad and he is under three years old. But he doesn't know how to send an email or install an app. When he is my age, if Moore's law still holds true and computer processers continue doubling in power every two years, then the games he played as a child will seem as outdated then as Sonic the Hedgehog seems now. Does this make anyone a digital-native? Is it really possible to claim that all this technology has become natural to us in just one or two generations?

Labelling the internet as a cultural repository is, again, untenable without a proper understanding of what we mean by culture. The internet is no more a source of culture and authentic language than a newspaper is. There are obvious differences between the two, and the internet is much more diverse and widely available. But, if we are not interacting with it as a social entity then we might as well just print out the pages we intend to use and revert back to the 'classic' definition of authenticity. Even with videos and other interactive media, we must be careful that what we are doing invokes a social-constructivist aspect of language use and engages students in a process of personal meaning making, otherwise it is very likely that the technology is just a more instantly gratifying version of a textbook built on behaviouristic principles.

Games and Authenticity

G. Cook (1997, 2000) points out that to say that language use is about achieving some communicative function is a misrepresentation of the reality of everyday interactions. People are not always speaking as a form of transaction. People learn languages to acquire cultural capital, and cultural capital is linked to linguistic capital, but not all use of language is based on exchanges of power. Learning is like this too. We do not always learn something to gain power, although people do say knowledge is power. People also say language is power. And yet, people often use language simply because it is natural for humans to do so. Language can be playful and it is not always identifiable as being driven by specific motives. By the same token, learning too can be undertaken purely as a hobby or for the enjoyment of learning. It may sound hard to believe, and even more difficult to convince a room full of students, but Csikszentmihalyi (1997) argues that learning should be its own reward. Some recent innovations in education are starting to take games and fun very seriously (Lazzaro, 2009). Games, especially online games, are beginning to create interest in the field of English language teaching (Chik, 2011; Cornillie *et al.*, 2012; Henry, 2013; Reinders, 2012; Reinhardt & Sykes, 2014). Naturally, both motivation and authenticity are being heavily referenced in the central justification for the adoption of learning scenarios that make use of online games, and so this is not surprising. The implications for these online types of environment could be very significant, and indeed herein lies another potential area of inquiry for authenticity. However, I can only briefly mention such environments, as the focus of this volume is on being able to frame authenticity from the very broad perspective of English as an international language.

Conclusion

The place of technology in today's world is quite unprecedented in terms of scale and intensity. Human ingenuity has always been involved with the advancement of technology, and so in some ways there is nothing new about technology in that sense. However, in another sense technology is always new, and in fact the newness of a piece of technology is one of the reasons we label it 'technology'. Recently, education has been entangled in a culture of innovation-seeking which can seem to be progressing at a very rapid pace, despite the cyclical nature of educational trends (Howatt & Widdowson, 2004). Like many textbooks needing to constantly produce new editions, there is a certain degree of maintaining face involved in the constant need to update technology in order to keep up with current trends. This is one of the reasons why I have avoided discussing any single innovation or trend in this chapter, for fear of dating the discussion prematurely. And yet, it is inevitable to mention certain trends and usages, as they have become natural to everyday life. And, at the same time, the power of new technologies seems to have simultaneously raised and lowered our expectations. On the one hand we expect technology to hold answers, and on the other we further distance ourselves from the actual process of taking onus for things that need to be done. British satirist and comedian Charlie Brooker shares a rather telling anecdote about people's faith in technology:

> When I was making the series How TV Ruined Your Life, we went out and asked members of the public to comment on a new invention we were claiming was real: a mobile phone that allowed you to call through

time, so you could speak to people in the past or future. Many people thought it was real: not so much a testament to gullibility, but an indicator of just how magical today's technology has become. We take miracles for granted on a daily basis. (Brooker, 2011)

The comments above suggest that rather than making people 'stupid', it makes people step away from the world more with the expectation that technology will be a reliable stand-in. In some ways then, technology takes people into auto-pilot and as a result they may find themselves less able to 'be there' as Heidegger had feared. In this sense, the existential side of authenticity is foregrounded when discussing technology. Online interactions and social networking are part of the fabric day-to-day life for a very large number of humans on the planet, making the phenomena of technology and communication a very rich area for further inquiry. The scepticism sewn throughout this chapter comes from my own conviction that such forms of new media have potentially damaging consequences, and that as a result we may be moving away from things that are naturally good for us in a short-sighted dash to make things easier. However, as far as education and language learning are concerned, the opportunities for technology to enhance authenticity are very exciting.

8 Conclusion

As a teacher I have been through many stages in my 10 years of full-time experience, and I have had to constantly re-imagine myself and adapt to new surroundings. I have only ever taught in Japan and England, in both countries I have only taught in either private language schools or universities. I have never worked in contexts where English is spoken as a second official language, I have never worked in developing countries, most of my experience is with university-level (and thus somewhat privileged) learners and teachers. Furthermore much of my research and experience is based in Japan, a unique EFL context which, although representative on some levels, will not reflect the idiosyncrasies of other local contexts. I am confessing all this (at the end of the book, I admit) in order to be authentic, or perhaps 'sincere' as Trilling (1972) would prefer. I confess this now in order to make sure that what I have said in this book is received with due diligence and criticism. When writing about the need to reconceptualise the idea of authenticity in journal articles, I was asked by editors and reviewers to clearly establish the need to do so, and I will admit that some editors rejected my papers because they felt I had not been able to do so. However, I was lucky that in my position I was able to see the gap between what had been an established opening up of authenticity that began with Widdowson (1978) and the rise in prominence of communicative language teaching, and the rather old-fashioned view which I still saw being held to by teachers and students in the language classrooms even to this day. However, these observations were mainly based in Japan. Works such as Holliday (2005) and Lee (1995) did help me to conclude and affirm that this problem was not isolated to Japan, and that rather than being a clear-cut problem of 'people think that "native speakers" are more authentic' the issue was actually multi-faceted. Most EFL textbooks still present the 'native speaker' as the dominant authentic model, and even those that claim to give the L2 speaker some stage-room (such as Macmillan's Global) still tend to relegate the L2 model to the side. Worse still, L2 learners and even L2 teachers further perpetuate the problem by holding to the self-effacing belief that countries in Kachru's inner-circle, at the so-called 'centre' are at the top of the authenticity hierarchy (Myhill, 2003). This was often something that remained implied within discussions of authenticity. It was, of course, very unfavourable to define authenticity according to 'native speakers' and so it seemed that people assumed the problem of authenticity had gone away by switching to the world 'real' instead of 'native'. This actually made the problem harder to challenge, because being only implied it was easy to deny and hard to demonstrate. I have tried to demonstrate that the implication of the problematic notion of the 'native speaker' is still there in discussions of authenticity, but I have also tried to show that this is not really the fault of any particular group or ideology. If anything is to blame, it is the complexity of authenticity as a concept. The discussions about authenticity were just too convoluted to really make sense to any ordinary practitioner, and so as a result the definition of authenticity tended to fall back to the 'classic' definition of something produced in a context where the language being learned is used by people who do not need to learn anymore. In other words, the real world, where people talk and communicate to get things done. I have also attempted to show why the 'real' definition is problematic in itself, regardless of the implicit shadow of the 'native speaker'. This is because by defining one context as the 'real', we seem to imply that the other context (in this case, the teaching context) is not real. This is especially problematic when English is viewed as an international language from a pedagogical perspective, because for many learners the classroom may well be the only context where they actually get a chance to 'experience' the English language in any authentic sense. Conversely, there are many other contexts where the opposite is true, where English is a part of people's everyday life and therefore a part of their reality. For them, turning this language into a subject to be taught at school creates what Henry (2013) labelled an 'authenticity gap'.

Although authenticity was already recognised as a complex issue, I have tried to establish that this is perhaps a more natural and dynamic type of complexity than has previously been acknowledged. Also, in order to write this book I have spent several years researching, reading new and old discussions on the subject, and it is even the focus of my PhD research. Not all of us have the time (or the inclination) to do so, and those who have are notable for having dedicated a large part of their careers to doing so. Therefore I have attempted in this book to provide an easy access route, and to provide the ideas and information in formats which will hopefully be easy to disseminate. I am hopeful that this book will be further simplified and communicated to practitioning language teachers in various contexts, and my real aim is to do away with the pervasive notion that newspapers are equal to authentic materials. Relevance to individuals in contexts which are socially dynamic might not have the same ring to it, but I think that this is a much better way of describing authenticity in language acquisition. This definition should not be limited to materials, but also other domains of authenticity as well.

Directions for Research

One of the fundamental arguments I have tried to put forward in this book is the idea that authenticity is not simple, it is not a case of 'authentic' or 'inauthentic' and it is not an inherent property of some text or activity owing to the cultural origins of any one person or thing. It is intensely personal and relates to the individual and sense of Self, and yet it also relates to, relies on and is influenced by society and social relationships. If we look at the 'small culture' of the classroom (Holliday, 1999) then this process of interaction happens on a relatively small scale, but it must be remembered that this is merely just one context and that the phenomenon of language learning exists and continues well beyond the walls of the institution or classroom. Small cultures can also be used to describe much larger contexts and social settings. Therefore authenticity is as relevant to the outside world as it is to the classroom, and the two contexts are not mutually exclusive. On the contrary, authenticity is and always has been about breaking down the walls of the classroom and exposing the learners to some form of reality of language in use and to provide an experience. By this I do not mean to imply that the classroom is not real, in fact quite the opposite. I mean that the classroom should be a valid reality where language is both learned *and* used *and* experienced. The problem is that in trying to understand authenticity it has nearly always been compartmentalised, reduced into something that fits under a microscopic lens. Quite often, when authenticity has been looked at from a wider perspective it has been as part of something else. This is something I think makes sense, and if we ascribe to the complex dynamic systems approach to applied linguistics which is currently reshaping the theoretical landscape (N.C. Ellis & Larsen-Freeman, 2009; Kramsch, 2011; Larsen-Freeman & Cameron, 2008a, 2008b; Mercer, 2011) then this would seem to be a promising perspective. In other words we cannot look at something in isolation, rather we must step back and try to see the whole system at work. It is necessary to get a holistic understanding of the dynamic nature of the process of second language acquisition.

Research into authenticity might be as much about a person's mental state as it is about their emotional state as well, because people are not merely products of their own minds but they also have more fundamental features imbedded within themselves, which identify and define them too. So, forming a genuine connection with people as humans is part of the authentic experience, and this might be a real challenge for people teaching and learning in language classrooms around the world, particularly in contexts where English is taught in large compulsory classes as a subject of study more than an actual living and breathing language with a tangible influence on the learner's lives. As I have argued before, language is an identifying and innate trait of being human, and one creates his or her identity through social interactions which utilise language. Therefore, it may well be almost impossible to have an authentic connection with a second language unless someone is able to express themselves. This is further complicated by the fact that in learning a new language, people are often engaged in a process of self-change or reinvention, and as such the L2 self may be very different to the L1 self. Either way, expression of the Self relies to some degree on having invested in the language enough to want to say something personal, or to be able to go through the process of self-creation or self-alteration on top of the challenge of speaking a foreign language. In this way, authenticity may very well be contingent to some degree on proficiency levels. However, this does not mean the language classroom cannot be authentic for low-level learners, it just means that the way it is structured will have to take into account that these learners need support in expressing themselves and maintaining authenticity will require negotiation, scaffolding, motivation, autonomy and patience.

Authenticity is an individual trait and research methods which seek to understand it must utilise techniques which are designed to better understand the Self. Sometimes this work is done by the researcher themselves, say in autoethnographic works (Simon-Maeda, 2011), and sometimes the research may be a learner or a teacher also. Research may also be ethnographic, and draw on a vast array of emerging methodologies for gaining deeper understandings and meaningful insights (Rodriguez & Ryave, 2002), but I think that essentially classroom-based research into authenticity needs to take into account both social and individual components. Authenticity as it relates to SLA cannot simply provide a deeper understanding of the L2 Self-concept and highlight each and every learner as an individual; in order to be truly useful and meaningful as a concept it still needs to be practical for teaching and learning languages. As such, authenticity should find a way of seeking to understand the human essence of the language classroom, and to build on the concept that introspection on a personal level does not take place in a vacuum, but in fact it belongs to the broader endeavour of human self-reflection. We are trying to build a sense of ourselves as individuals that belong to society, and that is never an easy thing. There are so many people in the world now, so many cultures and sub-cultures which are amalgamating, reacting, rejecting or even polarising themselves from each other. Society is on the brink of global energy shortages and environmental issues unprecedented in the whole of human history, and yet we have the technology and the knowledge of the accumulated millennia of our species' existence at our fingertips. The world is profligate with information now too, some of it can unlock the nature of the cosmos for us, and some of it is just celebrity gossip or even utterly false in its logic and facts. The need for critical thinking has never been so high, and yet the media is able to bombard our minds with incredibly influential messages with very few boundaries. Social problems are rife and at the same time social networks and innumerable entertainment channels keep us isolated, while at the same time ensuring we need never be alone. In a nutshell I am saying that society has probably never been so complicated or so complex, and hence investigating something like the nature of authenticity in language learning is likely to require a view that encompasses a great deal of flexibility and incorporates the ever-changing reality of identity construction.

Authenticity can be a powerful concept to empower both learners and teachers, because authenticity connects the individual learner to the content used for learning. It connects the students to the teacher, and also to other learners, which in turn influences classroom dynamics of interaction, and therefore affects how learners engage with tasks and how much they invest themselves in the learning. It is also an integral part of how learners conceptualise themselves in relation to the wider social context in which the target language will be used. In other words, nobody can tell us what is authentic, we have to find it for ourselves.

References

Abbott, S. (ed.) (2013) Authentic learning. The glossary of education reform. See http://edglossary.org/authentic-learning/ (accessed 16 September 2015).
Agger, B. (2012) *Oversharing: Presentations of Self in the Internet Age*. New York: Routledge.
Allan, R. (2009) Can a graded reader corpus provide 'authentic' input? *ELT Journal* 63 (1), 23–32.
Allwright, D. (2003) Exploratory practice: Rethinking practitioner research in language teaching. *Language Teaching Research* 7 (2), 113–141.
Allwright, D. (2005) Developing principles for practitioner research: The case of exploratory practice. *The Modern Language Journal* 89 (3), 353–366.
Allwright, D. and Bailey, K.M. (1991) *Focus on the Language Classroom: An Introduction to Classroom Research for Language Teachers*. Cambridge: Cambridge University Press.
Allwright, D. and Hanks, J. (2009) *The Developing Language Learner: An Introduction to Exploratory Practice*. Basingstoke: Palgrave Macmillan.
Alsagoff, L., McKay, S.L., Hu, G. and Renandya, W.A. (eds) (2012) *Principles and Practices for Teaching English as an International Language*. Oxon: Routledge.
Altbach, P.G. (1981) The university as center and periphery. *The Teachers College Record* 82 (4), 601–621.
Altbach, P.G. (2004) Globalisation and the university: Myths and realities in an unequal world. *Tertiary Education and Management* 10 (1), 3–25.
Ammon, U. (ed.) (2001) *The Dominance of English as a Language of Science: Effects on Other Languages and Language Communities*. Berlin: de Gruyter.
Amor, S. (2002) *Authenticity and Authentication in Language Learning: Distinctions, Orientations, Implications*. Frankfurt: Peter Lang.
Anderson, B. (2006) *Imagined Communities: Reflections on the Origin and Spread of Nationalism* (Revised ed.). London: Verso.
Anderson, C.E. (2011) CLIL for CALP in the multilingual, pluricultural, globalized knowledge society: Experiences and backgrounds to L2 English usage among Latin American L1 Spanish-users. *Latin American Journal of Content & Language Integrated Learning* 4 (2), 51–66.
Appadurai, A. (1990) Disjuncture and difference in the global cultural economy. *Public Culture* 2 (2), 1–24.
Apple, M.T., Da Silva, D. and Fellner, T. (eds) (2013) *Language Learning Motivation in Japan*. Bristol: Multilingual Matters.
Arnold, E. (1991) Authenticity revisited: How real is real? *English for Specific Purposes* 10 (3), 237–244.
Arthur, C. (2014, 29th September) Ten things to know about BlackBerry – and how much trouble it is (or isn't) in. *Technology*. Online. See http://www.theguardian.com/technology/2014/sep/29/ten-things-to-know-blackberry-john-chen (accessed 10 March 2015).

Árva, V. and Medgyes, P. (2000) Native and non-native teachers in the classroom. *System* 28 (3), 355–372.
Atkinson, D. (ed.) (2011) *Alternative Approaches to Second Language Acquisition*. London: Routledge.
Atkinson, T. and Claxton, G. (eds) (2000) *The Intuitive Practitioner: On the Value of Not Always Knowing What One is Doing*. Bristol: Taylor & Francis.
Auerbach, D. (2012) The stupidity of computers. *n + 1, Issue 13: Machine Politics*.
Bachman, L.F. (1991) What does language testing have to offer? *TESOL Quarterly* 25 (4), 671–704.
Bachman, L.F. and Palmer, A.S. (1996) *Language Testing in Practice: Designing and Developing Useful Language Tests*. Oxford: Oxford University Press.
Badger, R. and MacDonald, M.N. (2010) Making it real: authenticity, process and pedagogy. *Applied Linguistics* 31 (4), 578–582.
Bailey, J. (2011, 24 Febuary) The problem with detecting translated plagiarism. See https://www.plagiarismtoday.com/2011/02/24/the-problem-with-detecting-translated-plagiarism/ (accessed 17 April 2015).
Bailey, K. (2007) Akogare, ideology, and 'charisma man' mythology: Reflections on ethnographic research in English language schools in Japan. *Gender, Place & Culture* 14 (5), 585–608.
Bandura, A. (2001) Social cognitive theory: An agentic perspective. *Annual Review of Psychology* 52 (1), 1–26.
Barkhuizen, G. (2011) Narrative knowledging in TESOL. *TESOL Quarterly* 45 (3), 391–414.
Barkhuizen, G. (ed.) (2013) *Narrative Research in Applied Linguistics*. Cambridge: Cambridge University Press.
Barkhuizen, G., Benson, P. and Chik, A. (2014) *Narrative Inquiry in Language Teaching and Research*. New York: Routledge.
Batibo, H. (2005) *Language Decline and Death in Africa: Causes, Consequences, and Challenges*. Clevedon: Multilingual Matters
Beatty, K. (2013) *Teaching and Researching: Computer-Assisted Language Learning* (2nd edn). New York: Routledge.
Bell, J. and Gower, R. (2011) Writing course materials for the world: A great compromise. In B. Tomlinson (ed.) *Materials Development in Language Teaching* (2nd edn, pp. 135–150). Cambridge: Cambridge University Press.
Benson, P. (2013a) Drifting in and out of view: Autonomy and the social individual. In P. Benson and L. Cooker (eds) *The Applied Linguistic Individual* (pp. 75–89). Bristol: Equinox Books.
Benson, P. (2013b) *Teaching and Researching: Autonomy in Language Learning*. London: Routledge.
Benson, P. and Cooker, L. (eds) (2013) *The Applied Linguistic Individual*. Bristol: Equinox.
Benson, P. and Reinders, H. (eds) (2011) *Beyond the Language Classroom*. Basingstoke: Palgrave Macmillan.
Benson, P. and Voller, P. (eds) (1997) *Autonomy and Independence in Language Learning*. London: Longman.
Beppu, H. (2005) English dominance and self-orientalism [英語支配とセルフ・オリエンタリズム]. In K. Tsuda (ed) *English Dominance over Language, Information, and Culture [言語・情報・文化の英語支配]* (pp. 36–43). Tokyo: Akashi Shoten.
Bhardwaj, V. (2015) Luis Suarez memes flood Twitter after Barcelona striker bags first-half brace against Manchester City, *Metro*. See http://metro.co.uk/2015/02/24/luis-suarez-memes-flood-twitter-after-barcelona-striker-bags-first-half-brace-against-manchester-city-5077866/ (accessed 24 February 2015).
Blitz, M. (2014) Understanding Heidegger on technology. *The New Atlantis* 41 (Winter), 63–80.

Block, D. (2007) *Second Language Identities* (Bloomsbury classics in linguistics ed.). London: Bloomsbury.

Blommaert, J. (2010) *The Sociolinguistics of Globalization*. Cambridge: Cambridge University Press.

Blommaert, J. and Rampton, B. (2012) Language and superdiversity. *MMG Working Paper (Max Planck Institute for the Study of Religious and Ethnic Diversity)* 12 (05).

Blommaert, J. and Varis, P. (2011) Enough is enough: The heuristics of authenticity in superdiversity *Working Papers in Urban Language & Literacies* (Vol. 76): King's College, London, Albany, Gent, Tilburg.

Bolton, K. (2008) World Englishes today. In B.B. Kachru, Y. Kachru and C. Nelson (eds) *The Handbook of World Englishes* (pp. 240–270). Oxford: Wiley-Blackwell.

Bonnett, M. and Cuypers, S. (2003) Autonomy and authenticity in education. In N. Blake, P. Smeyers, R.D. Smith and P. Standish (eds) *The Blackwell Guide to the Philosophy of Education* (pp. 326–340). London: Blackwell.

Borg, S. (2006) The distinctive characteristics of foreign language teachers. *Language Teaching Research* 10 (1), 3–31.

Bourdieu, P. (1977) The economics of linguistic exchanges. *Social Science Information* 16 (6), 645–668.

Bourdieu, P. (1991) *Language and Symbolic Power* (G. Raymond and M. Adamson, Trans.). Cambridge, MA: Harvard University Press.

Braine, G. (2004) The nonnative English-speaking professionals' movement and its research foundations. In L.D. Kamhi-Stein (ed.) *Learning and Teaching from Experience: Perspectives on Nonnative English-Speaking Professionals* (pp. 9–24). Ann Arbor, MI: University of Michigan Press.

Braine, G. (2010) *Nonnative Speaker English Teachers: Research, Pedagogy, and Professional Growth*. London: Routledge.

Breen, M.P. (1985) Authenticity in the language classroom. *Applied Linguistics* 6 (1), 60–70.

Breiteneder, A. (2005) The naturalness of English as a European lingua franca: The case of the 'third person–s'. *VIEWS (Vienna English Working Papers)* 14, 3–26.

Brooker, C. (2011) The dark side of our gadget addiction. *The Guardian, Technology, 1 December*. See http://www.theguardian.com/technology/2011/dec/01/charlie-brooker-dark-side-gadget-addiction-black-mirror (accessed 10 March 2015).

Buzzfeed Community Member (2012) 25 stupid newspaper headlines. See http://www.buzzfeed.com/babymantis/25-stupid-newspaper-headlines-1opu (accessed 26 February 2015).

Campbell, J. (1949) *The Hero with a Thousand Faces* (1993 ed.). London: Fontana Press.

Canagarajah, A.S. (1993) Critical ethnography of a Sri Lankan classroom: Ambiguities in student opposition to reproduction through ESOL. *TESOL Quarterly*, 27 (4), 601–626.

Canagarajah, A.S. (1999a) Interrogating the 'native speaker fallacy': Non-linguistic roots, non-pedagogical results. In G. Braine (ed.) *Non-native Educators in English Language Teaching* (pp. 77–92). London: Routledge.

Canagarajah, A.S. (1999b) *Resisting Linguistic Imperialism in English Teaching*. Oxford: Oxford University Press.

Canagarajah, A.S. (2005) *Reclaiming the Local in Language Policy and Practice*. London: Routledge.

Canagarajah, A.S. (2013) *Translingual Practice: Global Englishes and Cosmopolitan Relations*. New York: Routledge.

Cassell, J. and Tversky, D. (2005) The language of online intercultural community formation. *Journal of Computer-Mediated Communication* 10 (2).

Chatfield, T. (2013a, 7 October) The attention economy. *Aeon Magazine*.

Chatfield, T. (2013b) *Netymology: From Apps to Zombies – A Linguistic Celebration of the Digital World*. London: Quercus Books.

Chik, A. (2011) Learner autonomy development through digital gameplay. *Digital Culture & Education* 3 (1), 30–45.
Chun, C.W. (2015) *Power and Meaning Making in an EAP Classroom: Engaging with the Everyday*. Bristol: Multilingual Matters.
Clandinin, D.J. and Connelly, F.M. (2000) *Narrative Inquiry: Experience and Story in Qualitative Research* (Vol. 6). San Francisco: Jossey-Bass.
Clark, E. and Paran, A. (2007) The employability of non-native-speaker teachers of EFL: A UK survey. *System* 35 (4), 407–430.
Clarke, D. F. (1989) Materials adaptation: why leave it all to the teacher? *ELT Journal* 43 (2), 133–141.
Cobb, R. (ed.) (2014) *The Paradox of Authenticity in a Globalized World*. New York: Palgrave Macmillan.
Coetzee-Van Rooy, S. (2006) Integrativeness: Untenable for world Englishes learners? *World Englishes* 25 (3–4), 437–450.
Cogo, A. and Dewey, M. (2006) Efficiency in ELF communication: from pragmatic motives to lexico-grammatical innovation. *Nordic Journal of English Studies* 5 (2), 59–94.
Cogo, A. and Dewey, M. (2012) *Analysing English as a Lingua Franca: Corpus-driven Investigation*. London: Continuum.
Cogo, A. and Jenkins, J. (2010) English as a lingua franca in Europe: A mismatch between policy and practice. *European Journal of Language Policy* 2 (2), 271–293.
Coleman, J. A. (2006) English-medium teaching in European higher education. *Language Teaching* 39 (01), 1–14.
Collier, V. P. (1992) The Canadian bilingual immersion debate. *Studies in Second Language Acquisition* 14 (01), 87–97.
Cook, G. (1997) Language play, language learning. *ELT Journal* 51 (3), 224–231.
Cook, G. (2000) *Language Play, Language Learning*. Oxford: Oxford University Press.
Cook, G. (2001) 'The philosopher pulled the lower jaw of the hen'. Ludicrous invented sentences in language teaching. *Applied Linguistics* 22 (3), 366–387.
Cook, V. (1999) Going beyond the native speaker in language teaching. *TESOL Quarterly* 33 (2), 185–209.
Cook, V. (2002) Background to the L2 user. In V. Cook (ed.) *Portraits of the L2 User* (pp. 1–28). Clevedon: Multilingual Matters.
Cook, V. and Singleton, D.M. (2014) *Key Topics in Second Language Acquisition*. Bristol: Multilingual Matters.
Cornillie, F., Thorne, S.L. and Desmet, P. (2012) ReCALL special issue: Digital games for language learning: Challenges and opportunities. *ReCALL* 24 (03), 243–381.
Coulthard, M. (2004) Author identification, idiolect, and linguistic uniqueness. *Applied Linguistics* 25 (4), 431–447.
Council of Europe (2002) *Common European Framework of Reference For Languages: Learning, Teaching, Assessment*. Strasbourg: Language Policy Unit.
Cowie, C. (2007) The accents of outsourcing: The meanings of 'neutral' in the Indian call centre industry. *World Englishes* 26 (3), 316–330.
Cowie, N. and Sakui, K. (2011) Crucial but neglected: English as a foreign language teachers' perspectives on learner motivation. In M. Garold, X. Gao and T.E. Lamb (eds) *Identity, Motivation and Autonomy in Language Learning* (pp. 212–228). Bristol: Multilingual Matters.
Coyle, D. (2006). Developing CLIL: Towards a theory of practice *CLIL in Catalonia: from theory to practice* 6, (pp. 5–29). Barcelona: APAC Monographs.
Coyle, D. (2007) Content and language integrated learning: Towards a connected research agenda for CLIL pedagogies. *International Journal of Bilingual Education and Bilingualism* 10 (5), 543–562.
Coyle, D., Hood, P. and Marsh, D. (2010) *CLIL: Content and Language Integrated Learning*. Cambridge: Cambridge University Press.

Creese, A., Blackledge, A. and Takhi, J.K. (2014) The Ideal 'native speaker' teacher: Negotiating Authenticity and legitimacy in the language classroom. *The Modern Language Journal* 98 (4), 937–951.
Crystal, D. (2003) *English as a Global Language*. Cambridge: Cambridge University Press.
Crystal, D. (2008) Two thousand million? *English Today* 24 (01), 3–6.
Csikszentmihalyi, M. (1990) *Flow: The Psychology of Optimal Experience*. New York: Harper & Row.
Csikszentmihalyi, M. (1997) Intrinsic motivation and effective teaching. In J.L. Bess (ed.) *Teaching Well and Liking It: Motivating Faculty to Teach Effectively* (pp. 72–89). Baltimore: John Hopkins University Press.
Csikszentmihalyi, M. (2013) *Flow: The Psychology of Happiness*. New York: Random House.
Dafouz, E. and Smit, U. (2014) Towards a dynamic conceptual framework for English-medium education in multilingual university settings. *Applied Linguistics* (Advanced Access), 1–20.
Dalton-Puffer, C. (2007) *Discourse in Content and Language Integrated Learning (CLIL) Classrooms* (Vol. 20). Philadelphia: John Benjamins.
Dantas-Whitney, M. and Rilling, S. (eds) (2010) *Authenticity in the Language Classroom and Beyond: Children and Adolescent Learners*. Virginia, USA: TESOL Inc.
Darwin, C. (1871) *The Descent of Man* (2004, Concise ed.). London: Penguin Classics.
Davies, A. (2003) *The Native Speaker: Myth and Reality* (2nd edn). Clevedon: Multilingual Matters.
Davies, A. (2004) The native speaker in applied linguistics. In A. Davies and C. Elder (eds) *The Handbook of Applied Linguistics* (pp. 431–450). Oxford: Blackwell.
Davies, J.B., Sandström, S., Shorrocks, A. and Wolff, E.N. (2008) *The World Distribution of Household Wealth*: WIDER Discussion Papers, World Institute for Development Economics (UNU-WIDER).
Davis, A., Sumara, D.J. and Kieren, T.E. (1996) Cognition, co-emergence, curriculum. *Journal of Curriculum Studies* 28 (2), 151–169.
de Bot, K. (2008) Introduction: Second language development as a dynamic process. *The Modern Language Journal* 92 (2), 166–178.
de Swaan, A. (2001) *Words of the World: The Global Language System*. Cambridge: Polity Press.
de Zarobe, Y.R. and Catalán, R.M.J. (eds) (2009) *Content and Language Integrated Learning: Evidence from Research in Europe*. Bristol: Multilingual Matters.
Deane, L. (2013) Why am I banned from following my teachers on Facebook and Twitter? *The Guardian, Technology, 19 March*. See http://www.theguardian.com/technology/the-northerner/2013/mar/19/facebook-schools-social-media-policy (accessed 10 March 2015).
Deci, E.L., Kasser, T. and Ryan, R.M. (1997) Self-determined teaching: Opportunities and obstacles. In J.L. Bess (ed.) *Teaching Well and Liking it: Motivating Faculty to Teach Effectively* (pp. 57–71). Baltimore: Johns Hopkins University Press.
Deci, E.L. and Ryan, R.M. (1985) *Intrinsic Motivation and Self-Determination in Human Behavior*. New York: Plenum.
Dewey, M. and Jenkins, J. (2010) English as a lingua franca in the global context: Interconnectedness, variation and change. In M. Saxena and T. Omoniyi (eds) *Contending with Globalization in World Englishes* (pp. 72–92). Bristol: Multilingual Matters.
Doiz, A., Lasagabaster, D. and Sierra, J.M. (2012) *English-Medium Instruction at Universities: Global Challenges*. Bristol: Multilingual Matters.
Dörnyei, Z. (2007) *Research Methods in Applied Linguistics*. Oxford: Oxford University Press.
Dörnyei, Z. (2009) The L2 motivational self system. In Z. Dörnyei and E. Ushioda (eds) *Motivation, Language Identity and the L2 Self* (pp. 9–42). Bristol: Multilingual Matters.

Dörnyei, Z., MacIntyre, P. and Henry, A. (eds) (2015) *Motivational Dynamics in Language Learning*. Bristol: Multilingual Matters.
Dörnyei, Z. and Ushioda, E. (2011) *Teaching and Researching: Motivation* (2nd edn). Harlow: Longman Pearson.
Dörnyei, Z. and Ushioda, E. (eds) (2009) *Motivation, Language Identity and the L2 Self*. Bristol: Multilingual Matters.
Eagleton, T. (2008) *Literary Theory: An Introduction* (25th Anniversary ed.). Minneapolis: University of Minnesota Press.
Edge, J. (2011) *The Reflexive Teacher Educator in TESOL: Roots and Wings*. London: Routledge.
Edidin, P. (2005, 28 August) Confounding machines: How the future looked. *New York Times*.
Education First (2014) English proficiency index (4th edn). http://www.ef.co.uk/epi/: Education First.
Ellis, N.C. and Larsen-Freeman, D. (eds) (2009) *Language as a Complex Adaptive System*. Sussex: John Wiley & Sons.
Ellis, R. (2008) *The Study of Second Language Acquisition* (2nd edn). Oxford: Oxford University Press.
Ellis, R. (2012) *Language Teaching Research and Language Pedagogy*. Sussex: Wiley-Blackwell.
Enriquez, J. and Gullans, S. (2010) *Homo Evolutis*. New York: New Word City.
Fairclough, N. (2001) *Language and Power* (2nd edn). Harlow: Longman.
Farrell, T.S.C. (2011) Exploring the professional role identities of experienced ESL teachers through reflective practice. *System* 39 (1), 54–62.
Flowerdew, J. (2001) Attitudes of journal editors to nonnative speaker contributions. *TESOL Quarterly* 35 (1), 121–150.
Fong, V., Lim, L. and Wee, L. (2002) 'Singlish': Used and abused. *Asian Englishes* 5 (1), 18–39.
Fromkin, V., Rodman, R. and Hyams, N.M. (2001) *An Introduction to Language* (8th edn). Hampshire: Heinle Cengage.
Galtung, J. (1971) A structural theory of imperialism. *Journal of Peace Research* 8 (2), 81–117.
Gao, X. and Lamb, T. (2011) Exploring links between identity, motivation and autonomy. In M. Garold, X. Gao and T.E. Lamb (eds) *Identity, Motivation and Autonomy in Language Learning* (pp. 1–8). Bristol: Multilingual Matters.
García, O. (2009) *Bilingual Education in the 21st Century. A Global Perspective*. London: Wiley Blackwell.
GB-GIL Trans-global (2002) Singaporean Government Denies Singlish its Basic Rights. *Sciforums*. See http://www.sciforums.com/threads/singaporean-government-denies-singlish-its-basic-rights.7633/ (accessed 19 May 2015).
Gieve, S. and Miller, I.K. (2006) What do we mean by 'quality of classroom life'?. In S. Gieve and I.K. Miller (eds) *Understanding the Language Classroom* (pp. 18–46). Basingstoke: Palgrave Macmillan.
Gilmore, A. (2004) A comparison of textbook and authentic interactions. *ELT Journal* 58 (4), 363–374.
Gilmore, A. (2005) Getting more out of English language teaching in Japanese universities. 研究論集 *[Journal of Inquiry and Research]* 82, 157–174.
Gilmore, A. (2007a) Authentic materials and authenticity in foreign language learning. *Language Teaching* 40 (02), 97–118.
Gilmore, A. (2007b) Getting Real in the Language Classroom: Developing Japanese Students' Communicative Competence with Authentic Materials. Doctoral Thesis, University of Nottingham, Nottingham.
Gilmore, A. (2011) 'I prefer not text': Developing Japanese learners' communicative competence with authentic materials. *Language Learning* 61 (3), 786–819.
Gilmore, A. (2012) Comparative book reveiw: Materials evaluation and design in language teaching. *Language Teaching* 45 (02), 250–262.

Glatthorn, A.A. (1975) Teacher as person: The search for the authentic. *English Journal*, 37–39.
Glatthorn, A.A. (1999) *Performance Standards and Authentic Learning*. New York: Eye on Education.
Golomb, J. (1995) *In Search of Authenticity: Existentialism from Kierkegaard to Camus*. London: Routledge.
González, O. G. (1990) *Teaching Language and Culture with Authentic materials*. (EdD), West Virginia University, Morgantown, West Virginia. Available from http://worldcat.org /z-wcorg/database (UMI-DA9121862).
Graddol, D. (1997) *The Future of English?: A Guide to Forecasting the Popularity of the English Language in the 21st Century*. London: British Council.
Graddol, D. (2003) The decline of the native speaker. In G. Anderman and M. Rogers (eds) *Translation Today: Trends and Perspectives* (pp. 152–167). Clevedon: Multilingual Matters.
Graddol, D. (2006) *English Next : Why Global English May Mean the End of 'English as a Foreign Language'*. London: British Council.
Graddol, D. (2007) *Changing English* (Revised ed.). Abingdon: Routledge.
Gregersen, T. and MacIntyre, P. (2013) *Capitalizing on Language Learners' Individuality: From Premise to Practice* (Vol. 72). Bristol: Multilingual Matters.
Grove, J. (2014) Sinister buttocks? Roget would blush at the crafty cheek. *Times Higher Education*.
Guariento, W. and Morley, J. (2001) Text and task authenticity in the EFL classroom. *ELT Journal* 55 (4), 347–353.
Guignon, C.B. (ed.) (1993) *The Cambridge Companion to Heidegger*. Cambridge: Cambridge University Press.
Gupta, A.F. (1994) The truth about Singapore English. *English Today* 10 (2), 15–17.
Hale, K., Krauss, M., Watahomigie, L.J., Yamamoto, A.Y., Craig, C., Jeanne, L.M. and England, N.C. (1992) Special issue on endangered languages. *Language* 68 (1), 1–42.
Hanna, B.E. and De Nooy, J. (2009) *Learning Language and Culture via Public Internet Discussion Forums*. New York: Palgrave Macmillan.
Hannay, A. (2003) *Kierkegaard: A Biography*. Cambridge: Cambridge University Press.
Harlow, R. (1998) Some languages are just not good enough. In L. Bauer and P. Trudgill (eds) *Language Myths* (pp. 9–14). London: Penguin UK.
Harmer, J. (2008) *The Practice of English Language Teaching* (4th edn). London: Pearson/Longman.
Harper, D. (2013) Online etymology dictionary (2001–2013). See http://www.etymonline.com (accessed 4 June 2013).
Harris, R. A. (1993) *The Linguistics Wars*. Oxford: Oxford University Press.
Hedge, T. (2000) *Teaching and Learning in the Language Classroom*. Oxford: Oxford University Press.
Henry, A. (2013) Digital games and ELT: Bridging the authenticity gap. In E. Ushioda (ed.) *International Perspectives on Motivation* (pp. 133–155). London: Palgrave Macmillan.
HESA (2015) *Statistical First Release 210*. Cheltenham: Higher Education Statistics Agency. See https://www.hesa.ac.uk/ (accessed 12 March 2015).
Holec, H. (1981) *Autonomy and Foreign Language Learning*. Oxford: Pergamon.
Holliday, A. (1994a) *Appropriate Methodology and Social Context*. Cambridge Cambridge University Press.
Holliday, A. (1994b) The house of TESEP and the communicative approach: the special needs of state English language education. *ELT Journal* 48 (1), 3–11.
Holliday, A. (1999) Small cultures. *Applied Linguistics* 20 (2), 237–264.
Holliday, A. (2003) Social autonomy: Addressing the dangers of culturism in TESOL. In D. Palfreyman and R.C. Smith (eds) *Learner Autonomy Across Cultures: Language Education Perspectives* (pp. 110–126). London: Palgrave Macmillan.

Holliday, A. (2005). *The Struggle to Teach English as an International Language*. Cambridge: Cambridge University Press.
Holliday, A. (2006) Native-speakerism. *ELT Journal* 60 (4), 385–387.
Holt, K. (2012) Authentic journalism? A critical discussion about existential authenticity in journalism ethics. *Journal of Mass Media Ethics* 27 (1), 2–14.
Houghton, S.A. and Rivers, D.J. (eds) (2013) *Native-Speakerism in Japan: Intergroup Dynamics in Foreign Language Education*. Bristol: Multilingual Matters.
House, J. (1999) Misunderstanding in intercultural communication: Interactions in English as a lingua franca and the myth of mutual intelligibility. In C. Gnutzmann (ed.) *Teaching and Learning English as a Global Language* (Vol. 8, pp. 73–89). Tüumbingen, Germany: Stauffenburg Verlag.
Howatt, A.P.R. and Widdowson, H.G. (2004) *A History of English Language Teaching* (2nd edn). Oxford: Oxford University Press.
Hu, G. (2012) Assessing English as an international language. In L. Alsagoff, S.L. McKay, G. Hu and W.A. Renandya (eds) *Principles and Practices for Teaching English as an International Language* (pp. 123–143). Oxon: Routledge.
Huang, K.-M. (2011) Motivating lessons: A classroom-oriented investigation of the effects of content-based instruction on EFL young learners' motivated behaviours and classroom verbal interaction. *System* 39 (2), 186–201.
Hung, D. and Victor Chen, D.-T. (2007) Context–process authenticity in learning: implications for identity enculturation and boundary crossing. *Educational Technology Research and Development* 55 (2), 147–167.
IIE (2013) Open Doors Report on International Educational Exchange 2013. In A.E. Goodman and P. Blumenthal (eds) *International Students in the United States and Study Abroad by American Students are at All-Time High* (Online ed., pp. 1–8): Institute of International Education.
Ikeda, M. (2013) Does CLIL Work for Japanese secondary school students? Potential for the 'weak' version of CLIL. *International CLIL Research Journal* 2 (1), 31–43.
Illés, É. (2009) What makes a coursebook series stand the test of time? *ELT Journal* 63 (2), 145–153.
Irie, K. and Brewster, D.R. (2014) Investing in Experiential capital: self-efficacy, imagination and development of ideal L2 selves. In K. Csizér and M. Magid (eds) *The Impact of Self-Concept on Language Learning* (pp. 171–188). Bristol: Multilingual Matters.
Isokallio, M. and Grönholm, A. (2007) Final report of project group for joint application of degree programmes conducted in a foreign language at polytechnics: Finnish Ministry of Education and Culture.
Izumi, S., Watanabe, Y. and Ikeda, M. (eds) (2012) *CLIL: New Challenges in Foreign Language Education at Sophia University* (Vol. 2: Practice and Applications). Tokyo: Sophia University Press.
Jenkins, J. (2000) *The Phonology of English as an International Language: New Models, New Norms, New Goals*: Oxford University Press, USA.
Jenkins, J. (2002) A sociolinguistically based, empirically researched pronunciation syllabus for English as an international language. *Applied Linguistics* 23 (1), 83–103.
Jenkins, J. (2004) Research in teaching pronunciation and intonation. *Annual Review of Applied Linguistics* 24 (109–125).
Jenkins, J. (2005) Implementing an international approach to English pronunciation: The role of teacher attitudes and identity. *TESOL Quarterly* 39 (3), 535–543.
Jenkins, J. (2006) Current perspectives on teaching world Englishes and English as a lingua franca. *TESOL Quarterly* 40 (1), 157–181.
Jenkins, J. (2014) *English as a Lingua Franca in the International University: The Politics of Academic English Language Policy*. London: Routledge.

Jenkins, J. (2015) *Global Englishes: A Resource Book for Students* (3rd edn). London: Routledge.
Jenkins, J., Cogo, A. and Dewey, M. (2011) Review of developments in research into English as a lingua franca. *Language Teaching* 44 (03), 281–315.
Johnson, K.E. and Golombek, P.R. (eds) (2002) *Teachers' Narrative Inquiry as Professional Development*. Cambridge: Cambridge University Press.
Jungwirth, B. and Bruce, B.C. (2002) Information overload: Threat or opportunity? *Journal of Adolescent & Adult Literacy* 45 (5), 400–406.
Kachru, B.B. (1985) Standards, codification and sociolinguistic realism: The English language in the outer circle. In R. Quirk, H.G. Widdowson and Y. Cantù (eds) *English in the World: Teaching and Learning the Language and Literatures* (pp. 11–30). Cambridge: Cambridge University Press.
Kachru, B.B. (1986) *The Alchemy of English: The Spread, Functions, and Models of Non-Native Englishes*. Oxford: Pergamon.
Kachru, B.B. (1988) The sacred cows of English. *English Today* 4 (04), 3–8.
Kachru, B.B. (1991) Liberation linguistics and the Quirk Concern. *English Today* 7 (01), 3–13.
Kachru, B.B. (2006) The English language in the outer circle. In K. Bolton and B.B. Kachru (eds) *World Englishes: Critical Concepts in Linguistics* (pp. 241–255). London: Routledge.
Kachru, B.B. and Thumboo, E. (2001) *The Three Circles of English : Language Specialists Talk about the English Language*. Singapore: UniPress.
Kanno, Y. and Norton, B. (2003) Imagined communities and educational possibilities: Introduction. *Journal of Language, Identity & Education* 2 (4), 241–249.
Kiczkowiak, M. (2015) Native speakers only. *IATEFL Voices, March–April* (243), 8–9.
Kienbaum, B. E., Russell, A. J. and Welty, S. (1986) *Communicative Competence in Foreign Language Learning with Authentic Materials. Final Project Report*. See http://files.eric.ed.gov/fulltext/ED275200.pdf (Retrieved 16 March 2016 from Hammond)
Kimura, Y. (2014) ELT motivation from a complex dynamic systems theory perspective: A longitudinal case study of L2 teacher motivation in Beijing. In K. Csizér and M. Magid (eds) *The Impact of Self-Concept on Language Learning* (pp. 310–332). Bristol: Multilingual Matters.
Kramsch, C. (1985) Literary texts in the classroom: A discourse. *The Modern Language Journal* 69 (4), 356–366.
Kramsch, C. (1997) The privilege of the non-native speaker. *PMLA (Modern Language Association)* 112 (3), 251–262.
Kramsch, C. (1998) *Language and Culture*. Oxford: Oxford University Press.
Kramsch, C. (2000) Social discursive constructions of self in L2 learning. In J.P. Lantolf (ed.) *Sociocultural Theory and Second Language Learning* (pp. 133–154). Oxford: Oxford University Press.
Kramsch, C. (2011) Why is everyone so excited about complexity theory in applied linguistics? *Melanges CRAPEL* 2 (33), 9–24.
Kramsch, C. and Lam, W.S.E. (1999) Textual identities: The importance of being non-native. In G. Braine (ed.) *Non-Native Educators in English Language Teaching* (pp. 57–72). London: Routledge.
Krashen, S. (1985) *The Input Hypothesis: Issues and Implications*. London: Longman.
Külekçi, E. (2015) 'Authenticity' in English Language Teaching and Learning: A Case Study of Four High School Classrooms in Turkey. (PhD Doctoral Thesis), University of Warwick, Coventry, UK.
Lai-kun, A.C. (2014) Authenticity in task design for vocational English teaching and learning: A case study of a project-based learning module. In X. Deng and R. Seow (eds) *Alternative Pedagogies in the English Language & Communication Classroom* (pp. 142–154). Singapore: Centre for English Language Communication, National University of Singapore.

Larsen-Freeman, D. (1997) Chaos/complexity science and second language acquisition. *Applied Linguistics* 18 (2), 141–165.

Larsen-Freeman, D. and Cameron, L. (2008a) *Complex Systems and Applied Linguistics*. Oxford: Oxford University Press.

Larsen-Freeman, D. and Cameron, L. (2008b) Research methodology on language development from a complex systems perspective. *The Modern Language Journal* 200–213.

Lasagabaster, D. (2011) English achievement and student motivation in CLIL and EFL settings. *Innovation in Language Learning and Teaching* 5 (1), 3–18.

Lasagabaster, D. and Sierra, J.M. (2005a) The nativeness factor: An analysis of students' preferences. *ITL Journal of Applied Linguistics* 148, 21–43

Lasagabaster, D. and Sierra, J.M. (2005b) What do students think about the pros and cons of having a native speaker teacher? In E. Llurda (ed.) *Non-Native Language Teachers* (Vol. 5, pp. 217–241). New York: Springer.

Lazzaro, N. (2009) Why we play: Affect and the fun of games. In A. Sears and J.A. Jacko (eds) *Human–Computer Interaction: Designing for Diverse Users and Domains* (pp. 155–176). Florida: CRC Press (Taylor Francis Group).

Lee, W.Y.c. (1995) Authenticity revisited: Text authenticity and learner authenticity. *ELT Journal* 49 (4), 323–328.

Levitt, T. (1983) The globalization of markets. *The Harvard Business Review* (May–June), 92–102.

Levy, M. (2009) Technologies in use for second language learning. *The Modern Language Journal* 93 (Issue Supplement S1), 769–782.

Levy, M. and Stockwell, G. (2006) *CALL Dimensions: Options and Issues in Computer-Assisted Language Learning*. New York: Lawrence Erlbaum Associates.

Lewkowicz, J.A. (2000) Authenticity in language testing: Some outstanding questions. *Language Testing* 17 (1), 43–64.

Lindholm, C. (2008) *Culture and Authenticity*. Oxford: Wiley-Blackwell.

Linguistics at MIT (2014). See http://web.mit.edu/linguistics/ (accessed 11 August 2014).

Little, D. (2004) Democracy, discourse and learner autonomy in the foreign language classroom. *Utbildning & Demokrati* 13 (3), 105–126.

Little, D., Devitt, S. and Singleton, D. (1988) *Learning Foreign Languages from Authentic Texts: Theory and Practice*. Dublin: Authentik in association with CILT.

Little, D. and Ushioda, E. (1998) Designing, implementing and evaluating a project in tandem language learning via e-mail. *ReCALL* 10 (01), 95–101.

Long, M.H. (1993) Assessment strategies for second language acquisition theories. *Applied Linguistics* 14 (3), 225–249.

Lorenz, E.N. (1963) The predictability of hydrodynamic flow. *Transactions of the New York Academy of Sciences* 25 (4 Series II), 409–432.

Lorenzo, F., Casal, S. and Moore, P. (2010) The effects of content and language integrated learning in European education: Key findings from the Andalusian bilingual sections evaluation project. *Applied Linguistics* 31 (3), 418–442.

Lynch, B.K. (1996) *Language Program Evaluation: Theory and Practice* (2003 digital print ed.). Cambridge: Cambridge University Press.

Macmillan. (2010) Global Coursebook. See http://www.macmillanglobal.com/about/the-course (accessed 20 March 2013).

Mahboob, A. and Golden, R. (2013) Looking for native speakers of English: Discrimination in English language teaching job advertisements. *Voices in Asia Journal* 1 (1), 72–81.

Marsh, D. (2002) CLIL/EMILE: The European Dimension: Actions, Trends and Foresight Potential *Public Services Contract EG EAC*. Strasbourg: European Commission.

Marshall, A. (2014) Japan enters the era of smartphones and 'dumbwalking', *BBC Magazine*. See http://www.bbc.com/news/magazine-28208144?OCID=fbasia&ocid=socialflow_facebook (accessed 14 July 2014).

Matsuda, A. (2002) Representation of users and uses of English in beginning Japanese EFL textbooks. *JALT Journal* 24 (2), 182–200.

Matsuda, A. (2003) Incorporating World Englishes in Teaching English as an International Language. *TESOL Quarterly* 37 (4), 719–729.

Matsuda, A. (2011) 'Not everyone can be a star': Student's and teacher's beliefs about English teaching in Japan. In P. Seargeant (ed.) *English in Japan in the Era of Globalization* (pp. 38–59). Basingstoke: Palgrave Macmillan.

Matsuda, A. (ed.) (2012) *Principles and Practices of Teaching English as an International Language*. Bristol: Multilingual Matters.

Matsuda, P.K. (2003) Proud to be a Nonnative English speaker. *TESOL Matters* 13 (4), 15.

Matthews, R. (2003) Madness' of Nietzsche was cancer not syphilis, comment, *The Telegraph*. See http://www.telegraph.co.uk/education/3313279/Madness-of-Nietzsche-was-cancer-not-syphilis.html (accessed 4 May 2003).

McDonough, J., Shaw, C. and Masuhara, H. (2012) *Materials and Methods in ELT* (3rd edn). Oxford: Wiley Blackwell.

McKay, S.L. (2002) *Teaching English as an International Language: Rethinking Goals and Approaches*. Oxford: Oxford University Press.

McMahon, R.J. (1994) *The Cold War on the Periphery: The United States, India, and Pakistan*. New York: Columbia University Press.

McVeigh, B.J. (2002) *Japanese Higher Education as Myth*. London: Routledge.

McWhorter, J.H. (2015, 2 January) What the world will speak in 2115. *The Wall Street Journal*, January.

Meddings, L. (2006) Embrace the parsnip. *The Guardian*, Education, 20 January. See http://www.theguardian.com/education/2006/jan/20/tefl4 (accessed 12 March 2015).

Meddings, L. and Thornbury, S. (2003) Dogme still able to divide ELT. *The Guardian*, Education, 17 April. See http://www.theguardian.com/education/2003/apr/17/tefl.lukemeddings (accessed 4 February 2015).

Meddings, L. and Thornbury, S. (2009) *Teaching Unplugged: Dogme in English Language Teaching*. Surrey: Delta Publishing.

Medgyes, P. (1994) *The Non-Native Teacher* (revised ed.). London: Macmillan.

Medgyes, P. (2005) Facts and beyond – teaching English in Hungary. In G. Braine (ed.) *Teaching English to the World: History, Curriculum, and Practice* (2011 ed., pp. 47–58). London: Routledge.

Medgyes, P. and László, M. (2001) The foreign language competence of hungarian scholars: Ten years later. In U. Ammon (ed.) *The Dominance of English as a Language of Science: Effects on Other Languages and Language Communities* (pp. 261–286). Berlin: de Gruyter.

Mehisto, P. (2012) *Excellence in Bilingual Education: A Guide for School Principals*. Cambridge: Cambridge University Press.

Mehisto, P., Frigols, M.J. and Marsh, D. (2008) *Uncovering CLIL: Content and Language Integrated Learning and Multilingual Education*. Oxford: Macmillan.

Menezes, V. (2013) Chaos and the complexity of second language acquisition. In P. Benson and L. Cooker (eds) *The Applied Linguistic Individual* (pp. 59–74). Bristol: Equinox.

Mercer, S. (2011) Language learner self-concept: Complexity, continuity and change. *System* 39 (3), 335–346.

Mercer, S. (2015) Dynamics of the self: A multilevel nested systems approach. In Z. Dörnyei, P. MacIntyre and A. Henry (eds) *Motivational Dynamics in Language Learning* (pp. 139–163). Bristol: Multilingual Matters.

Mercer, S. and Williams, M. (eds) (2014) *Multiple Perspectives on the Self in SLA*. Bristol: Multilingual Matters.

Mesthrie, R. (2008) English circling the globe. *English Today* 24 (01), 28–32.

MEXT (2012) *Selection for the FY2012 Project for Promotion of Global Human Resource Development*. Tokyo: Ministry of Education, Culture, Sports, Science and Technology. See http://www.mext.go.jp/english/highered/1326675.htm. (Retrieved 16 March 2016).

Mishan, F. (2000) Authenticity in Language Learning Materials Design. (PhD Doctoral Thesis), University of Limerick, Limerick.

Mishan, F. (2004) Authenticating corpora for language learning: a problem and its resolution. *ELT Journal* 58 (3), 219–227.

Mishan, F. (2005) *Designing Authenticity into Language Learning Materials*. Bristol: Intellect Books.

Mishan, F. (2011a) Whose learning is it anyway? Problem-based learning in language teacher development. *Innovation in Language Learning and Teaching* 5 (3), 253–272.

Mishan, F. (2011b) Withstanding washback: Thinking outside the box in materials development. In B. Tomlinson and H. Masuhara (eds) *Research for Materials Development in Language Learning: Evidence For Best Practice* (pp. 353–368). London: Continuum.

Mishan, F. and Chambers, A. (eds) (2010) *Perspectives on Language Learning Materials Development* (Vol. 1). Bern, Switzerland: Peter Lang.

Morgan, B. and Ramanathan, V. (2009) Outsourcing, globalizing economics, and shifting language policies: issues in managing Indian call centres. *Language Policy* 8 (1), 69–80.

Morrow, K. (1977) Authentic texts and ESP. In S. Holden (ed.) *English for Specific Purposes* (pp. 13–17). London: Modern English Publications.

Moussu, L. and Llurda, E. (2008) Non-native English-speaking English language teachers: History and research. *Language Teaching* 41 (03), 315–348.

Muir, C. and Dörnyei, Z. (2013) Directed motivational currents: Using vision to create effective motivational pathways. *Studies in Second Language Learning and Teaching* 3 (3), 357–375.

Mukherjee, J. (2004) Bridging the gap between applied corpus linguistics and the reality of English language teaching in Germany. *Language and Computers* 52 (1), 239–250.

Murray, D.E. (2001) New technology: New language at WORK? In A. Burns and C. Coffin (eds) *Analysing English in a Global Context: A Reader* (pp. 38–53). London: Routledge.

Murray, G. (ed.) (2014) *Social Dimensions of Autonomy in Language Learning*. London: Palgrave Macmillan.

Murray, G., Gao, X. and Lamb, T.E. (eds) (2011) *Identity, Motivation and Autonomy in Language Learning*. Bristol: Multilingual Matters.

Myhill, J. (2003) The native speaker, identity, and the authenticity hierarchy. *Language Sciences* 25 (1), 77–97.

Navés, T. (2009) Effective content and language integrated learning (CLIL) programmes. In Y.R. de Zarobe and R.M. Jiménez Catalán (eds) *Content and Language Integrated Learning: Evidence from Research in Europe* (pp. 22–40). Bristol: Multilingual Matters.

Nietzsche, F. (1974) *The Gay Science (the Joyful Wisdom)* (W. Kaufmann, Trans. 2009 ed.). New York: Vintage.

Nitta, R. and Baba, K. (2015) Self-regulation in the evolution of the ideal L2 self: a complex dynamic systems approach to the L2 motivational self system. In Z. Dörnyei, P. MacIntyre and A. Henry (eds) *Motivational Dynamics in Language Learning* (pp. 367–396). Bristol: Multilingual Matters.

Norton, B. (2013) *Identity and Language Learning: Extending the Conversation* (2nd edn). Bristol: Multilingual Matters.

Norton, B. and Kamal, F. (2003) The imagined communities of English language learners in a Pakistani school. *Journal of Language, Identity & Education* 2 (4), 301–317.

Norton Peirce, B. (1995) Social identity, investment, and language learning. *TESOL Quarterly* 29 (1), 9–31.

Nunan, D. (1989) *Designing Tasks for the Communicative Classroom*. Cambridge: Cambridge University Press.

Nunan, D. (2003) The impact of English as a global language on educational policies and practices in the Asia–Pacific Region. *TESOL Quarterly* 37 (4), 589–613.

Nunan, D. and Richards, J.C. (eds) (2015) *Language Learning Beyond the Classroom*. London: Routledge.

O'Dowd, R. (2007) Evaluating the outcomes of online intercultural exchange. *ELT Journal* 61 (2), 144–152.

O'Keeffe, A., McCarthy, M. and Carter, R. (2007) *From Corpus to Classroom: Language Use and Language Teaching*. Cambridge: Cambridge University Press.

Ono, H. and Zavodny, M. (2008) Immigrants, English ability and the digital divide. *Social Forces* 86 (4), 1455–1479.

Paikeday, T. (1985) *The Native Speaker is Dead*. Toronto: Paikeday.

Palfreyman, D. and Smith, R.C. (eds) (2003) *Learner Autonomy Across Cultures: Language Education Perspectives*. New York: Palgrave Macmillan.

Pan, J. (2015) Group seeks legal end to language policy. *Taipei Times*, 30 January, 3. See Taepeitimes.com website: http://www.taipeitimes.com/News/taiwan/archives/2015/01/30/2003610426 (accessed 12 February 2015).

Pavlenko, A. (2002) Poststructuralist approaches to the study of social factors in second language learning and use. In V. Cook (ed.) *Portraits of the L2 User* (pp. 277–302). Clevedon: Multilingual Matters.

Pavlenko, A. (2007) Autobiographic narratives as data in applied linguistics. *Applied Linguistics* 28 (2), 163–188.

Pavlenko, A. and Blackledge, A. (eds) (2004) *Negotiation of Identities in Multilingual Contexts*. Clevedon: Multilingual Matters.

Peacock, M. (1996) The Motivation of Adult EFL Learners with Authentic Materials and Artificial Materials. PhD Doctoral Thesis, University of Essex.

Peacock, M. (1997a) Comparing learner and teacher views on the usefulness and enjoyableness of materials. *International Journal of Applied Linguistics* 7 (2), 183–196.

Peacock, M. (1997b) The effect of authentic materials on the motivation of EFL learners. *ELT Journal* 51 (2), 144–156.

Peacock, M. (1998) Usefulness and enjoyableness of teaching materials as predictors of on-task behavior. *TESL-EJ* 3 (2), 2–8.

Pennycook, A. (1989) The Concept of method, interested knowledge, and the politics of language teaching. *TESOL Quarterly* 23 (4), 589–618.

Pennycook, A. (1994) *The Cultural Politics of English as an International Language* (Reprint 2013 ed.). Oxon: Routledge.

Petraglia, J. (1998a) The real world on a short leash: The (mis) application of constructivism to the design of educational technology. *Educational Technology Research and Development* 46 (3), 53–65.

Petraglia, J. (1998b) *Reality by Design: The Rhetoric and Technology of Authenticity in Education*. London: Routledge.

Phillipson, R. (1992) *Linguistic Imperialism*. Oxford: Oxford University Press.

Phillipson, R. (1996) Linguistic imperialism: African perspectives. *ELT Journal* 50 (2), 160–167.

Phillipson, R. (2009) *Linguistic Imperialism Continued*. Hyderbad: Orient Blackswan (Routledge).

Piller, I. (2015) Access denied. *Language On The Move*. See http://www.languageonthemove.com/education/access-denied (accessed 25 March 2015).

Pinner, R.S. (2013) Authenticity and CLIL: Examining authenticity from an international CLIL perspective. *International CLIL Research Journal* 2 (1), 44–54.

Pinner, R.S. (2014a) The authenticity continuum: Empowering international voices. *English Language Teacher Education and Development* 16 (1), 9–17.

Pinner, R.S. (2014b) The authenticity continuum: Towards a definition incorporating international voices. *English Today* 30 (4), 22–27.

Pinner, R.S. (2015) Authenticity in a global context: Learning, working and communicating with L2 teachers of English. In J. Angouri, T. Harrison, S. Schnurr and S. Wharton (eds) *Learning, Working and Communicating in a Global Context* (pp. 135–139). London: Scitsiugnil Press for the British Association for Applied Linguistics.
Porter, D. and Roberts, J. (1981) Authentic listening activities. *ELT Journal* 36 (1), 37–47.
Prator, C. (1968) The British heresy in TESL. In J.A. Fishman, C. Ferguson and J. Das Gupta (eds) *Language Problems in Developing Nations* (pp. 459–476). New York: John Wiley.
Prensky, M. (2001) Digital natives, digital immigrants part 1. *On the Horizon* 9 (5), 1–6.
Quirk, R. (1985) The English language in a global context. In R. Quirk, H.G. Widdowson and Y. Cantu (eds) *English in the World: Teaching and Learning the Language and Literatures* (pp. 1–6). Cambridge: Cambridge University Press for the British Council.
Quirk, R. (1990) Language varieties and standard language. *English Today* 6 (1), 3–10.
Quirk, R., Greenbaum, S., Leech, G. and Svartvik, J. (1985) *A Comprehensive Grammar of the English language*. London: Longman.
Ramanathan, V. (2005) *The English-Vernacular Divide: Postcolonial Language Politics and Practice*. Clevedon: Multilingual Matters.
Ramanathan, V., Norton, B. and Pennycook, A. (2009) Preface. In P. Seargeant (ed.) *The Idea of English in Japan* (pp. xi–xv). Bristol: Multilingual Matters.
Rampton, B. (1990) Displacing the 'native speaker': Expertise, affiliation, and inheritance. *ELT Journal* 44 (2), 97–101.
Rebuck, M. (2008) The effect of excessively difficult listening lessons on motivation and the influence of authentic listening as a "lesson selling" tag'. *JALT Journal* 30 (2), 197–223.
Reinders, H. (ed.) (2012) *Digital Games in Language Learning and Teaching*. Basingstoke: Palgrave Macmillan.
Reinhardt, J. and Sykes, J.M. (2014) Digital game and play activity in L2 teaching and learning. *Language, Learning & Technology* 18 (2), 2–8.
Reves, T. and Medgyes, P. (1994) The non-native English speaking EFL/ESL teacher's self-image: An international survey. *System* 22 (3), 353–367.
Richards, J.C. and Schmidt, R.W. (2013) *Longman Dictionary of Language Teaching and Applied Linguistics*. Harlow: Routledge.
Richards, K. (2006) 'Being the teacher': Identity and classroom conversation. *Applied Linguistics* 27 (1), 51–77.
Rico García, M. and Vinagre Arias, F. (2000) A comparative study in motivation and learning through print-oriented and computer-oriented tests. *Computer Assisted Language Learning* 13 (4–5), 457–465.
Rilling, S. and Dantas-Whitney, M. (2009a) Authenticity, creativity, and localization in language learning. In S. Rilling and M. Dantas-Whitney (eds) *Authenticity in the Language Classroom and Beyond: Adult Learners* (pp. 1–8). Virginia: TESOL Inc.
Rilling, S. and Dantas-Whitney, M. (eds) (2009b) *Authenticity in the Language Classroom and Beyond: Adult Learners*. Virginia: TESOL Inc.
Rodriguez, N.M. and Ryave, A. (2002) *Systematic Self-Observation: A Method for Researching the Hidden and Elusive Features of Everyday Social Life* (Vol. 49). London: Sage.
Rogers, P.S. (1998) National agendas and the English divide. *Business Communication Quarterly* 61 (3), 79–85.
Römer, U. (2004) Comparing real and ideal language learner input: the use of an EFL textbook corpus in corpus linguistics and language teaching. In G. Aston, S. Bernardini and D. Stewart (eds) *Corpora and Language Learners* (pp. 151–168). Amsterdam: John Benjamins.
Rost, M. (2002) *Teaching and Researching Listening*. London: Longman.
Rui, Y. (2014) China's Removal of English from Gaokao. *International Higher Education* 75 (Spring), 12–13.

Ryan, S. and Irie, K. (2014) Imagined and possible selves: Stories we tell ourselves about ourselves. In S. Mercer and M. Williams (eds) *Multiple Perspectives on the Self in SLA* (p. 109) Bristol: Multilingual Matters.

Salaberry, M.R. (2001) The use of technology for second language learning and teaching: A retrospective. *The Modern Language Journal* 85 (1), 39–56.

Sartre, J.-P. (1992) *Notebooks for an Ethics*. Chicago: University of Chicago Press.

Schön, D.A. (1983) *The Reflective Practitioner: How Professionals Think in Action*. New York: Basic Books.

Scovel, T. (1978) The effect of affect on foreign language learning: A review of the anxiety research. *Language Learning* 28 (1), 129–142.

Seargeant, P. (2005) 'More English than England itself': the simulation of authenticity in foreign language practice in Japan. *International Journal of Applied Linguistics* 15 (3), 326–345.

Seargeant, P. (2009) *The Idea of English in Japan: Ideology and the Evolution of a Global Language*. Bristol: Multilingual Matters.

Seargeant, P. (ed.) (2011) *English in Japan in the Era of Globalization*. Basingstoke: Palgrave Macmillan.

Seidlhofer, B. (2004) Research perspectives on teaching english as a lingua franca. *Annual Review of Applied Linguistics* 24 (1), 209–239.

Seidlhofer, B. (2005) English as a lingua franca. *ELT Journal* 59 (4), 339.

Seidlhofer, B. (2012) Corpora and English as a lingua franca. In K. Hyland, C.M. Huat and M. Handford (eds) *Corpus Applications in Applied Linguistics* (pp. 135–149). London: Continuum.

Selwyn, N. (2008) 'Not necessarily a bad thing …': a study of online plagiarism amongst undergraduate students. *Assessment & Evaluation in Higher Education* 33 (5), 465–479.

Siegel, A. (2014) What should we talk about? The authenticity of textbook topics. *ELT Journal* 68 (4), 363–375.

Siegel, J. (2013) Second language learners' perceptions of listening strategy instruction. *Innovation in Language Learning and Teaching* 7 (1), 1–18.

Simon-Maeda, A. (2011) *Being and Becoming a Speaker of Japanese: An Autoethnographic Account*. Bristol: Multilingual Matters.

Smith, L.E. (1976) English as an International Auxiliary Language. *RELC Journal* 7 (2), 38–42.

Snyder-Parampil, K. and Hensley, J. (2009) I Tube… do YouTube? Virtual portfolios for reflective learning and peer review. In S. Rilling and M. Dantas-Whitney (eds) *Authenticity in the Language Classroom and Beyond: Adult Learners* (pp. 223–229). Virginia, USA: TESOL Inc.

Stewart, I. (2011) Sources of uncertainty in deterministic dynamics: an informal overview. *Philosophical Transactions of the Royal Society A: Mathematical, Physical and Engineering Sciences* 369 (1956), 4705–4729.

Stipe, M. and Yasen, L. (2009) Climate change and other hot topics on campus: project-based learning. In S. Rilling and M. Dantas-Whitney (eds) *Authenticity in the Language Classroom and Beyond: Adult Learners* (pp. 129–142). Virginia, USA: TESOL Inc.

Suzuki, A. (2011) Introducing diversity of English into ELT: student teachers' responses. *ELT Journal* 65 (2), 145–153.

Swaffar, J.K. (1985) Reading authentic texts in a foreign language: A cognitive model. *The Modern Language Journal* 69 (1), 15–34.

Swain, M. (1974) French immersion programs across Canada: Research findings. *Canadian Modern Language Review* 31 (2), 117–129.

Tahira, M. (2012) Behind MEXT's new course of study guidelines. *The Language Teacher* 36 (3), 3–8.

Takahashi, K. (2013) *Language Learning, Gender and Desire: Japanese Women on the Move*. Bristol: Multilingual Matters.

Tan, M. (2005) Authentic language or language errors? Lessons from a learner corpus. *ELT Journal* 59 (2), 126–134.

Taylor, D. (1994) Inauthentic authenticity or authentic inauthenticity? *TESL-EJ* 1 (2), 1–12.

Thompson, D. (2013, 28th February) How Airline ticket prices fell 50% in 30 years (and Why nobody noticed). *The Atlantic*.

Thumboo, E. (2005) Poems. See https://courses.nus.edu.sg/course/ellthumb/site/poems/may1954.html (accessed 28 October 2015).

Tomlinson, B. (ed.) (2008) *English Language Learning Materials: A Critical Review*. London: Continuum.

Tomlinson, B. (2011a) Introduction: Principles and procedures of materials development. In B. Tomlinson (ed.) *Materials Development in Language Teaching* (pp. 1–34). Cambridge: Cambridge University Press. (Reprinted from: 2011).

Tomlinson, B. (ed.) (2011b) *Materials Development in Language Teaching*. Cambridge: Cambridge University Press.

Tomlinson, B. (ed.) (2013) *Applied Linguistics and Materials Development*. London: Bloomsbury Academic.

Tomlinson, B. and Masuhara, H. (2010) Applications of the research results for second language acquisition theory and research. In B. Tomlinson and H. Masuhara (eds) *Research for Materials Development in Language Learning: Evidence for Best Practice* (pp. 399–409). London: Continuum.

Torikai, K. (2011) 国際共通語としての英語 *[English as a Common Language]*. Tokyo: Kodansha.

Trabelsi, S. (2010) Developing and trialling authentic materials for business English students at a Tunisian university. In B. Tomlinson and H. Masuhara (eds) *Research for Materials Development in Language Learning: Evidence for Best Practice* (pp. 103–120). London: Continuum.

Trilling, L. (1972) *Sincerity and Authenticity: The Charles Eliot Norton Lectures, 1969–1970*. Cambridge, MA: Harvard University Press.

Trudgill, P. (2002) *Sociolinguistic Variation and Change*. Edinburgh: Edinburgh University Press.

Tudor, I. (2003) Learning to live with complexity: Towards an ecological perspective on language teaching. *System* 31 (1), 1–12.

Ushioda, E. (1993) Redefining motivation from the L2 learner's point of view. *Teanga (Journal of the Irish Association of Applied Linguistics)* 13, 1–12.

Ushioda, E. (1996) Developing a dynamic concept of L2 motivation. In T. Hickey and J. Williams (eds) *Language, Education and Society in a Changing World* (pp. 239–245). Clevedon: Multilingual Matters.

Ushioda, E. (2000) Tandem language learning via e-mail: From motivation to autonomy. *ReCALL* 12 (02), 121–128.

Ushioda, E. (2007) Motivation, autonomy, and socio-cultural theory. In P. Benson (ed.) *Learner Autonomy 8* (pp. 5–24). Dublin: Authentik.

Ushioda, E. (2009) A person-in-context relational view of emergent motivation, self and identity. In E. Ushioda and Z. Dörnyei (eds) *Motivation, Language Identity and the L2 Self* (pp. 215–228). Bristol: Multilingual Matters.

Ushioda, E. (2011a) Language learning motivation, self and identity: Current theoretical perspectives. *Computer Assisted Language Learning* 24 (3), 199–210.

Ushioda, E. (2011b) Motivating learners to speak as themselves. In G. Murray, X. Gao and T.E. Lamb (eds) *Identity, Motivation and Autonomy in Language Learning* (pp. 11–25). Bristol: Multilingual Matters.

Ushioda, E. (2011c) Why autonomy? Insights from motivation theory and research. *Innovation in Language Learning and Teaching* 5 (2), 221–232.

Ushioda, E. (2013a) Motivation and ELT: Global issues and local concerns. In E. Ushioda (ed.) *International Perspectives on Motivation: Language Learning and Professional Challenges* (pp. 1–19). New York: Palgrave Macmillan.

Ushioda, E. (2015) Context and complex dynamic systems theory. In Z. Dörnyei, P. MacIntyre and A. Henry (eds) *Motivational Dynamics in Language Learning* (pp. 47–54). Bristol: Multilingual Matters.

Ushioda, E. (ed.) (2013b) *International Perspectives on Motivation: Language Learning and Professional Challenges*. New York: Palgrave Macmillan.

Ushioda, E. and Dörnyei, Z. (2009) Motivation, language identities and the L2 self: A theoretical overview. In Z. Dörnyei and E. Ushioda (eds) *Motivation, Language Identity and the L2 Self* (pp. 1–8). Bristol: Multilingual Matters.

Valdés, C. (2000) Reception factors in translated advertisements. In A. Chesterman, N.G. San Salvador and Y. Gambier (eds) *Translation in Context: Selected papers from the EST Congress, Granada 1998* (pp. 271–280) Amsterdam: John Benjamins.

Van De Mieroop, D. and Clifton, J. (2012) The interplay between professional identities and age, gender and ethnicity (Introduction to the special issue). *Pragmatics* 22 (2), 193–201.

van Lier, L. (1988) *The Classroom and the Language Learner: Ethnography and Second-Language Classroom Research*. London: Longman

van Lier, L. (1996) *Interaction in the Language Curriculum: Awareness, Autonomy and Authenticity*. London: Longman.

van Lier, L. (1998) The relationship between consciousness, interaction and language learning. *Language Awareness* 7 (2–3), 128–145.

van Lier, L. (2007) Action-based teaching, autonomy and identity. *Innovation in Language Learning and Teaching* 1 (1), 46–65.

Vasagar, J. and Williams, M. (2012) Teachers warned over befriending pupils on Facebook. *The Guardian*, Education, 23 January. See http://www.theguardian.com/education/2012/jan/23/teacher-misconduct-cases-facebook (accessed 10 March 2015).

Vertovec, S. (2007) Super-diversity and its implications. *Ethnic and Racial Studies* 30 (6), 1024–1054.

Vertovec, S. (2010) Towards post-multiculturalism? Changing communities, conditions and contexts of diversity. *International Social Science Journal* 61 (199), 83–95.

Vygotsky, L.S. (1964) *Thought and Language* (E. Hanfmann, G. Vakar and A. Kozulin, Trans. A. Kozulin Ed. Revised and expanded ed.). Cambridge, MA: The MIT Press.

Vygotsky, L.S. (1978) *Mind in Society: The Development of Higher Psychological Processes* (A. Luria, R. and M. Lopez-Morollas, Trans. V. John-Steiner and M. Cole Eds. Revised ed.). Cambridge, MA: Harvard University Press.

Walker, J. (2009) *The World's English Mania*. February 2009. TED.Com: TED Conferences. See http://www.ted.com/talks/jay_walker_on_the_world_s_english_mania.html (accessed 20 March 2013).

Warschauer, M. (1996) Comparing face-to-face electronic discussion in the second language classroom. *CALICO Journal* 13 (2), 7–26.

Warschauer, M. and Healey, D. (1998) Computers and language learning: An overview. *Language Teaching* 31 (02), 57–71.

Warschauer, M., Turbee, L. and Roberts, B. (1996) Computer learning networks and student empowerment. *System* 24 (1), 1–14.

Watanabe, Y., Ikeda, M. and Izumi, S. (eds) (2011) *CLIL: New Challenges in Foreign Language Education at Sophia University* (Vol. 1: Principles and Methodology). Tokyo: Sophia University Press.

Wenger, E. (1998) *Communities of Practice: Learning, Meaning, and Identity* (2003 ed.). Cambridge: Cambridge University Press.

Widdowson, H.G. (1978) *Teaching Language as Communication*. Oxford: Oxford University Press.

Widdowson, H.G. (1979) *Explorations in Applied Linguistics* (Vol. 2). Oxford: Oxford University Press
Widdowson, H.G. (1990) *Aspects of Language Teaching*. Oxford: Oxford University Press.
Widdowson, H.G. (1996) Comment: Authenticity and autonomy in ELT. *ELT Journal* 50 (1), 67–68.
Widdowson, H.G. (2001) Interpretations and correlations: A reply to Stubbs. *Applied Linguistics* 22 (4), 531–538.
Widmer, R., Oswald-Krapf, H., Sinha-Khetriwal, D., Schnellmann, M. and Böni, H. (2005) Global perspectives on e-waste. *Environmental Impact Assessment Review* 25 (5), 436–458.
Williams, M. and Burden, R.L. (1997) *Psychology for Language Teachers*. Cambridge: Cambridge University Press.
Wittgenstein, L. (1953) *Philosophical Investigations* (P.M.S. Hacker and J. Schulte, Trans. 4th ed.). Sussex: Wiley-Blackwell.
Wurman, R.S. (1989) *Information Anxiety*. New York: Doubleday.
Yacobi, B.G. (2012) The limits of authenticity. *Philosophy Now* 92, 28–30.
Yamagami, M. and Tollefson, J. (2011) Elite discourses of globalization in Japan: The role of English. In P. Seargeant (ed.) *English in Japan in the Era of Globalization* (pp. 15–37). Basingstoke: Palgrave Macmillan.
Yano, Y. (2011) English as an international language and 'Japanese English'. In P. Seargeant (ed.) *English in Japan in the Era of Globalization* (pp. 125–142). Basingstoke: Palgrave Macmillan.
Yoshida, K. (2001) The need for a qualitative change in the teaching of English in Japan in the 21st century. In A. Furness, G. Wong and L. Wu (eds) *Penetrating Discourse: Integrating Theory and Practice in Second Language Teaching* (pp. 159–172). Hong Kong: Hong Kong University of Science and Technology.
Yoshida, K. (2009) The new course of study and the possibilities for change in Japan's English education. In K. Namai and Y. Fukuda (eds) *Toward the Fusion of Language, Culture and Education from the Perspectives of International and Interdisciplinary Research [言語・文化・教育の融合を目指して―国際的・学際的研究の視座から]* (pp. 387–398) Tokyo: Kaitakushya.
Zhang, J. (2011) Language Policy and Planning for the 2008 Beijing Olympics: An Investigation of the Discursive Construction of an Olympic City and a Global Population. (PhD Doctoral Thesis), Macquarie University, Sydney.
Zimmerman, D.H. (1998) Identity, context and interaction. In C. Antaki and S. Widdicombe (eds) *Identities in Talk* (pp. 87–106). London: Sage.

Author Index

Agger, Ben, 153
Allan, Rachel, 93
Allwright, Dick, 30, 91, 106
Alsagoff, Lubna, 41
Altbach, Philip G., 133
Ammon, Ulrich, 6, 121
Amor, Stuart, 80, 82, 95–96, 100
Anderson, Benedict, 101, 127, 138, 144
Appadurai, Arjun, 133–34, 144
Apple, Matthew, 51, 144
Arnold, Ewen, 70
Atkinson, Dwight, 87
Atkinson, Terry, 5, 30

Baba, Kyoko, 17
Bachman, Lyle F, 69–70, 73, 84, 101
Badger, Richard, 73
Bailey, Kathleen M, 30, 122, 159
Bandura, Albert, 87
Barkhuizen, Gary, 8, 31
Benson, Phil, 14, 49, 65–67, 69, 122, 157, 160
Block, David, 17, 20–21, 122
Blommaert, Jan, 5, 37, 67
Bolton, Kingsley, 41, 68
Bonnett, Michael, 14
Borg, Simon, 28
Bourdieu, Pierre, 23
Braine, George, 47, 49
Breen, Michael P, 1, 3, 14, 69–71, 73, 80, 122
Brewster, Damon, 156

Cameron, Lynne, 29–31
Campbell, Joseph, 128
Canagarajah, A. Suresh, 33, 37, 39, 42, 49, 55, 65, 92, 148
Chatfield, Tom, 145, 147, 155
Chomsky, Noam, 18
Clandinin, D Jean, 8

Clark, Elizabeth, 44
Clarke, David, 107
Cobb, Russell, 79
Coetzee-Van Rooy, Susan, 146
Cogo, Alessia, 40
Cook, Guy, 3, 75–77, 146, 162
Cook, Vivian, 35, 39, 44–5, 146
Cooker, Lucy, 14
Cowie, Neil, 50, 111
Coyle, Do, 7, 137–39, 143, 155
Crystal, David, 39, 41, 56
Csikszentmihalyi, Mihaly, 3, 31, 110, 163
Cuypers, Stefaan, 14

Dalton-Puffer, Christiane, 137, 139
Dantas-Whitney, Maria, 15, 90
Darwin, Charles, 18
Davies, Alan, 39, 42, 44
de Bot, Kees, 28
Deci, Edward, 109
de Swaan, Abram, 34, 37, 71
Dewey, Martin, 40,
Dörnyei, Zoltán, 17, 28, 30–31, 84, 86–87, 90, 97, 104, 111, 122

Eagleton, Terry, 75, 79
Edge, Julian, 8, 45
Ellis, Nick, 28–29, 122, 167
Ellis, Rod, 19, 36, 48, 97, 107

Fairclough, Norman, 5, 99, 145
Farrell, Thomas, 8
Flowerdew, John, 43
Fong, Vivienne, 60
Fromkin, Victoria, 74

Galtung, Johan, 133
Gilmore, Alex, 4, 32, 44, 63, 69–71, 81–84, 86–89, 92, 96, 98, 102, 114

Golomb, Jacob, 12, 64, 67, 151
Golombek, Paula R., 8, 31
González, Olgalucía Gaitán, 86
Graddol, David, 34, 40–41, 43, 113, 142, 149

Hanks, Judith, 91
Harmer, Jeremy, 2–3, 68–69, 77, 84, 86, 127
Harper, Douglas, 65, 75, 144
Hedge, Tricia, 3, 84
Heidegger, Martin, 7, 13–14, 98, 147, 164
Henry, Alastair, 6, 53, 159, 163, 166
Holec, Henri, 65
Holliday, Adrian, 5, 37, 44–45, 65, 68, 111, 129, 165, 167
Houghton, Stephanie Ann, 44, 46
Howatt, Anthony Philip Reid, 134
Huang, Kuei-Min, 143
Hung, David, 71–72, 118, 124–28, 139, 153

Ikeda, Makoto, 138
Illés, Éva, 98
Irie, Kay, 17, 117, 156

Jean-Paul Sartre, 13–15
Jenkins, Jennifer, 34, 40–42, 53–55, 65, 88, 93, 133, 136, 141
Johnson, Karen E., 8, 31

Kachru, Braj, 37–42, 61, 121, 165
Kiczkowiak, Marek, 51
Kierkegaard, Søren, 7, 13
Kimura, Yuzo, 30, 112
Kramsch, Claire, 4, 20, 31, 43, 70, 82, 122, 128, 167
Krashen, Stephen, 80
Külekçi, Erkan, 97, 110, 120

Larsen-Freeman, Diane, 4, 28–32, 87, 122, 167
Lasagabaster, David, 43, 52, 138, 143
László, Mònika, 121
Lazzaro, Nicole, 3, 110, 163
Levitt, Theodore, 35
Lewkowicz, Jo, 69–70, 84
Lindholm, Charles, 12
Lorenz, Edward, 29
Lorenzo, Francisco, 140, 143

MacDonald, Malcolm, 73
MacIntyre, Peter, 16
Mahboob, Ahmar, 2
Marsh, David, 137–38

Masuhara, Hitomi, 76–77, 80, 90, 110, 122, 156
Matsuda, Aya, 36, 41, 44–46, 52, 68, 92
Matsuda, Paul Kei, 45
McKay, Sandra Lee, 41
Meddings, Luke, 56, 116, 131, 156, 158
Medgyes, Péter, 43, 47, 53, 121
Mehisto, Peeter, 134, 137–38
Menezes, Vera, 14, 20–21, 28, 122
Mercer, Sarah, 4, 20, 167
Mishan, Freda, 3, 15, 18–19, 63–64, 66, 71–73, 78–80, 83, 87–90, 93, 128, 142, 144, 153, 156
Morrow, Keith, 69, 71, 81, 85, 88, 102, 155
Muir, Christine, 87
Mukherjee, Joybrato, 93
Murray, Garold, 14, 122, 148
Myhill, John, 53, 55, 91, 165

Navés, Teresa, 137–38
Norton. Bonny, 20–23, 41, 52, 101, 122, 128
Nunan, David, 41, 49, 69, 121

O'Dowd, Robert, 157
O'Keeffe, Anne, 93

Paikeday, Thomas, 39, 44
Palfreyman & Smith, 129
Palmer, Adrian, 73, 101–2
Pavlenko, Aneta, 8, 20, 31, 71, 146
Peacock, Matthew, 85–86, 96
Pennycook, Alastair, 37, 65, 133–34
Petraglia, Joseph, 125, 139, 142
Phillipson, Robert, 37, 65, 130, 133–34
Piller, Ingrid, 99, 112
Pinner, Richard, 37, 45, 68, 84, 102, 104–5, 115, 138
Prator, Clifford, 37, 41
Prensky, Marc, 161–62

Quirk, Randolph, 37–40, 42, 60–61

Ramanathan, Vaidehi, 35, 121
Rampton, Ben, 45, 160, 163
Reves, Thea, 47
Richards, Jack C., 2, 15, 22
Richards, Keith, 22
Rilling, Sarah, 15, 90
Rivers, Damian, 44
Rodriguez & Ryave, 168
Rousseau, Henri, 12, 15, 98

Rousseau, Jean-Jacques, 12
Ryan, Richard, 104
Ryan, Stephen, 17, 117, 156

Sakui, Keiko, 111
Schmidt, Richard. W., 2, 67
Schön, Donald A., 8
Scovel, Tom, 47
Seargeant, Philip, 39, 46, 50, 91–92, 122
Seidlhofer, Barbara, 36, 40, 93
Siegel, Aki, 88, 92
Simon-Maeda, Andrea, 168
Smith, Jack C., 2, 49, 67
Smith, Richard C., 129
Snyder-Parampil, 90
Suzuki, Ayako, 37, 43–44, 60, 68
Swaffar, Janet K, 69
Swain, Merrill, 137
Sweet, Henry, 75

Takahashi, Kimie, 20, 120
Tan, Melinda, 44, 93
Taylor, David, 73, 83, 102
Thompson, Derek, 147
Thornbury, Scott, 56, 116, 156, 158
Thumboo, Edwin, 41, 96
Tollefson, James W., 50, 141
Tomlinson, Brian, 56, 76–77, 80, 89–90, 107, 110, 116, 122, 156
Trabelsi, Soufiane, 91, 96
Trilling, Lionel, 165
Trudgill, Peter, 40
Tudor, Ian, 4–5, 24, 97

Ushioda, Ema, 4, 7, 14–15, 18, 20–22, 31, 85, 87, 90, 104, 122, 142–43, 145–46, 149, 157

Valdés, Christina, 131
van Lier, Leo, 1, 5, 14, 22, 24, 27, 30, 65, 69, 71, 73, 95–96, 102, 121
Vasagar, Jeevan, 154–55
Vertovec, Steven, 5
Victor Chen, Der-Thanq, 71, 124–28
Vygotsky, Lev, 24, 80, 143

Warschauer, Mark, 157–59
Watanabe, Yoshinori, 138
Wenger, Etienne, 126
Widdowson, Henry, 1–3, 14, 65–66, 69, 71–73, 75, 95, 102, 108, 121, 128, 134–35, 137, 155, 165
Williams, Marion, 17, 102, 125, 155
Wittgenstein, Ludwig, 126

Yacobi, Ben, 12, 15, 98
Yamagami, Mai, 50, 141
Yano, Yasutaka, 51
Yoshida, Kensaku, 136

Zhang, Jie, 99, 112
Zimmerman, Don H., 15, 21–22, 154

Subject Index

accents, 50, 161
affective factors, 14, 90, 97
Africa, 37, 149
age, 13, 73, 79, 109, 144, 162
agency, 7, 15, 91
American Association of Applied Linguistics, 47
American culture, 6
American English, 59, 61
Americanised, 134
Americans, 51
American Sign Language, 19
American varieties, 43
Anglo-American orientations, 51
Anglo-centric focus, 78
Anglo-global models, 156
Anglo-global world, 5
applied linguistics, 15, 18, 22, 28, 30, 42–43, 47, 62, 66–67, 69, 93–96, 167
approaches
  ecological, 5, 125
  educational, 125, 137
  practical, 2, 66
  sociocultural, 7, 15
Australia, 59, 136
authenticating, 137, 142
authentication, 14, 95–96, 100, 120, 128
authentic content, 67, 80
authentic examples, 93, 151
authentic experience, 92, 167
authentic input, 49, 88
authenticity
  classic definition, 2, 8, 64, 67–69, 71, 73, 82, 85, 88, 103–4, 115, 117, 130, 161–62, 166
  complexity of, 4, 115, 166
  context-process, 126
  degree of, 72, 77, 107

dimensions of, 118, 120
element of, 155–56
personal, 12, 15, 20, 129
professional community, 126
reconceptualise, 104
social, 129
surrounding, 6, 67, 69
theme of, 15, 66, 83
understanding, 11, 28, 33
authenticity and motivation, 7, 17, 85–86, 97, 114, 117
Authenticity and second language acquisition, 87
authenticity continuum, 8, 99, 101, 103–9, 111–15, 117–19, 121, 123–25, 127, 129, 155
authenticity debate, 3, 8, 77, 95, 99–100, 102, 104
authenticity hierarchy, 55, 91, 165
Authenticity in Bilingual Educational Contexts, 131, 133, 135, 137, 139, 141, 143
Authenticity in research literature, 93
authenticity of purpose, 7, 135, 137, 139–40, 143, 155
authentic language, 4–5, 46, 48, 51, 53, 64, 71, 73, 77, 81, 92, 140, 162
authentic materials, 2–3, 46, 62–63, 67–68, 70, 72, 76, 78, 80, 83, 85–89, 91, 108–14, 157, 160
authentic model, 45–46, 53
authentic self, 7, 11–12, 15–17, 21, 121
authentic texts, 67–68, 75–77, 80, 87, 139–40
autonomy, 6–8, 14–16, 26–27, 64–67, 87, 90, 98, 101, 104, 107, 109, 118, 122, 129, 157–58
social, 14

Bangladesh, 38
Barcelona, 74
beliefs, 13, 30, 43, 47, 85–86, 91, 125
　affective, 50
　common, 110
　personal, 5, 77
　shared, 118
bilingual, 7–8, 62, 130, 132, 135, 137, 142–43, 146
bilingual education, 136–38
Bilingual Educational Contexts, 131, 133, 135, 137, 139, 141, 143
bilingualism, 53, 138, 142
bilingual models, 134, 140
bilingual models of education, 134–35, 138
Brazil, 145
Britain, 43, 61, 131
British English, 57, 61

Canada, 38, 136–37
careers, 6, 42, 99, 166
chaos, 28–29, 65
chaos/complexity theory, 4, 7, 10, 24, 28–30, 63, 82
chaos theory, 28–29
Chinese, 19, 51, 58
circles, 38, 53
citations, 83–84, 106
class, 22, 25, 47, 49, 52, 54–55, 59, 61, 107–11, 113–14, 118–19, 140, 142, 155, 157
classroom, 21–22, 25–26, 30–31, 48–49, 65, 68, 70–73, 77–78, 101–2, 112–19, 126, 139–40, 154–56, 159–61, 166–67
CLIL (Content and Language Integrated Learning), 7, 134, 137–40, 142–43
Common European Framework of Reference for Languages, 48
communicative language teaching, 3, 135, 139, 165
community
　international, 70, 101, 120
　professional, 126–27
complex dynamic systems, 10, 28–31, 69, 87, 167
complexity theory, 28–31, 65, 97
complex system, 1, 7, 29, 31
compulsory language classes, 7, 104
computers, 121, 133, 144–49, 157–59
content, 1, 4–5, 25, 27, 104, 108, 111–12, 115, 118–19, 125, 137–40, 143, 153, 156, 158

Content and Language Integrated Learning. *See* CLIL
Content-Based Instruction, 137
contexts, 11–12, 17–19, 21, 23, 28–31, 35–37, 74–77, 89–93, 100–105, 112–14, 119–20, 124–27, 129–31, 136–37, 165–67
continuum, 6–7, 23, 31, 89, 95, 99–102, 104–8, 111, 113–22, 124–27, 130
control, 6–7, 88, 155
cultural capital, 23, 41–42, 122, 124, 132, 134–35, 162
cultural products, 3, 78–79, 128, 153
culture
　target language, 1, 7, 70, 103, 140
　target-language, 70
currency, 23, 78–79, 144

Dasein, 14
definition of authenticity, 46, 48, 64–65, 67, 69, 71–73, 91, 93, 103–4, 112–13, 115, 117, 127, 129–30, 161–62
discourse, 5, 21–22, 37, 40, 92, 95–96, 99, 112, 124, 128–29, 139, 154
domains, 1, 7, 19, 28, 65, 70–71, 73, 81, 100–102, 104, 115–19, 121, 128, 145, 155
domains of authenticity, 1, 80–81, 166
dynamic components, 7, 27, 31, 69, 111

ecological perspectives, 24, 97
educational models, 7–8, 130, 132, 134–35, 142–43
EFL
　classroom, 92
　contexts, 7, 41, 104, 165
　learners, 44
　methodologies, 139
　textbooks, 92, 165
EIL. *See* English as an International Language
ELF (English as a Lingua Franca), 36–37, 40–41, 50, 61, 69, 71, 93
ELT. *See* English language teaching
ELT industry, 44, 65
ELT materials, 66, 78
ELT publishers, 131, 156
EMI (English as a Medium of Instruction), 7, 134, 136–38, 141–43
English as a Foreign Language (EFL), 8
English as a Lingua Franca. *See* ELF
English as a Medium of Instruction. *See* EMI

English as an International Language (EIL), 37, 44, 69, 91–92, 103–4, 117, 124, 127, 163
Englishes, 54–55, 61, 69
English language, 2, 4–6, 36–37, 43, 50–53, 63, 71, 79, 96, 122, 143, 150, 156, 159–60, 166
English language classroom, 44
English language education, 37, 62, 142
English language learners, 49
English language learning, 24, 34
English language teachers, 42, 51
English language teaching (ELT), 2, 7, 14, 27, 31, 42–44, 46, 100, 104, 107, 110, 115, 117, 120, 139–40
English proficiency, 6, 42, 113, 149
English teaching and English language learning, 34
enjoyment, 3, 110, 161, 163
environment, 20, 31, 67, 99, 118, 121, 125, 150, 157, 163
  changing, 146
  monolingual classroom, 55
  multilingual, 138
  organic, 24
  social, 1, 77
Europe, 48, 136–38, 142
exams, 109–10, 113
Existential, 10–11, 13–15, 17, 19, 21, 23, 25, 27, 29, 31, 33
existentialists, 11–12, 14, 32, 147
existential philosophy, 4, 10, 98
experience, 25, 28, 30, 61–62, 67–68, 76–78, 80, 110, 113–14, 117, 120–21, 143, 149, 156–57, 165–67

Facebook, 146, 150, 153, 155
first language, 6, 40, 48, 55, 62–63, 68, 103, 121, 136–37, 140
flow theory, 3, 110
foreign language, 1, 17, 48, 51, 62–63, 65, 67, 97, 100, 102, 112–13, 129–30, 135–37, 139, 142–43
foreign language identity, 17
foreign language learning context, 124
Foreign Language Major, 61
foreign language teacher self-efficacy, 113
fun, 109–10, 123, 163

gap, 25, 44, 165
Global English, 24, 34–37, 39, 41–42, 50, 53–54, 56, 59, 71

globalisation, 5, 33–35, 79, 98, 122, 129, 132, 141–42, 145, 147–50
globalisation of discourse, 5, 99, 145
Global Language, 2, 4, 6–8, 12, 14, 16, 18, 20, 22, 32, 34–62, 78, 82, 98–100, 156
Graded Readers, 93, 117
Grammar-Translation and Communicative Language Teaching, 135

Hacktivism, 161
Haitian Creole, 50
Harvard, 135
hegemonic dominance, 44
hierarchies, 12, 37, 47, 53, 55
  reconceptualised, 54
  traditional, 34
Higher Education, 137
high-school students, 51
Hindi, 37
Hiroshima, 91
human essence, 168
human existence, 17, 128
Human ingenuity, 163
humanity, 13, 131, 147
humans, 17–18, 147–48, 154, 163–64, 167
husband, 20, 22, 146

ICT, 114, 142, 148–49
identity, 1, 4, 7, 10, 14–15, 17–18, 20–23, 46–47, 53, 55, 60, 101, 119–20, 122, 154–55
  constructed, 17
  dependent, 16, 21
  doctor/patient, 21
  individual, 7, 14
  latent, 21
  layered, 21
  multiple, 104
  national, 5
  negotiating, 7
  prescriptive, 99
  professional, 108
  situated, 22
  teacher/student, 21
  transportable, 15, 21–22, 154
identity change, 20–21
ideologies, 35, 55, 103, 124, 166
idiolect, 19–20, 24–25
IELTS, 88, 141
images, 26, 121–22, 124
Imagined Communities, 145

imbalance, 42, 90, 135
imperialism, 133
   linguistic, 41, 103–4
implications, 20–21, 31, 38, 40, 61, 65, 68, 129, 142, 149, 163, 166
   philosophical, 63, 137
   practical, 30
   social, 104
inauthenticity, 12, 151
India, 37–38, 50, 133
Indian English, 57
information age, 148
information overload, 147
information technology, 149
Inner Circle, 38
input, 63, 65, 72, 78, 80, 88, 128, 159–60
intention, 12, 35, 99, 105, 114, 121, 127, 136, 148, 160
interactions, 14–16, 29–30, 48, 69, 71, 73, 77, 100, 102, 110, 117, 119–20, 125–26, 154–55, 167–69
international communication, 2, 37, 53, 100
international language, 39, 50, 91–92, 103, 117, 127, 166
international models, 34, 41, 55, 60
international students, 133, 135–36, 141
internet, 26, 129, 148, 150–51, 153–54, 160–62
internet age, 153
internet memes, 151
internet users, 151
introversion, 47, 141
intuition, 5, 30
investment, 8, 23, 52, 160

Japan, 20, 24–25, 41, 43, 50–51, 53, 55, 57, 91–92, 131, 136, 138, 141, 146–47, 165
Japan Association of Language Teaching (JALT), 66
Japanese education, 112
Japanese English language school, 123
Japanese high school teachers, 36, 45, 105
Japanese society, 24, 36
Japanese teachers, 19, 24, 51, 54, 60, 111
Japanese university, 25, 53, 92
joke, 13, 18, 144, 150
journal editors, 8, 43
journals, 8, 64, 66–67, 93–94, 138

journey, 12, 32
Judeo-Christian ethos, 39
justifications, 2, 16, 41, 78, 80, 137, 163

Korea, 38, 116

language
   connect, 114
   decontextualised, 76
   disembodied, 35, 92, 104, 156
   human, 18
   hyper-central, 37
   hyper-centralised, 34
   learned foreign, 104
   native, 59, 120
   second, 6–7, 16, 20, 23, 34–36, 40–41, 43–44, 55, 70–71, 99, 107, 127, 134, 136, 138
language change, 144–45
language classroom, 6–7, 11, 17, 23, 36, 63, 77, 80, 82, 110, 112, 130, 134, 165, 167–68
language education, 14, 18, 127, 130, 133–34, 140, 143, 148–49
language learners, 20, 22, 80, 136, 138
language learning, 5, 8, 10, 18, 20–21, 23–25, 28, 31–32, 71, 73, 76–78, 84, 93–97, 137–40, 158–61
Language Learning Materials, 77, 96
language teachers, 25, 28, 75, 79–80, 82, 97, 102, 104, 108, 114, 121–22, 127, 129–30, 136–39, 160–61
language teaching, 3–4, 7, 14, 16–17, 28, 32, 55–56, 61–62, 64–66, 68, 82, 84, 93, 136, 138
learner autonomy, 14, 66, 136
learners, 6–8, 15–17, 20–25, 40–42, 47–50, 61–63, 71–80, 87–91, 98–101, 104–5, 107–9, 121–22, 135–40, 158–60, 165–69
   individual, 1, 105, 119, 169
learning materials, 7, 40, 63–64, 78, 99–100, 107, 115, 120, 143
lessons, 19, 22, 25, 30, 40, 45–47, 59, 66–67, 74, 79, 107, 109–10, 113–14, 139
lingua franca, 36–37, 61, 90, 92
linguistic fingerprinting, 19
literacy, 74, 142, 144–45
   digital, 149
literature, 3–4, 9, 11, 13–14, 16, 32, 66, 86, 94–97, 100, 121, 128, 137, 139

Lithuania, 50
the living textbook, 79

Mandarin, 60
materials, 2–3, 5, 7–8, 16, 45–46, 67–68, 79–81, 89–90, 104–5, 107–9, 111, 114, 119, 130, 153
　authenticity of, 114
models, 21, 31, 39, 41, 48, 53–54, 57, 60–61, 64, 68, 87, 90–91, 134, 165
　all-encompassing, 136
　authenticity and international, 34, 55
　best, 68, 105
　centre/periphery, 134
　dynamic, 30, 120
　expanding circle, 43
　glamour, 124
　global, 131
　inclusive, 135
　learner-apprentice, 125
　native-speakerist, 136
　non-native speaker, 98
　second-language, 37
　social, 48
　successful, 156
　unrealistic native, 59
monocentrism, 39
motivation, 1, 3–4, 6–8, 15, 17, 22–23, 30–31, 41, 43, 84–87, 90, 97–98, 104, 111, 157
　conceptualising, 104
　extrinsic, 23
　personal, 101
　positive, 109
　result, 49
motivational, 109, 143
motivational benefits, 143
motivational challenges, 143
motivational flow theory, 31
motivational force, 7
motivational inertia, 117
motivational push, sustained, 49
motivational theory, 97
multilingual, 101, 114, 134, 146
multilingualism, 130
multilingual people, 121
multilingual society, 99, 140

native speaker (NSs), 34, 37–38, 40–48, 51–53, 55–57, 59, 61–62, 68–71, 73, 88, 91–93, 98, 112–13, 130, 165–66
native-speakerism, 34, 44, 46–47, 53, 98, 103

native-speakerist, 45–46, 103
native-speakerist assumptions, making, 88
native-speakerist biases, 46
native speaker label, 45
native speaker models, 44, 59, 141
native speakers, 34, 37–41, 43–48, 51–53, 56–57, 59, 61–62, 68–71, 73, 88, 91–93, 98, 113, 130, 165–66
native speaker teachers, 43–44
native speaker varieties, 43, 48, 59
native varieties, 57
natural language, 68, 73–77
nature, 15, 18, 32, 44, 67, 71, 73, 76, 95, 115, 151, 157, 168–69
　changing, 79
　complex, 96
　cyclical, 134, 163
　deictic, 75
　dynamic, 15, 28, 167
　human, 14–15
　individual, 71
　organic, 119
　social, 17
nature of authenticity, 17, 90, 102, 139
Newcastle, 57
newspapers, 2–3, 24, 46, 67–68, 70, 73–74, 77, 85, 88, 109–10, 112, 124, 160, 162, 166
New York, 148
New Zealand, 38, 136
Nietzsche, Friedrich, 13
Nirvana, 79
NNS. *See* non-native speaker
non-native speaker (NNS), 38–39, 42–45, 47–48, 52–53, 55–56, 59, 95, 98, 112–13
non-native speaker teachers, 44, 53
North American, 60
Nova, 123
NSs. *See* native speaker

official language, 60
　second, 165
online, 6, 75, 86, 149, 151, 154–55, 157–58, 160
online bullying, 151
online communication, 155
Online Corpus, 93
online exchanges, 156–57
　classroom-based, 156
online games, 6, 159, 163

Online interactions and social
    networking, 164
online language learning, 159
online learning materials, 158
online security, 153
online self, 155
Online self-access centres (OSACs), 158
online translation software, 158–59
optimistic, 87, 92, 104, 108
Orwell, George, 55
OSACs (Online self-access centres), 158
Osaka, 45, 106–10
othering, 51, 103, 124, 140
overpopulation, 91
overseas, 133, 141, 156
oversharing, 153
ownership, 7, 39, 41–42, 62, 90
Oxford, 135

Pakistan, 96
paradox, 67, 98, 127–28
paradox of authenticity, 2, 79, 111, 127, 151
Pareto efficiency, 42
Paris, 52
PARSNIPS, 131, 140
peak attention, 147
peak oil, 147
pedagogical, 143
pedagogical purposes, 67, 139, 155
pedagogical rationale, 80
pedagogical sources, 106
pedagogic contrivance, 72
pedagogic rationale, 78
pedagogic value, 107
person in-context, 7
perspective, 2, 32, 34, 75, 78, 104, 163, 167
Philippines, 38, 50
philosophers, 11, 13, 16, 75
    existentialist, 7, 12–13, 15
Philosophical, 10–11, 13, 15, 17, 19, 21, 23, 25, 27, 29, 31, 33
plagiarism, 159
PlayStation, 162
pluralist, 19
pluricentric, 38
pluricentrism, 39
podcast TEFLology, 68
poetry, 95, 128
policy
    educational, 54
    home country's, 22

illegitimate, 60
official, 43
school's, 154
power, 23, 34, 39, 41–42, 45, 110, 133, 154, 162–63
    economic, 40, 132
    political, 40, 42, 61, 133
practice, exploratory, 30, 90–91, 106
practitioners, 2, 11, 85, 90, 100
pragmatics, 31, 40, 75
prejudices, 7–8, 43–44, 46, 91, 98
pressure, 51, 141, 143, 149
    institutional, 51, 99
    personal, 51
    social, 6, 51, 62, 112, 134
problem-based learning, 125, 135, 142
problems, 25, 31–32, 43–44, 47, 53–54, 61–62, 64, 67, 124–25, 127–28, 149, 153, 156, 158–59, 165–67
process, 3–4, 7–9, 14–15, 23–24, 27–32, 79–80, 82, 100, 102, 104, 110, 120, 128, 162–63, 167–68
    collective, 79
    emergent, 126
    mediated, 24, 30
    situated, 79
    social, 119
proficiency, 45, 113, 136, 157, 159–60
    advanced, 25
proficiency levels, 168
programmes, 135–36, 138, 141
    complicated grooming, 154
    educational, 141
    television, 159

Queen Elizabeth II, 57–59
Queen's English, 53, 59

reality, 27, 36, 38, 42, 44, 51, 71–73, 88, 91, 98, 102, 112–14, 125–26, 162, 166–67
real world, 48, 67–68, 76, 113, 118, 125–26, 129, 166
references, 5, 16, 48, 83, 88, 94, 96, 127, 132, 144
    cultural, 73
    implicit, 161
    semantic, 75, 144
    special, 10
religions, 13, 131, 145
research, 6, 8–9, 15–16, 19, 21, 26, 28, 31, 42–43, 78, 85–91, 94–97, 105–7, 111, 165–68

action, 91
   classroom-based, 168
   empirical, 64, 83, 90, 94, 97
   mixed-methods, 88
   motivational, 28, 30, 87
   practitioner, 90–91
   qualitative, 90
   third-party, 91
Rogeting, 159
Russian, 19

Saudi Arabia, 22, 38
scaffolding, 20, 114, 137, 140, 168
schemata, 128
   cultural, 74–75, 80, 128
schema theory, 78
scholars, 17, 19, 33, 39–41, 45, 65, 72–73, 77, 82–83, 96, 99, 102, 121, 129–30, 133
school community, 127
school curriculum, 135
schools, 6, 25, 48, 53, 61–62, 91, 112, 114, 131, 135, 139, 141, 154, 166
Schwarzenegger, Arnold, 58–59
second language acquisition. *See* SLA
Second World War, 144
Sega Mega Drive, 162
self, 2, 7, 10, 12, 14–16, 18, 20–23, 32, 63, 65, 104, 108, 117, 153, 167–68
   empowered, 121
   individual, 6
   natural, 12, 98
self-access learning, 158
self-alteration, 168
self-awareness, 129
self-change, 168
self-concepts, 17, 168
Self-confidence, 47
Self-Directed Learning, 66
self-discrimination, 43, 113
self-efficacy, 45, 98
self-expression, 17
self-image, 7, 17, 21, 43, 45–46
self-observations, 8
self-orientalism, 51
self system, 104
self-volition, 98
semantic shifting, 75
Senegal, 50
sentence, 19, 66, 72, 74–76, 97, 158–59
   contrived, 75–77
   invented, 75, 77
sexual predators, 154

Shakespeare, 127
Simpsons, 29
Singapore, 38, 59, 96
Singaporean, 57, 96
Singaporean English, 37, 57
Singlish, 37, 60
Skinner, Burrhus Frederic, 18
Skype, 146
SLA (second language acquisition), 1, 4–5, 7, 10–11, 14–17, 19–20, 24, 28, 31–32, 62–66, 78, 95–97, 145, 148, 167–68
smartphones, 147
SNS, 150, 154
social context, 1, 4, 14–15, 25, 89, 145, 154, 169
social networks, 150, 153–54, 168
society, 2, 4, 10–16, 18, 24–25, 32, 63, 79, 82, 99, 108, 133, 167–69
sociocultural context, 76
sociocultural theory, 24
son, 6, 62, 146–47, 153, 162
Sonic, 162
Sophia University, 56, 138, 145
South Africa, 136
Sri Lanka, 38, 92
Standard English, 61, 161
state-of-the-art paper, 4, 66
stereotypes, 13
story, 21, 24, 29–30, 34, 42, 145–47, 151
Street Fighter, 162
stresses, 17, 79, 118, 126
student empowerment, 157
student feedback, 89
student motivation, 109, 111
students, 4–6, 11, 21–22, 25–27, 35–36, 40–43, 51–59, 61, 79–81, 92, 107–14, 117–18, 133–36, 140–43, 153–60
studies, 21, 24, 29, 43, 45–48, 51–52, 63–64, 83–89, 92–94, 96–97, 105, 107, 135–36, 140–41, 157
subject, 2, 6, 10–11, 28, 61–62, 66, 81, 85–86, 91, 95, 97, 99, 134–38, 142–43, 166–67
Sweden, 6, 53, 159
Swiss watch, 47, 64
syntax, 31, 158
synthesis, 64, 69, 99, 121

Taipei, 60
Taiwan, 157
Taiwanese National Party, 60
target culture, 71, 100, 161

target language, 1–2, 16, 20–21, 23, 25, 48, 70, 76–78, 118, 124, 130, 136, 139, 161, 169
target language use (TLU), 25, 70, 101, 104
Task Based Learning, 125, 135, 139
tasks, 11, 16, 22, 25, 30, 55–56, 59, 63, 69–70, 80–81, 107–9, 111, 114–16, 118–19, 125
  communicative, 55
  complicated, 30
  computer-based, 149
  individual, 139
  language test, 101
  real-world, 149
teacher cognition, 98
teachers, 1–2, 4–6, 24–25, 27–30, 43–47, 52–56, 64–69, 104–5, 107, 109–14, 128–29, 136–38, 154–55, 159–61, 165
  bilingual, 53
  guiding, 104
  harm, 98
  ideal, 44
  non-native, 45–46
  speaking, 45
teacher self-efficacy, 43
teacher/student fraternisation, 154
teacher training, 56–57, 60
teaching approaches, 77
teaching career, 25, 118
teaching context, 5, 166
teaching journals, 67
teaching licence, 56, 105
teaching self-efficacy, 113
teaching strategies, 54
technology, 13–15, 18, 133, 143–44, 147–49, 154, 159–60, 162–64, 168
  communicative, 18, 118, 147
  dislike, 13
  new, 133, 163
  update, 163
technology-enhanced learning, 157
TED.com, 35–36, 148
teen pregnancy, 73
televised news coverage, 35
televisions, 13, 53, 60, 85, 146, 150
Terminator, 158
TESOL Quarterly, 23
tests, 6, 42, 51–52, 64, 88, 101, 113, 136, 158, 160
  computer-based, 159
  gate-keeping, 88
  high-stakes, 112
  large stan-dardised institutional, 141
  multiple-choice, 136
textbook grammar presentation, 40
text book producers, 86
textbooks, 46, 48–49, 56, 76–77, 79, 84, 88, 92, 109, 112–13, 116, 119, 122, 158, 162–63
  international, 116
  localised, 107
textbook writers, 67
texts, 24, 64, 67, 69, 71–72, 77, 79–81, 86, 94–95, 100, 117, 119, 124, 128, 139
Textual Identity, 20
Tibet, 58
TLU. *See* target language use
TOEFL, 88, 136, 141
Tokyo, 46, 56, 106–7, 110–14, 147
too elusive to be useful, 71, 114
tool, 2, 18, 20, 37, 48–50, 76, 100–101, 111, 114, 143, 146
topics, 1, 3, 11, 66, 73, 79, 83, 92, 94, 96, 100, 111, 114, 116, 118
Treasure Island Dizzy, 162
Trojan virus, 98
troll, 75
trolling, 151, 161
truth, 11, 13, 104, 128, 161
Tunisia, 91
Turkey, 131
Turkish, 22
Twitter, 74, 150, 154

UK, 5, 20, 38, 52, 101, 114, 131, 133–36, 154
Ulysses, 96
United Nations, 50
United States, 146
universities, 6, 54, 57, 88, 96, 121, 133, 136, 141–42, 157, 160, 165
Urdu, 120

validity, 6, 41, 60, 71, 73, 84
  instructional, 110
  perceived, 1
varieties, standard, 34, 39, 42, 61
videos, 25, 35–36, 57, 86, 146, 150, 157–58, 161–62
vocabulary size, 48
voices, 22, 34, 39, 70, 93
Vygotskyian, 76, 80

washback, 134, 156
washing powder, 131

water, 3
web, 5, 153–54
web-based sources, 88
Western educational ideology, 129
whitewashing, 131
world, 4–6, 17–18, 26–27, 34, 36–38, 40–43, 49–50, 55–56, 71–72, 98–100, 108, 128–29, 135–36, 145–47, 166–68
  developed, 131–32, 149
World Englishes, 34, 37–38, 41, 60–61, 69, 108

World Englishes debate, 37, 39
world hunger, 25–26
world's wealth, 42

Xbox, 144

Yahoo Answers, 151
Yale, 135
Yemen, 131
YouTube, 26, 90, 118

ZPD, 80

For Product Safety Concerns and Information please contact our EU Authorised Representative:

Easy Access System Europe

Mustamäe tee 50

10621 Tallinn

Estonia

gpsr.requests@easproject.com

www.ingramcontent.com/pod-product-compliance
Lightning Source LLC
Chambersburg PA
CBHW070609300426
44113CB00010B/1473